English Revision for Leaving Certificate

English Revision for Leaving Certificate

ORDINARY LEVEL

FIFTH EDITION
FOR 2010 AND 2011 EXAMINATIONS

Anne Gormley

GILL & MACMILLAN

Gill & Macmillan Ltd
Hume Avenue
Park West
Dublin 12
with associated companies throughout the world

© Anne Gormley 2002, 2003, 2007, 2009, 2010
978 0 7171 4522 5

Print origination in Ireland by O'K Graphic Design, Dublin

The paper used in this book is made from the wood pulp of managed forests.
For every tree felled, at least one tree is planted, thereby renewing natural resources.

All rights reserved.
No part of this publication may be copied, reproduced or transmitted in any form or by any means without written permission of the publishers or else under the terms of any licence permitting limited copying issued by the Irish Copyright Licensing Agency.

Note: The texts, films and poems discussed in this book are prescribed choices for the Ordinary Level Leaving Certificate Examinations in June 2010 and June 2011.

Contents

Acknowledgments	viii
Preface	ix

1. Revision Techniques	1
2. Examination Techniques in Paper I	2
3. Comprehension	3
Features of comprehension passages	3
Types of prose writing	3
Structure and form of comprehension passages	6
The language of comprehension	8
Characteristics of well-written answers in comprehension	9
Comprehension vocabulary	10
Exercises on style	12
4. Composition	16
General notes on writing	16
Solving problems	16
Preparation	17
Planning	21
The paragraph	22
5. The Types of Language	31
Narrative writing	31
State Examinations Commission criteria for assessment	36
The language of argument	40
The language of information	48
Persuasive writing	61
Descriptive writing: The aesthetic use of language	71
Answering Question B, Paper I	78
6. Samples of Paper I with Model Answers	83
Structure of Paper I	83
First sample paper: Holidays and pleasure	84
Second sample paper: Strong characters	89
Third sample paper: Fashionable trends	95
Fourth sample paper: Healthy living	102
7. Examination Techniques in Paper II	110
Prescribed texts for examination 2010	110

Prescribed texts for examination 2011	112
Structure of Paper II	113
Answering literature questions	114

8. The Study of a Single Text — 116
How to answer a question on the in-depth study of a text	116
Sample questions and answers	116
Wuthering Heights (2010 and 2011 exams)	116
Lies of Silence (2010 exam)	117
How Many Miles to Babylon? (2011 exam)	119
Possible questions on the study of a single text	121

9. The Comparative Study of Texts — 122
What is a comparative study?	122
Answering a question on the comparative study of texts	123
Sample questions and answers	123

10. Notes on Some Prescribed Texts — 128
Lies of Silence (2010 exam and 2011 comparative study only)	128
Circle of Friends (2010 comparative study only and 2011 exam)	130
The Plough and the Stars (2011 exam)	133
How Many Miles to Babylon? (2011 exam)	135
A Whistle in the Dark (2010 comparative study only and 2011 exam)	137
Dancing at Lughnasa (2010 exam and 2011 comparative study only)	140
Lamb (2010 exam and 2011 comparative study only)	143
Panther in the Basement (2010 exam)	145
Sive (2010 exam and 2011 comparative study only)	146
The Blackwater Lightship (2010 exam)	148
The Grapes of Wrath (2010 and 2011 exams)	152
The Secret Life of Bees (2011 exam)	155

11. Notes on Films — 159
Characteristics of films	159
Inside I'm Dancing (2010 and 2011 exams)	160
Richard III (2010 exam)	164
Il Postino (2010 and 2011 exams)	167
The Truman Show (2010 exam)	169
As You Like It (2011 exam)	173
Billy Elliott (2010 and 2011 exams)	177
Casablanca (2010 and 2011 exams)	182
The Constant Gardener (2011 exam)	187

12. Unseen Poetry — 194
Approaching the unseen poem	194
The language of poetry	195
Method of answering questions on an unseen poem	200
Sample questions and answers	201

13. Prescribed Poetry	208
Approaching the question	208
Sample questions and answers	208
14. Examination Papers	214
Leaving Certificate 2009	214

Acknowledgments

For permission to reproduce copyright material in this book, grateful acknowledgment is made to the following:

Merlin Publishing for an extract from 'Three Lambs' by Liam O'Flaherty and two extracts from 'The Fairy Goose' by Liam O'Flaherty; Penguin Books Ltd for two extracts from 'My Oedipus Complex' by Frank O'Connor; HarperCollins Publishers US for an extract from *Empire of the Sun* by J.G. Ballard; Bloomsbury Publishing for two extracts from *Lies of Silence* by Brian Moore; Faber and Faber Ltd for an extract from 'Journey of the Magi' by T.S. Eliot; John Murray (Publishers) for an extract from *Wheels Within Wheels* by Dervla Murphy; PFD Literary Agents for 'Courtesy' by Hilaire Belloc; Anne Dean for her poem 'Fittings'; A.P. Watt Ltd on behalf of Michael B. Yeats for 'The Wild Swans at Coole' by W.B. Yeats; 'Child of our Time' by Eavan Boland from *New Collected Poems*, published by Carcanet Press Limited. Reproduced by kind permission of Carcanet Press Limited.

The publishers have made every effort to trace all copyright holders, but if they have inadvertently overlooked any they will be pleased to make the necessary arrangements at the first opportunity.

Picture Credits

175, 182, 189 © Rex Features; 161, 165, 168, 170, 178 © The Kobal Collection.

Preface

In this revision book, guidelines are set out clearly that will enable you to revise for the Leaving Certificate course at Ordinary Level. The book gives a series of practical guidelines on how to tackle both Paper I and Paper II. There are notes on the different types of language genres, together with sample material and commentary, which will help you in dealing with questions on Paper I. There are also a number of samples of Paper I. These follow the same form – that is, comprehension and composition – as the examination on Paper I.

The book also deals with Paper II. There are guidelines on how to prepare for the question on both the single study of a text and the comparative study of texts. The notes on all texts are specifically designed for Ordinary Level.

Guidelines are also given on answering questions on both the prescribed and the unseen poetry. The method of answering poetry questions in both the prescribed and the unseen section is clearly outlined. In addition, there are sample answers on both unseen poetry and some of the prescribed poetry on the course.

I hope the practical approach adopted throughout this book will enable you to prepare in an efficient and focused manner for all aspects of this new course.

Anne Gormley

Revision Techniques

1. Make sure you are completely familiar with the syllabus and the requirements for Ordinary Level. Know exactly how many questions you have to answer on each paper and roughly how much time you have for answering each one. Know what sections or questions are compulsory.
2. Prepare yourself for Paper I, which covers *comprehension* and *composition*, by reading material on topics you are interested in. Gather ideas on these topics and write them up in a notebook.
3. Study unseen passages for the comprehension section and practise writing answers to these. It is useful to compare your own answers with sample answers in this book.
4. Practise writing compositions in the different types of language genres.
5. Identify clearly which play or novel you will choose for the in-depth question on a single text, as you will need to know this in detail.
6. Decide which three texts you are studying for the comparative question. Remember that you can study a film for this question. If you take a film for study in the comparative section, watch it several times and familiarise yourself with the central issues and techniques.
7. Know your texts, whether book or play, very well. You cannot read your texts often enough. There is no substitute for your own personal interaction with the text. Understand what you are reading. Follow what is happening. If you miss a connection in the story, you will find yourself increasingly puzzled as you read on. Ask yourself the following questions: Why are the characters behaving in this way? How is the plot constructed? Study key passages and sections in great detail. Take note of important quotations, and familiarise yourself with the plot and the main features of the characters.
8. Practise writing essays on the single text which you are studying in depth, and also on the three texts which you are studying for the comparative question. Give yourself the same amount of time as you would have in the exam.
9. You have two questions to answer on the poetry, so remember to practise the techniques used for answering a question on the unseen poem, and a question on the prescribed poets.

Examination Techniques in Paper I

1. The total number of marks for this paper is 200, which is half the total for the examination. There are 100 marks for the comprehension and 100 marks for the composition assignment.
2. Four comprehension texts are given, each followed by two questions: question A and question B. You must answer *two* questions: question A on *any text* and question B on *any other text*. You cannot answer two questions on the same text.
3. In addition, you must answer one question on a composition or writing assignment.
4. The time limit for this paper is two hours and fifty minutes.
5. Spend eighty-five minutes on the comprehension and eighty-five minutes on the writing assignment.
6. Give yourself approximately forty minutes on each comprehension question.
7. Answer the comprehension questions first, since they are less demanding than the composition.

Comprehension 3

FEATURES OF COMPREHENSION PASSAGES

In the comprehension passage, always look for the following:
- **Theme:** The subject matter of the writing.
- **Tone:** The relationship between the writer and the reader; *how* the writer is saying what is in the passage.
- **Intention or purpose:** *Why* the writer wrote the passage.

All three features are related. If a writer's intention is to condemn violence, the theme will reflect that intention. A writer may wish to tell a story, so the subject matter will be written in the form of a narrative. Another writer may wish to persuade the reader about something and will therefore use a persuasive style of writing.

TYPES OF PROSE WRITING

Autobiographical writing

In this kind of writing we get an insight into the mind of the writer. The use of the subjective 'I' is a feature of autobiographical writing, i.e. writing about oneself.

> Until we moved to Toronto I was happy.
>
> Before that we didn't really live anywhere; or we lived so many places it was hard to remember them. We spent a lot of the time driving, in our low-slung, boat-sized Studebaker, over back roads or along two-lane highways up north, curving past lake after lake, hill after hill, with the white lines going down the middle of the road and the telephone poles along the sides, tall ones and shorter ones, the wires looking as if they were moving up and down.
>
> I sit by myself in the back of the car, among the suitcases and the cardboard boxes of food and the coats, and the gassy, dry-cleaning smell of the car upholstery. My brother Stephen sits in the front seat, beside the partly open window. He smells of peppermint LifeSavers; underneath that is his ordinary smell, of cedarwood lead pencils and wet sand. Sometimes he throws up into paper bags, or beside the road if my father can stop the car in time. He gets carsick and I do not, which is why he has to sit in the front. It's his only weakness that I know of.
>
> (Margaret Atwood, *Cat's Eye*)

COMMENT

This is an example of autobiographical writing where the writer tells us many things about her personal life. Here we get some details about the writer's life when she was a child.

Argument writing

Argument or discursive writing presents information in a logical and organised manner. The method of the writer here is detached and logical.

> **The need for parents to understand drugs**
> Drug abuse can occur in any family. The prospect of a son or daughter becoming involved in drug abuse is frightening. It is important for parents to be informed about drugs and to be vigilant without being over-anxious.
>
> Young people are exposed to a variety of drugs today. They must be able to handle this exposure. Parents need to be aware of influences on young people and to develop an understanding of adolescence. For some, adolescence is a time of questioning established values, pushing out boundaries and experimenting with the forbidden. This often means coming in contact with drugs.

COMMENT

This piece of writing is written in the style of argument. The writer wishes to persuade parents of the need to know more about drugs so that they will be better able to help their child if need be.

Informative writing

The purpose of this type of writing is to inform or convey certain facts in a clear and terse manner.

> We are eating more low-fat products than ever before, yet still becoming a fatter nation by the day, so something is clearly very wrong with our eating habits. Cheese has been an important part of the human diet for thousands of years. Rich in essential nutrients for the growth and repair of body cells, it's especially useful in the growing years. Even more important, perhaps at a time when osteoporosis affects one in four women over the age of sixty and one in two over seventy, cheese should be an everyday food for older people, because it is rich in calcium and vitamin D.

COMMENT

The above paragraph is an informative piece of writing about the importance of cheese in our diet.

Narrative writing

In narrative writing, the writer is telling a story. There is a definite arrangement of ideas or sequence of events. Narrative prose puts an emphasis on description: describing people, actions and events in detail.

> He woke with a start frightened. Over his head in the loft a cock was crowing. It was a weird sound in the enclosed space of the kitchen. He heard a voice calling and arms were reaching with a stick. He felt very tired still. The straw and its covering where he slept was warm. Beside him the four little boys were sleeping, head to toe like oat-sheaves in a cart. They looked very young and innocent, their hair tousled, their young faces and brows untroubled.
>
> Then he saw Mairtin at the door. He came over to him. 'You are awake,' he said. 'Rise up fast. There are boats crossing the loch.' Dualta felt his heart sinking as he pushed aside the blanket.
>
> (Walter Macken, *The Silent People*)

COMMENT

This is a short piece of narrative writing which gives us a description about Dualta and where he slept one night. There is a strong emphasis on highlighting certain details in description, such as 'the four little boys were sleeping, head to toe like oat-sheaves in a cart.' The use of such description makes the writing more immediate and vivid.

Persuasive writing

The purpose of persuasive writing is to sway the reader towards a certain viewpoint on the strength of feeling and emotion.

> Thoughts of warm winter sunshine are just the thing to chase the blues of an Irish summer away. If you're planning a break during a month with an R in it, now is a good time to book, to avail of early special offers. Carefree Holidays has launched a new winter programme, which offers a vast amount of good value breaks.
>
> Prices start at €199 for a week in self-catering apartments in Costa Del Sol. Holidays booked on or before July 27 can avail of a low booking deposit of €30 per person.
>
> For an extra €15 a day, holidaymakers can take an extended winter break for up to six weeks.
>
> For details call Carefree Holidays on 021–78664400.

COMMENT

This is an example of persuasive writing. The extract is obviously taken from a holiday brochure. The first sentence appeals to the emotions – the thought of warm sunshine, which will chase the blues away. The language is clear and urgent: 'prices start at', 'holidays booked on or before 27 July can avail of a low booking deposit of €30 per person'.

This type of approach – calling for action – is a hallmark of persuasive writing.

Descriptive writing

In descriptive writing, there is a strong emphasis on describing things and/or people. Where narrative writing tells us what people and things *do*, descriptive writing tells us what people or things *are like*.

Descriptive writing:
- gives a clear picture
- selects details with great care
- uses precise vocabulary and avoids exaggeration
- appeals to the different senses of taste, touch, sight, etc.

> The rich colouring of the land was shorn away, or beaten down by wind and rain. On the hills the grey fields were like the faces of spent men; the leaves lay in sodden drifts in the loanens, and the water rose brownly in the wells. The men ran new runlets against the equinoctial storms, patched barns and byres, brerded hedges where the falling leaf revealed gaps and listened patiently to the indoor needs of the farmwife. The women felt the breast of fowls, laid fragrant apples in the loft, and in the comfortable farms drew out again voluminous half-finished embroidered cloths from parlour chests.
> (Sam Hanna Bell, *December Bride*)

COMMENT
The emphasis in the above passage is on colour and on drawing vivid pictures. Note, for example, the reference to the grey colouring in the first lines: 'the grey fields were like the faces of spent men'.

STRUCTURE AND FORM OF COMPREHENSION PASSAGES

A comprehension passage is made up of:
- paragraphs
- sentences
- words.

Paragraphs
A paragraph consists of one main sentence, usually called the *topic sentence*. The rest of the paragraph consists of support for that topic sentence. When studying paragraphs for comprehension, examine:
- the topic sentence: try to locate where exactly in the paragraph it comes. Usually topic sentences come at the beginning or end of a paragraph
- the linking devices used by the writer to tie up the different ideas in each paragraph.

Sentences
A sentence may be defined as a group of words that makes complete sense. A sentence can be:

- a **statement** or an **assertion**:

    A blinding sandstorm blew across the desert.

    We have enough fuel for the winter.

    It was a glorious September day.

- a **question**:
  Did you pass the examination?
  Who recommended that book?
  Where have you been?
- a **command**:
  Rule a line under that heading.
  Close the garage door.
  Wipe your feet on the mat before you come in that door.
- an **expression of surprise** or **shock**:
  How precious that supply of water was!
  What a lot you have bought!
  What an amazing piece of work that is!

Sentences can also be:
- **simple:** this type of sentence is made up of one subject and one object:
  The schoolboy broke the door handle.
- **compound:** two simple sentences connected by a conjunction:
  The young girl passed her oral test, and she was very pleased.
- **complex:** a simple statement followed by one or two clauses:
  As soon as I arrived in Canada, I telephoned my home in Ireland, where they were waiting anxiously for news.

The way a writer constructs sentences can reveal certain attitudes they may have towards the subject. Simple sentences anchor a writer's thoughts securely. A series of terse sentences can contribute to the flow of thought in a passage:

> What was I doing in the world's most radioactive environment? Inner cries of Help! rushed to the surface. I felt engulfed by a strong sense of panic. I couldn't breathe. My heart raced and felt as if it might burst. I looked at the Geiger counter in my hand and – my God! I saw the needle rise beyond what it was capable of registering. My fear was overwhelming. Feelings of sinking deep into a black hole rushed forth like a torrent of evil. I screamed silently. I was in my own private world of terror. I had just entered 'Death Valley', the exclusion zone surrounding Chernobyl.

Words

It is important to understand clearly how words are used in writing. The same word can be used to persuade, to argue or to describe something. A writer can also use words to draw pictures or images of certain things.

There are different kinds of words. *Pictorial* words draw an image or picture of something, e.g. a red coat, a black jacket, a pink sunset. *Concrete* words give a specific idea about something, e.g. a heavy man, a tall girl, an oval-shaped face, a hollow cheek, a green, ripe apple. *Abstract* is the opposite of concrete. It usually means something that is not specific, e.g. goodness, loyalty, whiteness, truth.

The context of words

Examine the context of certain words. The same word or set of words can be used to provoke a totally different type of reaction in the reader, depending on its particular context. For example, look at the following sentences:

He is a notable politician.

Notable criminals have been put on file.

The environmental lobby met with politicians in Dublin today.

He has built a large lobby onto the hotel.

Clouds loom on the horizon.

She uses a loom for her weaving.

The prospect of losing all his savings still looms.

The fishermen had a large haul of fish last night.

Gardaí haul in several suspects of the crime.

Cordon off the area because of a suspected bomb.

A cordon was constructed around the building site because of danger.

The physiotherapist manipulated the athlete's muscles.

He allowed himself to be easily manipulated.

The media manipulate the audience's responses.

Thus we can see that the particular context of words can affect their meaning in a passage.

Connotations

The connotation of a word is the emotive impact it may have on a reader. Word connotations suggest certain attitudes to an idea. Examine the following words, and consider the various connotations that spring to mind when you read them:

cool	obese
upbeat	foolish
traditional	raw
soap opera	

THE LANGUAGE OF COMPREHENSION

Style

Style is the ability to present the subject in a way that is best suited to achieving the writer's aim. It is important when understanding a passage to know how to 'read between the lines', i.e. to understand how language and imagery work together to create a certain tone or mood, and how they all add up to a coherent style.

Tone
Tone is the relationship a writer establishes with the reader: how the writer is saying what is in the passage.

Mood
Mood is the particular atmosphere of the piece of writing.

Imagery
Words can be combined to form *images* or *word pictures*. Images can be used:
- to illustrate a point:
  In the universal contamination of the environment, chemicals are the partners of radiation in changing the very nature of life.
- to create atmosphere:
  Today Chernobyl is beating in the heart of all Belarussians. It is in the deceivingly tranquil beauty of the forests, rivers and streams that no one may now enter.
- to provoke an emotional impact. Look at the following lines, which are taken from an advertisement on chocolate:
  Savour the tempting aroma of chocolate . . .
  . . . then abandon yourselves to the sensation of rich chocolate melting into delicious centres.

Remember, imagery is effective when it conveys what a writer intends in a vivid and economical way. The use of imagery can also help a writer to achieve originality of expression in writing.

CHARACTERISTICS OF WELL-WRITTEN ANSWERS IN COMPREHENSION

1. Your answers must reflect a clear understanding of the content of the passage.
2. Organise your thoughts clearly. Focus on exactly what you are asked. Avoid padding or digressing, i.e. introducing irrelevant points.
3. Show that you have a thorough grasp of the writer's intention in writing. Be able to understand whether the writing is persuasion, argument or narration.
4. Be able to follow a line of argument and evaluate the points objectively.
5. Your answers must show a basic knowledge of the elements of writing: how to structure sentences and paragraphs, how to use tone and imagery.
6. Use clear, correct English and lucid argument to support your statements.
7. Answers must be clear, logical, factual and precise.

Common errors in comprehension answers
1. Misunderstanding the content of the passage.
2. Using incorrect facts or information in answers.
3. Misunderstanding the questions. Distinguish between simple questions such as
   How does a writer reach the conclusion . . .?
   Why does a writer claim that this is the case?
   Demonstrate from your own experience . . .

4. Not giving reasons for answers when asked to do so.
5. Badly structured answers, where the main point is ignored and irrelevant points are introduced and developed.
6. Badly written answers, with faulty grammar, weak expression and poor punctuation.
7. Not answering the question asked, but rambling and going off the point.

Method of answering comprehension questions
1. Remember, you have *two* questions to answer on comprehension. These must be taken from *two different texts*.
2. Spend approximately forty minutes on each question.
3. Read the passage through several times in order to grasp the gist or general idea of what it is about. Try to examine what the primary purpose of the passage is: is it informative, narrative or persuasive?
4. Quickly scan the layout of the passage. If the text is divided into sub-headings, these headings can often provide you with an idea of what the passage is about and how the points are developed.
5. Sometimes it can help to write out one sentence or phrase on the main idea of the passage. This can help to focus your mind and keep to the point.
6. If the passage uses imagery, examine why it is used and what point is being made in the imagery.
7. Does the writer intrude in the text, and why?
8. In a passage that is factual or based on argument, know how to distinguish facts from opinions in the writing. Is evidence used to support the points made?
9. Before beginning to write your answers, work on a rough draft – getting your points down in note form – for each question.
10. Tackle every aspect of the question. Keep control of time. Stop when your allotted time is up.
11. Use your own words as much as possible.
12. When reading back, read your answers with a purpose. Check the question and then your answer. Have you answered the question asked? Have you used examples that are relevant and useful? Is your answer clear and logical, or is it repetitive and long-winded?

COMPREHENSION VOCABULARY

Learn the difference between the following words:

compare: show the similarities and the differences between things (**compare with:** make a comparison, **compare to:** suggest a similarity)
contrast: show the differences between things
criticise: point out mistakes and weaknesses in a balanced way
define: give the precise meaning of a concept
discuss: explain an item and give details, with examples
explain: offer a detailed and exact explanation of an idea or principle

illustrate: give examples that demonstrate and prove a point
justify: give the reasons for a position
prove: give answers that demonstrate the logical position
state: express the points briefly and clearly
summarise/outline: give only the main points, not details
trace: give a description in logical or chronological order of the stages of a process

Common vocabulary errors
Be aware of the difference in meaning between the following sets of words:

advance: progress, go forward:
   the advance of medicine, the advance of old age, the advance of time
advancement: promotion, helping forward:
   The Dáil are working for the advancement of education for inner-city children in our country.

affect (a verb): this word has different meanings:
pretend an effect on:
   The climate affected his health.
move or influence:
   The news affected relations with Japan.
   The film affected me deeply.
pretend something, pretend to feel:
   He affected shock at the news.
effect (when used as a noun): the result or consequence of an action:
   The effects of the nuclear fall-out were disastrous.
effect (when used as a verb): cause or bring about:
   The prisoners tried to effect an escape.

agree with: regard something with approval:
   I agree with the minister's new proposal.
agree to: give consent:
   They were forced to agree to the plans for the new building although they did not like them.
illusion: a false image:
   He has illusions of greatness.
delusion: a false belief with no basis in fact:
   He suffers from delusions ever since the accident.
   She is under the delusion that she can write well.

anecdote: a short story
antidote: a medicine used to counteract the effects of a poison or a disease

approve: give consent to:
   The committee has approved the budget.
approve of: think well of, to regard with favour:
   He did not approve of the plan to build an extension to the house.

assent/consent: both words mean 'agree to', and both take the preposition 'to'. Assent is immediate agreement; consent is agreement after some consideration

cancel: put off altogether
postpone: put off until a later date

its (a possessive pronoun):
  The cat is licking its paw.
  The world is using up its resources.
it's (a pronoun and a verb): the abbreviated form of 'it is':
  It's a fine day.

lose (a verb):
  I lose my keys frequently.
  I have lost my confidence in the government.
loose (an adjective):
  The door handle is loose.

stationery (a noun):
  The stationery shop is on the corner.
stationary (an adjective): at a standstill:
  The car is stationary.

EXERCISES ON STYLE

Examine the following sentences, then rewrite them correctly. You can compare your answers with those on pp. 14–15.

A. Correct the following sentences:
1. I shall attend the concert providing I am not too busy.
2. The rose is well known for it's scent.
3. The view she took was opposite of that taken by her friend.
4. The feet performed by the clown was absolutely incredulous.
5. The car accident did not effect his health.
6. He looses his keys frequently.

B. Correct the errors in each of the following sentences:
1. This shop sell's men's clothes.
2. He new less people than she did.
3. Not even one of the men were their.
4. Jane says she won't never come back to this country again.
5. Don't try and do too much before you are well again.
6. I haven't never seen them before.

C. Rewrite the following sentences and eliminate the repetition:

1. It is a realistic and entertaining programme, which is really entertaining.
2. On average children watch over three hours of TV per day, they watch cartoons that are very violent.
3. The action heroes that brutally murder are the heroes of our world.
4. Acting can give the average person in the street a great deal of self-confidence as the average person knows.
5. The teacher had difficulty with some students as the teacher did not know what to say.
6. It is not possible in this world of ours to find a completely honest person one you can trust.

D. Rewrite the following sentences and make the meaning more clear:

1. Second-hand car wanted to purchase by gentleman in good condition.
2. The teachers were invited to meet the parents but they did not arrive.
3. Good home wanted for kitten with children.
4. The President awarded him a medal for a very brave act.
5. She did not doubt whether her class would win.
6. I have got an idea for improving this room.

E. Rewrite the following sentences and correct the spelling and grammar:

1. Seventy per cent of young peoples thoughts are controlled by what they watch on TV today.
2. The Internet has a great affect on young people; it keeps you tuned in to whats happening.
3. The most interesting programme on TV has to be Friends.
4. She did not care weather he beccoming famous or not.
5. Books, their one of the most boring things on earth.
6. Everybodies sure to be their so lets hurry up and go.

F. Insert the apostrophe in the following sentences:

1. Joans friends are staying at the sea, whereas Michaels friend is staying at his uncles cottage in the country.
2. The girls shoes and the referees jacket were stolen.
3. The pupils classroom is bigger than the teachers staff room.
4. Marions sister formed a Girl Guides Club, and all the girls from the cities are members.
5. The babies nappies are hanging on the line, while the suns rays are shining on the grass.
6. Mens hats, boys shoes and ladies sportswear are sold in that shop.

A. Answers
1. I shall attend the concert provided I am not too busy.
2. The rose is well known for its scent.
3. The view she took was opposite to that taken by her friend.
4. The feat performed by the clown was absolutely incredible.
5. The car accident did not affect his health.
6. He loses his keys frequently.

B. Answers
1. This shop sells men's clothes.
2. He knew fewer people than she did.
3. Not even one of the men was there.
4. Jane says she won't ever come back to this country again. (Jane says she will never come back to this country again.)
5. Don't try to do too much before you are well again.
6. I have never seen them before.

C. Answers
1. It is a realistic and entertaining programme.
2. On average, children watch over three hours of TV per day. They watch cartoons that can be very violent.
3. Today's heroes are those people who carry out brutal murders.
4. Acting can give the average person in the street a great deal of self-confidence, as most people know.
5. The teacher had difficulty with some students as she did not know what to say.
6. It is not possible in this world of ours to find a completely honest person whom you can trust.

D. Answers
1. Second-hand car in good condition, wanted by gentleman.
2. The teachers were invited to meet the parents, but the parents did not arrive.
3. Good home with children, wanted for kitten.
4. He was awarded a medal by the President for bravery.
5. She did not doubt that her class would win.
6. I have got an idea on how to improve this room.

E. Answers
1. Seventy per cent of young people's thoughts are controlled by what they watch on TV today.
2. The Internet has a great influence on young people; it keeps you tuned in to what's happening.
3. The most interesting programme on TV is *Friends*.
4. She did not care whether he was becoming famous or not.
5. Books, they are one of the most boring things on earth.
6. Everybody's sure to be there, so let's hurry up and go.

F. Answers
1. Joan's friends are staying at the sea, whereas Michael's friend is staying at his uncle's cottage in the country.
2. The girl's shoes and the referee's jacket were stolen.
3. The pupils' classroom is bigger than the teachers' staff room.
4. Marion's sister formed a Girl Guides Club, and all the girls from the cities are members.
5. The babies' nappies are hanging on the line, while the sun's rays are shining on the grass.
6. Men's hats, boy's shoes and ladies' sportswear are sold in that shop.

Composition 4

GENERAL NOTES ON WRITING

How to write effectively
Successful writing involves taking a number of different things into account:
- knowing how to construct sentences so that they form effective and clear paragraphs
- the ability to construct paragraphs and to link them together to achieve a coherent unity and structure
- selecting the appropriate style for your reader
- the ability to master the conventions of spelling and punctuation
- polishing and revising what you have written.

Before you start writing, clearly establish:
- what the purpose of your communication is
- what your subject matter is
- the type of reader, and what expectations they have.

Your composition must be your own individual response to the subject. It is important, therefore, not to regurgitate material or to learn compositions off by heart. Nor is it advisable to write a composition simply 'off the top of your head', without any preparation whatever. Remember, the best compositions and writing are written on topics which you enjoy. Work at cultivating a variety of interests, and learn to identify your own style – your own particular way of writing.

SOLVING PROBLEMS

Content
One of the main problems is in knowing what exactly to write. Having to write on an unseen topic can be confusing and unsettling for many people. Gather ideas from daily newspapers or magazines that deal with current affairs, and jot down your ideas in a notebook.

Identify your style of writing and what type of writing appeals to you. The advice from your teacher can be invaluable here. Often you write best on subjects that you enjoy or feel strongly about.

Study the points on how to write in different types of language in Chapter 5. Know exactly what is required for each style. Also, study the sample material provided for each type of writing, and in particular the comment after each sample.

Writer's block and exam paralysis
Overcoming exam paralysis and actually putting pen to paper may be a problem. The solution is simply to pick up your pen and free-write (see page 20) until your thoughts become coherent.

Organising ideas
There is also the difficulty of organising ideas – of knowing exactly how to construct a paragraph, how to select relevant information and how to discard useless ideas. Many students have difficulty writing a suitable opening paragraph.

Some of the pre-writing strategies, such as brainstorming or writing a rough outline, can help you to structure your ideas and to organise your thoughts more clearly. The section on paragraphing, and especially on opening paragraphs, offers some useful guidelines and sample material to help you construct opening paragraphs.

Poor timing
Time and time management can be a further problem. Set deadlines for yourself when writing throughout the year. Work out exactly how much time you will have in the examination to write your composition, and make sure to keep to that limit in any writing you do.

Faulty style
Faulty style can be shown in many different ways: excessive repetition, poor spelling, bad grammar and sloppy handwriting.

Pay attention to small details such as spelling, handwriting and grammar. Correct all spelling errors, and check that every word you use is the right one. Read your work aloud if possible, as this can alert you to repetition not only of words but also of ideas. Study the exercises on style (pages 12–15) and learn how to eliminate common errors in grammar and spelling.

Misinterpreting the question or title of a composition
This can occur from a careless reading of the titles. Always read the questions and titles slowly. Remember the purpose of the task and the target audience.

PREPARATION

Pre-writing activities
The success of a piece of writing depends, to a great extent, on preparation. Much of the effect of the written product depends on learning pre-writing activities and how to use them. Some of the more important pre-writing activities include
- brainstorming
- clustering
- outlines
- free-writing.

Brainstorming

This is the process of trying to trigger as many ideas as possible on the topic. It literally means storming the topic with ideas or different thoughts. It can be very useful to use questions such as Why? How? Where? What? and When? to generate ideas on the topic.

Look at the following examples of trigger questions that you can use to brainstorm a topic.

Topic 1: Are we all born storytellers?
What is a storyteller?
Why do we need stories?
How can you tell a story is a good one?
When did storytelling begin?
How can storytelling help us?

Topic 2: Beauty in this world
Can beauty be defined clearly?
Who decides that something is beautiful or not?
Why do we need beauty in our world?
Where can beauty be found today?
How does beauty affect us?

Clustering

Answer the questions you have asked in your brainstorm. Draw together all the answers. Assemble these answers into points. This is what is known as clustering your ideas.

For example look at the topic 'Are we all born storytellers?' The 'clustered' answers to the trigger questions might look like this:

- Storytelling is the art of being able to tell a story that has a beginning, a middle and a conclusion.
- We need to hear stories because they offer us an escape from the problems and tensions of this world, and they help us to know about different things in a unique way.
- A good story is one that will keep the attention of the listener. It must be true to life, or about something that the listener can identify with and understand.
- Storytelling began many years ago as a form of entertainment and communication, before the invention of radio and television.
- Storytelling can help us in many ways. We can acquire knowledge about different customs and traditions. We can gain an insight into different types of people and their lifestyles. Stories can help us to deal with our everyday problems by offering us a means of entertainment and relaxation.

When you group these ideas together you will have the basis for an outline.

Outlines

Outlines form another part of pre-writing activities. The use of outlines can be very helpful when you are planning a writing activity, particularly a composition. Outlines have the following advantages:
- They organise your thoughts.
- They clarify exactly where you are going in the composition.
- They help to focus the flow of ideas in the composition.
- They help to overcome exam paralysis. Staring at a blank page can be a daunting experience, and the rough outline can be a life-saver here.
- They help you to organise and structure paragraphs.

Rough outlines help you to organise your thoughts; they show what needs to be emphasised and what needs to be eliminated, where repetition occurs, etc. Many common errors can be eliminated using a rough outline, such as:
- gaps in the logical development of ideas
- excessive repetition
- omission of central ideas and information on the subject
- going off the point
- insufficient evidence and examples.

The following is an example of how to brainstorm a topic, cluster the ideas together, and finally draw up an outline. Examine the method closely and try to follow it in your writing assignments.

Topic
Write a persuasive article for your school magazine on the topic 'Television is a mixed blessing'.

Sample brainstorm
- What exactly does 'mixed blessing' mean?
- How is television a mixed blessing?
- Does television raise awareness or create compassion fatigue?
- How unbiased is political coverage? For example, channels that are owned by rich magnates with their own agendas.
- Do the drawbacks of television outweigh the educational benefits of it?
- Is television a means or a barrier to communication?

Sample clustering of ideas
Television can be good in so far as it can help us in many ways. On the other hand, it can have disadvantages. This is what a mixed blessing means.

Television is a mixed blessing in many ways. On the one hand, it can offer genuine entertainment, and on the other it can create a culture of couch potatoes.

Television can raise awareness of important issues such as war, famine, earthquakes and injustice in many parts of the world.

Television is often used as a forum for political debates. Some of these, however, have little substance other than propaganda. Many powerful magnates control television channels and they influence what we hear and see.

Often the drawbacks of television can outweigh the educational advantages. It is important that people learn to use television properly, to serve them.

While television is an effective means to communicate current topics in many ways, it can also be a barrier to communication; for example, television can dominate family mealtimes.

Sample outline

Television is a mixed blessing?

Opening paragraph: Young children spending all morning at weekends watching TV.

Paragraph 2: When television was first launched it was seen to be a splendid advance on many fronts. Now, we have experienced some of the ill effects of TV, from increased aggression, to bad table manners, to limited vocabulary.

Paragraph 3: Television fans have praised its effectiveness in raising public awareness of topical issues. However, there is the danger of causing compassion fatigue within us; for example, the recent coverage of the most devastating earthquake in Turkey focused on images such as friendly three-year-olds being rescued and totally ignored the thousands who died or were seriously injured.

Paragraph 4: Powerful magnates own many TV channels and control the content of what is shown. Many debates on current and topical issues are superficial and focus on the packaging rather than offering real solutions to problems.

Paragraph 5: Television is potentially addictive. It can cause people, especially students, to waste a great deal of time and so neglect their study time.

Paragraph 6: Some people claim that TV facilitates communication. However, many families spend their meals in silence around the TV.

Concluding paragraph: All the advantages and disadvantages of TV must be weighed up clearly. We must remember that controllers of TV determine what we see. In order to benefit fully from TV we must be selective and discriminating about what we watch. In addition, we must question what we are being told and challenge what we hear, and not allow ourselves to passively accept all that is put before us. This is how we can make TV work to our advantage.

Free-writing

Free-writing can be a very helpful method of warming up before you actually begin writing in a formal and coherent manner. The main idea underlying this activity is to put pen to paper and to get going on the writing process immediately. Simply write about anything you choose and in whatever way you like, not caring about punctuation, spelling or structure. Write without stopping. Do not stop to plan, organise or edit. It can help to focus on a topic, though you should set a time limit to this activity.

Planning

1. Be decisive about selecting what topic or question you are going to write about.
2. Rephrase the title as a question if it is not already in the form of a question, as this will often help to generate ideas on the subject.
3. Brainstorm the topic using trigger questions such as Who? Why? How?
4. Cluster ideas that are related. Be clear about what particular direction your essay is taking. Do not introduce irrelevant material or go off the point.
5. Select material for paragraphs. Write out fully the topic sentence of each paragraph.
6. Your composition must have an overall unity. This will be shown in a logical development of thought between the paragraphs, and in a clear, conclusive and satisfactory ending.

Ten basic hints on writing a composition

1. Write every day. Write a paragraph on any topic in order to improve your expression and your flow of thought.
2. Cultivate your own ideas on current events. You can do this by having a notebook in which to collect ideas throughout the year.
3. Understand the topic fully; otherwise do not write on it.
4. Start with some of the pre-writing activities – brainstorming, clustering, drawing up outlines and free-writing – before writing seriously on the topic.
5. Avoid errors made in previous writing by learning spellings and correcting mistakes in grammar.
6. Identify your strengths and weaknesses in writing. Work at eliminating the weaknesses and improving the strong points.
7. Write simply. Choose a simple word instead of a more obscure one. Avoid using clichés, such as 'how and ever', 'few and far between', 'in the heel of the hunt', 'to tell you the truth'.
8. Work at writing interesting and catchy openings.
9. Draw up your own list of quotations and clever phrases, and use them in written work.
10. Do not make general or global statements without supporting them with clear and specific examples and evidence.

Ten do's

1. Write a paragraph every day on any topic. Leave it to 'cool', then come back later and correct it.
2. Always brainstorm your title, and always write rough drafts.
3. Organise your paragraphs, putting the most important ideas first.
4. Write interesting and exciting opening paragraphs.
5. Make your composition a reasonable length: three to four pages of A4 paper are usually sufficient.
6. Make sure the ideas you use are relevant. Use your own ideas.
7. Make your conclusion clear, fairly substantial and non-repetitive.

8. Vary the length and structure of your sentences.
9. Link your literature course to your composition; weave in quotations or ideas naturally and fluidly.
10. Read your composition aloud in order to hear your mistakes.

Ten don'ts
1. Don't go off the point: stick to the topic.
2. Don't use direct speech unless it is necessary.
3. Don't use two different ideas in one paragraph.
4. Avoid self-conscious expressions such as 'I hope to prove . . .' or 'I feel that I have shown . . .'.
5. Avoid the use of clichés and repetitive phrases.
6. Don't use quotation marks unless you are quoting.
7. Avoid the use of a definition in your opening paragraph.
8. Don't conclude your composition in mid-air.
9. Don't conclude on one sentence.
10. Don't reproduce compositions that you have learned off by heart.

THE PARAGRAPH

Paragraphs form the basic unit of any composition. A paragraph is like a miniature composition. It should have a clear beginning, a middle and a conclusion.

Each paragraph deals with one section of your subject. Each paragraph has one main idea or topic sentence, together with support or examples. The paragraph must have a unity: all ideas, examples, statistics and illustrations must be related to the main idea.

Paragraphs can be linked by transitional or linking devices such as *nevertheless, furthermore, however, if, or, so*. Paragraphs can be any length, but avoid extremes – don't make your paragraphs too long or too short. Generally speaking, there should be a variety in the construction of paragraphs within the composition.

Features of paragraphs
- Clarity.
- Unity.
- Emphasis.
- Coherence.
- Transitional or linking devices between paragraphs.

Clarity
Good writing aims at communicating effectively to your readers, and not merely impressing them. The topic sentence or main idea must be clear to your reader. The topic sentence usually comes either at the beginning or at the end of a paragraph.

The following paragraphs are an example of clear writing.

> Little Michael rose before dawn. He tried to make as little noise as possible. He ate two slices of bread and butter and drank a cup of milk, although he hated cold milk with bread in the morning. But on an occasion like this, what did it matter what a boy ate? He was going out to watch the black sheep having a lamb. His father had mentioned the night before that the black sheep was sure to lamb that morning, and of course there was a prize, three pancakes for the first one who saw the lamb.
>
> He lifted the latch gently and stole out. It was best not to let his brother John know he was going. He would be sure to want to come too. As he ran down the lane, his sleeves brushing against the evergreen bushes were wetted by the dew, and the tip of his cap was just visible above the hedge, bobbing up and down as he ran. He was in too great a hurry to open the gate and tore a little hole in the breast of his blue jersey climbing over it. But he didn't mind that. He would get another one on his thirteenth birthday.
>
> (Liam O'Flaherty, 'Three Lambs')

COMMENT

The main idea is set out clearly in the opening sentence: 'Little Michael rose before dawn.' The rest of the paragraph draws a clear picture of Michael's intentions as he sets off to see the black sheep, which is going to have a lamb.

Unity

Unity occurs in a paragraph when the main idea is clearly stated and all examples or supporting material are related to that main idea. Look at the following paragraph.

> The war was the most peaceful period of my life. The window of my attic faced southeast. My mother had curtained it, but that had small effect. I always woke with the first light and, with all the responsibilities of the previous day melted, feeling myself rather like the sun, ready to illumine and rejoice. Life never seemed so simple and clear and full of possibilities as then. I put my feet out from under the clothes – I called them Mrs Left and Mrs Right – and invented dramatic situations for them in which they discussed the problems of the day. At least Mrs Right did; she was very demonstrative, but I hadn't the same control of Mrs Left, so she mostly contented herself with nodding agreement.
>
> (Frank O'Connor, 'My Oedipus Complex')

COMMENT

The above extract from Frank O'Connor's short story 'My Oedipus Complex' is an example of a humorous paragraph. The topic or main sentence comes first, and then the writer gives us some humorous examples of how he amused himself during the war.

Emphasis

Emphasis comes from the position of the key sentence within the paragraph. The topic sentence can occur anywhere within the paragraph. The following two paragraphs show the effect of placing the topic sentence in a distinctive position within the paragraph.

> An old woman named Mary Wiggins got three goose eggs from a neighbour in order to hatch a clutch of goslings. She put an old clucking hen over the eggs in a wooden box with a straw bed. The hen proved to be a bad sitter. She was continually deserting the eggs, possibly because they were too big. The old woman then kept her shut up in the box. Either through weariness, want of air, or simply through pure devilment, the hen died on the eggs, two days before it was time for the shells to break.
>
> The old woman shed tears of rage, both at the loss of her hen, of which she was particularly fond, and through fear of losing her goslings. She put the eggs near the fire in the kitchen, wrapped up in straw and old clothes. Two days afterwards, one of the eggs broke and a tiny gosling put out its beak. The other eggs proved not to be fertile. They were thrown away.
>
> (Liam O'Flaherty, 'The Fairy Goose')

COMMENT

The main or topic sentence appears at the conclusion of the paragraph. The writer builds up tension and interest in the reader through this technique of placing the topic sentence at the end of the paragraph.

Coherence

Coherence means the logical flow of thought between ideas. All the sentences in a paragraph must relate to the topic sentence and to one another. There must be a link between one sentence and another, so that the reader will see clearly a logical progression and development in thought throughout the paragraph. There are different ways to achieve coherence within a paragraph. A writer can use linking or transition words such as *moreover*, *but*, *furthermore*. A writer may also use repetition of the same word, phrase or sentence to link the ideas within the paragraph. The following paragraph is an example of the smooth and logical flow of thought from one idea to another.

> For a long time it seemed certain that the gosling was on the point of death. It spent all the day on the hearth in the kitchen nestling among the peat ashes, either sleeping or making little tweaky noises. When it was offered food, it stretched out its beak without rising off its stomach. Gradually, however, it became hardier and went out of doors to sit in the sun, on a flat rock. When it was three months old it was still a yellowish colour with soft down, even though other goslings of that age in the village were already going to the pond with the flock and able to flap their wings and join in the cackle at evening time, when the setting sun was being saluted. The little gosling was not aware of the other geese, even though it saw them rise on windy days and fly with a great noise from their houses to the pond. It made no effort to become a goose, and at four months it still could not stand on one leg.
>
> (Liam O'Flaherty, 'The Fairy Goose')

Comment

The above paragraph is an example of coherence between one sentence and another. The paragraph traces the growth of the little gosling. Each sentence develops the main idea that the gosling seemed on the point of death, but gradually it began to grow stronger.

Remember, in order to achieve coherence within a paragraph:
1. Clearly establish your topic sentence.
2. Do not introduce two topic sentences or two different ideas in one paragraph.
3. Make sure that every point made in the paragraph has some relation to this topic idea.
4. Every sentence must develop or advance the previous ideas, or build up to a climax if the topic sentence comes at the end of the paragraph.
5. Do not introduce irrelevant statements into the paragraph.
6. Use linking devices to help provide a smooth and logical continuity within the paragraph.

Linking devices

Look at the following examples of how linking devices can be used in different ways:

To show contrast between ideas:
But
Nevertheless
Still
Although
Conversely
Yet
On the contrary

To emphasise a point:
For example
For instance
In fact
Indeed

To show the consequences of something:
Therefore
Thus
As a result
Accordingly

To show relations of time and sequence:
Then
Later
Afterwards
Next
Meanwhile
Soon

To sum up or conclude:
In conclusion
Finally
To sum up

Examine the following paragraphs, which are written on the subject of grief, and which have clear linking or transition devices both within and between them. Study the commentary carefully.

> On a hot July night 20 years ago, my husband Mark died. He was 24. Clever and witty, he had thick brown hair that he pushed off his forehead, and he loved me, of that I have no doubt. In all the pictures I have of him, he looks as though he's just said something funny. We were married for nine and a half months.
>
> At one precise moment I lost my world. I was not prepared, as no one can be. Grief is not a trip you can pack for. It's utterly lonely. What can I do? I asked recently, when out of the blue the telephone rang and news came of a friend's death. Do I call or write? Do I drop by the house? Do I take flowers? Food? What do I say?
>
> Because these questions came early to me, I have spent a good deal of time thinking about them. I've discovered there is an etiquette for grief. It is not so much a set of rules as a way of being; it requires accepting a place for sadness, for something that cannot be fixed. As a result, it runs counter to cultural assumptions that we must unlearn.
>
> *Reader's Digest*

COMMENT

The above extract taken from an article on grief is written in a personal and narrative style. Note the writer's use of certain linking devices between the sentences in the paragraph. The first few sentences are written in a short story format about the death of the writer's husband. The writer uses phrases such as 'On a night', 'He was', 'In all', 'We were' in order to develop the story line. Then the writer poses a series of questions to show the problems she experienced in trying to come to terms with and handle grief better: 'What can I do?', 'Do I?'. Note how the phrase 'Do I?' is repeated a few times for emphasis.

Note how the writer uses linking phrases in order to conclude or sum up the points made in the article: 'Because these questions', 'I've discovered', 'It is not so much', 'As a result'.

The introductory paragraph

The introductory and the concluding paragraphs are the two most important paragraphs in your composition.

The introductory paragraph has two main functions:
- to capture the attention of your reader
- to introduce your material and demonstrate your particular stance or approach to the subject.

The opening lines or paragraph of your composition must be interesting for your reader. Avoid openings that are predictable and dull, for example definition-style openings such as:

> Technology means . . .
> Fashion means the different styles that are around . . .

Make sure that your opening paragraph is original or takes an original slant on the topic. It can help to use an anecdote, a quotation or a surprising statistic.

Study the following paragraph, which is taken from students' work, and examine the commentary.

Write an opening paragraph on the most entertaining programme on television.

> To entertain is an attempt by the Director of a Program to keep the observer interested. What is the most entertaining program on TV? That is the question. I do believe the answer is an animated Cartoon headed *South Park*. The program is for adult viewing due to the scenes of Violence and use of language, which I feel, keeps the viewer interested. The hilarious use of Young school children and vulgar language adds to the affect of entertaining an adult more or less. For better or for worse it keeps you interested and tuned in to whats happening.
>
> Is *South Park* the most interesting program on TV? 'To be or not to be' you choose.

COMMENT

The above paragraph is an example of a very weak opening. The writer begins by attempting to define the word 'entertaining' and then asking the question what is entertainment? There are many errors in spelling and grammar. There is no clear topic sentence and no linked examples to back it up.

Rewritten version

> In my opinion, one of the most entertaining programmes on television is the cartoon *South Park*. This programme is for adults only, because many scenes are quite violent. The programme makes realistic use of young schoolchildren and the type of language they use. While some of the language may be quite vulgar, it serves to give the viewer a realistic insight into what is happening today. Some people may not find *South Park* to be the most entertaining programme, but for me it offers real amusement and escape from the troubles of my life.

The following two paragraphs are taken from a debate on the subject 'We are slaves of fashion'. Examine them and pay particular attention to the comment that follows.

> Fashions and dress codes are a big issue in today's society. Take any secondary school, which don't wear a uniform. If you were too look around in one particular room you

would notice a division. This division would have all different groups. People in one group will all have the same clothes on and people in another group will all have the same clothes on.

These divisions all have 'names'. Such names are 'the Jocks', 'The Nerds', 'The Easy Girls', 'The Rock Hard boys', and the 'Popular Group'. These names are given to because not only is the way we dress the name of the group we are in but also reflects the way in which we act. To proove my point, have you ever seen someone who dresses like a jock to be in the Nerd group? This is just one example of how 'we are slaves of fashion'.

COMMENT

These two paragraphs on the subject of fashion are very weak. There is no clear topic sentence in either paragraph. In addition, the writer uses many sentences that are not clear, and have weak grammar and spelling.

Rewritten version

Fashion and dress codes play a large part in our society today. Take, for example, the case of a secondary school where the students do not have a specific uniform. In such a situation, from the beginning, you would notice a clear division between the students. This division would be shown through many different groups of people. In one group, all the students will be wearing the same type of clothes, while in another group the same thing will happen.

Generally, all of these divisions in the way of dressing are given different names. For example, there are certain groups such as The Jocks, The Nerds, The Easy Girls, The Rock Hard Boys or The Popular Group. These names come into existence not only because of the particular style of dress used by the person in the group, but also because of the way in which they act. It is unheard of to have someone who dresses like a Jock belonging to the Nerd group. In other words, this proves my point that in many ways we are slaves of fashion.

The concluding paragraph

Your concluding paragraph is your final statement on the topic of your writing composition. It is the last impression left on your reader and therefore it is vitally important. A good conclusion has two purposes:
- to round off the main points or ideas in your composition satisfactorily
- to provide an overall unity of impression.

Avoid conclusions that repeat the main ideas of your composition in exactly the same words. On the other hand, avoid going to the other extreme by introducing a different approach or new ideas in your conclusion, because this will only serve to frustrate your reader. One happy medium between the two extremes is to refer back to the introductory paragraph and develop the anecdote or statistic, or simply the point that was made there. This method can ensure that there is a unity in your composition.

Examine the following two concluding paragraphs.

Write an article on what you consider to be the most entertaining programme on television.

> In my opinion then *South Park* definitely is the most entertaining programme on television because it helps you relax and just chill out before the box. There are few programmes on TV as good as *South Park*.

Rewritten version

> To conclude, therefore, I believe that for me one of the most enjoyable programmes on television is *South Park*. My weekend would not be the same without this truly entertaining programme. After a week of classes and homework, there is no greater pleasure than to sit before a glowing fire with a mug of steaming hot chocolate and watch this exciting and diverting show.

Write a debate on the subject 'We are slaves of fashion'.

> If you were asked to go into a room of two ladies – one a traveller and one an upper class lady and you were asked to identify which was which, do you think you'd be able? I think all you'd have to do is look at what each lady is wearing once again this prooves the point that we are what we wear.

Rewritten version

> Finally, I believe that in many ways what we wear truly reflects the type of person we really are. For example, would you be able to identify a person's background or profession from simply walking into a room? The answer is no, of course not. However, a careful study of the type of clothes and accessories they have would enable you to form a judgment of what type of person you are dealing with. Therefore, as we have seen from the many different types of examples, it can be said that 'we are what we wear'.

Rules for a good style

1. Write to communicate and not to impress. Know exactly what you want to say, then go ahead and say it.
2. Put your statements in a positive form. Make your assertions or ideas clear and definite.
3. Choose a specific and concrete word. Avoid the use of vague or abstract expressions.
4. Use an active verb rather than a passive one, e.g. 'Many people believe . . .' rather than 'It is believed by many people . . .'. Your writing is more effective and forceful when you use the active verb.
5. Avoid repeating yourself in the same words. Repetition has to be used correctly, otherwise it can weaken a piece of writing.

6. Vary the length and structure of your sentences. Every sentence must have a subject, a verb and an object.
7. Always consult a dictionary when you are not sure how to spell a word, or to check the meaning of a word.
8. Get used to writing and rewriting.
9. Learn the basic rules of correct punctuation thoroughly.
10. Know how to link your paragraphs correctly. The section on paragraphs (pages 22–9) gives examples of transition or linking devices and how to use them.

The Types of Language 5

Study the notes below on the different language types. In each section there are notes and guidelines on how to understand and write in different language types. Follow the advice given and use it to guide you through the exercises.

NARRATIVE WRITING

In narrative writing (the language of narration), the writer is telling a story.

Uses of narrative writing
Narrative writing is used in novels and short stories. Non-fictional narrative includes biography, autobiography and travel literature. A biography is the study of one person's life and achievements written by another person. In an autobiography a writer narrates an account of his or her own life and experiences. Generally these events are told in chronological sequence. Travel literature records details of journeys and the writer's impressions of places visited.

Features of narrative writing
1. The ability to tell a story that has a beginning, a middle and a conclusion that are all clearly defined. There must be a distinct arrangement in the sequence of events.
2. The story must have a definite location and context.
3. The story should be interesting and original. Avoid clichés and stereotyping.
4. In a good narrative, the writer introduces some personal commitment or experience to the narrative.
5. The description used must be both vivid and realistic.
6. Sometimes an anecdote can be used as part of a narrative. Here a single incident is told in the form of a short story. The incident almost always contains a definite point.
7. The characters presented must be realistic.
8. The story must have atmosphere. There has to be a certain setting, e.g. a country, a certain type of house or a distinct period in history.

Sample passages

> The Petrel was sinking at her moorings. Steam rose from her stern and midships, and Jim could see the queue of sailors standing in the bows, waiting to take their places in the ship's cutter. A Japanese tank moved along the Bund, its tracks striking sparks from the tramlines. It swivelled jerkily around an abandoned tram, and crushed a rickshaw against a telegraph pole. Sprung loose from the wreckage, a warped wheel careened across the roadway. It kept pace with the Japanese officer who commanded the assault troops, his sword raised as if whipping the wheel ahead of him. Two fighter aircraft streaked along the waterfront, the wash from their propellers stripping the bamboo hatches from the sampans and exposing hundreds of crouching Chinese. A battalion of Japanese marines advanced along the Bund, appearing like a stage army through the ornamental trees of the Public Gardens. A platoon with fixed bayonets raced to the steps of the British Consulate, led by an officer with a Mauser pistol.
>
> 'There's the car . . . we'll have to run!' Taking Jim and his mother by the hand, his father propelled him into the street. Immediately Jim was knocked to the ground by a coolie striding past. He lay stunned among the pounding feet, expecting the bare-chested Chinese to come back and apologize. Then he picked himself up, brushed the dust from his cap and blazer and followed his parents towards the car parked in front of the Shanghai Club. A group of exhausted Chinese women sat on the steps, sorting their handbags and choking on the diesel fuel that drifted across the river from the capsized hull of the Petrel.
>
> (J. G. Ballard, *Empire of the Sun*)

COMMENT

The above extract is taken from the novel *Empire of the Sun*. It recounts an incident that occurred one day when Jim was walking along the street. The writing is dramatic and filled with excitement and immediacy. Note how the writer uses a lot of small details in order to paint a vivid image of the whole scene: 'a warped wheel careened across the roadway . . .'. The Japanese army are described as 'appearing like a stage army through the ornamental trees of the Public Gardens'.

Question A [Comprehension]
(i) Identify two features of Jim's character. Support your answer with reference to the passage.
(ii) Show how the writer succeeds in building up a distinct type of atmosphere in the above extract.

Question B [Writing task]
Imagine you are a friend of Jim's. Write a conclusion to the above extract. Pay attention to drawing some realistic description of character and places in your story.

> There was a wealthy man in Okonkwo's village who had three huge barns, nine wives and thirty children. His name was Nwakibie and he had taken the highest but one title which a man could take in the clan. It was for this man that Okonkwo worked to earn his first seed yams.
>
> He took a pot of palm-wine and a cock to Nwakibie. Two elderly neighbours were sent for, and Nwakibie's two grown-up sons were also present in his obi. He presented a kola nut and an alligator pepper, which was passed round for all to see, and then returned to him. He broke it saying: 'We shall all live. We pray for life, children, a good harvest and happiness. You will have what is good for you, and I will have what is good for me. Let the kite perch and let the eagle perch too. If one says no to the other let his wing break.'
>
> After the kola had been eaten Okonkwo brought his palm-wine from the corner of the hut where it had been placed, and stood it in the centre of the group. He addressed Nwakibie, calling him 'Our Father.'
>
> 'Nna ayi,' he said, 'I have brought you this little kola. As our people say, a man who pays respect to the great, paves the way for his own greatness. I have come to pay you my respects and also to ask you a favour. But let us drink the wine first.'
>
> (Chinua Achebe, *Things Fall Apart*)

COMMENT
The above extract is taken from the novel *Things Fall Apart*. It is written in a simple narrative style. The writer describes the distinct customs and way of life in this community.

Question A [Comprehension]
(i) Pick out three features of the character of Okonkwo from the above extract.
(ii) Show how the writer uses small details to draw a vivid picture of the whole scene.

Question B [Writing task]
Write a short narrative of an imaginary trip that you made to the jungle in Africa.

Writing in the language of narration
The skills of good narrative composition come from practice. Writing a narrative composition means being able to write a short story. The story should have one point of view and there should be a definite arrangement of ideas. A story must be original and interesting for your reader. A good story springs from your own personal experience.

How to write a narrative composition or short story
1. Tell the story in one tense; generally the past tense is better.
2. It can help to put your own experience into the narrative: personal experience makes the narrative authentic.
3. The structure of your story can be straightforward and in chronological sequence, or it can be told in flashback. Remember, your story must have a shape: a clear beginning, middle and conclusion.

4. Use the third-person narrator to tell your story. Avoid the use of too much dialogue, as it can break up the flow of thought. Dialogue needs to be written very well in order to read well.
5. Take plot, characters, dialogue, mood and atmosphere into account when writing a narrative composition, and know how to use them correctly.

Plot
A plot can be defined as the series of events which make up a story. Plot is what gives rise to the storyline.

Features of plots
- The plot must move forward towards a definite conclusion.
- The plot must include some element of change. The situation at the beginning of the story must change as the story unfolds.
- All events of the plot must carry the narrative forward.
- There has to be a pace in the plot. Balance your beginning, middle and conclusion carefully to give your story a shape.

When planning your plot, don't forget to have:
- change in the story
- pace and movement in the narrative
- overall shape at the conclusion.

Characters
Because stories are about people, your characters must be real, recognisable figures. Your reader must be able to recognise the characters in your story; if not, they will not arouse any interest. You can reveal the true nature of your characters through dialogue and description. Focus on one or two significant features of a character when describing them rather than on several points.

When you are describing a character, do not tell everything at once. Instead, use implication or suggestion. Look, for example, at the following description of Michael Dillon's character, which is taken from the novel *Lies of Silence*.

> Tonight, the place was packed with celebrating students. He had to push his way through a jam of boys and girls, laughing, drinking, and arguing. Last year Andrea was one of this crowd, her degree fresh in her hand, with no notion that he even existed. Fear came over him again. Don't think about it.
>
> At the bar, there were four men serving. One of them, a temporary, saw him and went for Mickey. When Mickey brought the supplies list and put it in front of him, suddenly it was as though he had forgotten why he had come in here. Mickey was saying something, but the words were meaningless, as the muted mouthings of the newsreader on the television set above the bar. He signed the supplies list without looking at it, said good night to Mickey and in sudden panic, pushed his way out through the press of students. In the lobby he did not wait for the lift but ran up the winding staircase to his office on

> the mezzanine. He shut the door behind him and stood, feeling his heart thump. His office, lit by the yellow glow of a summer's evening, was still as a painting. He dialled her number.
>
> (Brian Moore, *Lies of Silence*)

COMMENT

This is a description of a man who is worried about something. The description only suggests certain things but does not state them clearly. We know, for example, that 'Fear came over him again.' The writer does not intrude and tell us things about the character involved in this extract. Instead, we are told that this man is distracted, that he hurries up the stairs instead of taking the lift, that he feels his heart thumping. All of this is an example of how a writer can use implication or suggestion in drawing a description of a certain character.

Dialogue

Learn how to write dialogue before beginning a narrative composition. One of the main functions of dialogue is to reproduce live speech. Never allow dialogue simply to slip into a conversation. It must have an object or purpose. Effective dialogue can convey conflict in a realistic manner. Conversation or good dialogue can add pace and variety to an otherwise dull story.

Learn how to punctuate dialogue correctly. Use quotation marks at the beginning and end of each section of direct speech. Separate the dialogue from the narrative by means of commas. The first word in every piece of direct speech begins with a capital letter. Use a new paragraph each time there is a change of speaker.

Study the following example of dialogue, which is taken from the short story 'My Oedipus Complex'.

> 'Mummy,' I shouted, 'I want a cup of tea, too.'
>
> 'Yes, dear,' she said patiently. 'You can drink from Mummy's saucer.'
>
> That night when she was putting me to bed she said gently: 'Larry, I want you to promise me something.'
>
> 'What is it?' I asked.
>
> 'Not to come in and disturb poor Daddy in the morning. Promise?'
>
> 'Poor Daddy' again! I was becoming suspicious of everything involving that quite impossible man. 'Why?' I asked.
>
> 'Because poor Daddy is worried and tired and he doesn't sleep well.'
>
> 'Why doesn't he, Mummy?'
>
> 'Well, you know, don't you, that while he was at the war Mummy got the pennies from the Post Office?'
>
> 'From Miss McCarthy?'
>
> 'That's right. But now, you see Miss McCarthy hasn't any more pennies, so Daddy must go and find us some. You know what would happen if he couldn't?'
>
> (Frank O'Connor, 'My Oedipus Complex')

Mood and atmosphere

Note the difference between the terms *mood* and *atmosphere*. Mood is the way the writer feels. Atmosphere is how the place and setting are described. Every story needs an atmosphere. Atmosphere is created in a narrative by a careful blending of people, events and setting. Your atmosphere must help to draw your reader into your story. While the use of imagination can help to build up an atmosphere, remember that the imagination must be controlled in writing. This is important in order to make your writing more realistic and authentic.

STATE EXAMINATIONS COMMISSION CRITERIA FOR ASSESSMENT

The tasks set for candidates in both Paper I and Paper II will be assessed in accordance with the following criteria:

Clarity of purpose (P), i.e. engagement with the set task.	30% of the marks available for the task
Coherence of delivery (C), i.e. ability to sustain the response over the entire answer.	30% of the marks available for the task
Efficiency of language use (L), i.e. management and control of language to achieve clear communication.	30% of the marks available for the task
Accuracy of mechanics (M), i.e. spelling and grammar.	10% of the marks available for the task

Sample compositions in the language of narration

The following compositions are written in the language of narration. They are taken from actual students' work and graded according to the standards required at Ordinary Level. Study them carefully and pay particular attention to the commentary that follows.

'And then I threw my mobile phone away forever.'

Write a short story ending with the above phrase.

> Grasping tightly onto my mobile phone, I stood outside the ostentatious home that was my employer's. As I stood there, several grotesque gargoyles stared at me through semi-precious stone eyes. Beside them I could see four large dishes perched on top of a Tudor-style turret.
>
> As I waited to be admitted to the oversized and sprawling monstrosity, I surveyed the surrounding mini kingdom, otherwise known as the garden. The long driveway up to the house was lined on each side by enormous bonsai trees pruned into the shapes of well-known, but rather randomly picked, animals, the cow, the elephant and the dog to name

a few. Merely a few minutes away from these were replicas of original Stone Age monuments varying from Stonehenge to miniature dolmens.

Behind the door I could hear approaching voices and the pitter-patter of little footsteps. It was soon opened by one of my three charges for the evening – a four year old girl who for the moment I shall call Mary. She was instantly joined by her brother John and Anne. They told me that their mother was just getting dressed and that she would be down shortly.

Sure enough, about two minutes later their mother waltzed into the playroom, where I was fruitlessly trying to convince the youngest that mashing chewing gum into the carpet would not make Mammy or Daddy happy. Mammy herself was dressed to kill. So much so, that if she were an assassin I could easily imagine her having more skill, weapons and gadgets than James Bond. As always she was wearing a dress that I knew I would never see on her again. Sitting on the low couch I had a great view of her Coca Chanel shoes, which probably cost more than my sister's first car. She was wearing diamond earrings and necklace that matched her outfit perfectly and sparkled and shimmered so brightly that I worried about the safety of my eyesight.

The mother proceeded to tell me how fortunate it was that I had made no plans for the evening, and that I had been able to come. I bit down hard on my tongue, so hard I feared I would bite it in two and plastered a silly smile on my face. She had called me on my mobile phone only half an hour before hand to baby-sit for the night. When I told her that I was just on my way out somewhere, she hummed and hawed so forcefully that I knew I would be out of a job if I wasn't on her doorstep in twenty minutes. So the bit about me 'having no plans for the evening' was the biggest lie I had heard in a long time.

So thanks to the fact that this woman was my sole source of income I miserably cancelled my plans and made my way to Mrs Lucy Fir's not so humble abode.

Mrs Fir gave me the usual run-down of what he children and I were allowed (and not allowed) to say, do, watch, eat, drink, touch, use or breathe near. This was followed by the usual typed list of each child's preferences, dislikes, allergies and mannerisms. I knew all this already but it was part of her satanic ritual. I already had a shoe box full of these sheets under my bed at home one for each time I had babysat. She also presented me with a list of emergency contacts, varying from the pediatrician, to her own number to that of the priest. I vaguely wondered if he performed exorcisms.

With that she was gone and I was left alone with the three children. After extracting chewing gum from the youngest's mouth, I threw the wet, sticky lump in the bin and decided that they needed something a little less plastic to nourish themselves on. We made our way into the industrial-sized kitchen and the children occupied themselves with some colouring, as I searched for something that fitted around all their respective dislikes and allergies.

I was just putting some sandwiches on the table when I felt my pants pocket vibrate. It was Mrs Fir. I pressed the green call button and before I even had time to greet her she was instructing me to find her little, green leather phonebook in the hall table. She needed her hairstylist's number. This, she informed me was not for herself. It was, she added in a hushed and conspiratorial tone for a friend who was desperate to hide her silver roots. I thought the last bit was said in a tone of malicious glee and superiority.

On my return to the kitchen I discovered the children had finished and had decided to try their hand at washing up. Unfortunately the kitchen looked as if it had been functioning as a boxing ring between Free Willy and Fungi. There was water everywhere. I knew it was going to be a long night.

Within the next two hours somehow I managed to clean up the deluge in the kitchen, get the children ready for bed and read their stories. However, all was not over. I had to deal with Mrs Fir for the rest of the night. I was constantly plagued by her calls on the mobile. Each time her demands became more complicated and more outrageous. I even found myself being told that I was by no means to use the Head and Shoulders on Princess her Parisian poodle. As I'm sure you can imagine her Highness was no more delighted with the arrangements than I was. She seemed as intent on destroying the rooms with water as the children had been. Soon the bathroom resembled a Biblical scene resembling something on the lines of Noah and his Ark.

They arrived home sometime after two and the children's father offered to drive me home. I declined, knowing that he usually drove like a bat out of hell on steroids. I walked home and when I arrived at the gates of my own home I welcomed them as if they were the pearly gates of heaven.

Suddenly I felt the all-too familiar vibrations in my pocket. I tensed up interiorly. Then something caught my eye – our big, black bin. I smiled to myself, decided to rid myself of all traces of Mrs Fir for good, all means through which she could ever contact me again and with that thought I threw my mobile phone away forever.

P: 28
C: 28
L: 27
M: 9
Total: 92 **Grade A1**

COMMENT
This composition is amusing and manages to meet the requirements of a short story at this level. The writer draws some original pictures of the house and its occupants, and also uses some very striking language to communicate the ideas.

Compose a narrative account of a city or country scene at night. Concentrate on the use of description, and give a title to your composition.

Misery
It is the middle of December and the bitter coldness of winter has engulfed the entire city with a blanket of ice. A blustery wind sweeps through the streets like a whetted knife, piercing every nook and cranny with a triumphant howl. The glow of neon signs and Christmas lights, which adorn the streets, illuminates the night sky, and highlights the sinister storm clouds that threaten the concrete jungle below. Strings of people mill around the various clubs and bars that are open, hoping to find shelter from the harsh

elements. In the distance, the faint wail of sirens rings out, muffled occasionally by the gusts of wind. For many, night has just begun.

I, however, have resigned myself to staying indoors on this depressing night. My only wish is to be home, instead of just beginning the long, arduous journey to my apartment. I pull the hood of my jacket tightly around my face, in a feeble effort to shut out the cold that bites at my nose. Across the street, three homeless men gather around a burning bin, soaking up the heat for all that it is worth. Society it seems, has an ugly habit of throwing its unwanted goods in the gutter – be it paper or people. I hurry on, hoping to spot a vacant taxi; instead cars stream past, splashing unwary passers-by with an unwelcome icy shower. My quickest way home now, is to head for the underground.

As I make my way down the grimy steps, I shiver as I begin to recall my last visit to the city under the city. I had ended up being mugged at knifepoint by a group of junkies. Ever since I had tried to refrain from using the underground. Today has been sheer misery at work, and I simply want to get home. I hurry along the various tunnels, festooned with posters advertising the many shows running in London's West End. In the main lobby, hundreds of people mill around like sewer rats, waiting to go in their various directions. Over an intercom a voice bellows out a warning about pickpockets and other lowlights who operate at the various stations. I quickly get my ticket and move on my way.

After a short wait on the platform, the train arrives; a bit of pushing and shoving, and I am inside the stuffy carriage. Getting a seat is something similar to finding a fish in the desert. The clinging humidity is as unwelcome as the coldness outside. I look around and observe my fellow passengers. Some are business people and others are students, reading books as they rock from side to side. This is the bit I don't like, the long climb back outside.

Back on the street I am only a few hundred yards from my apartment. Ahead of me to the rear of the apartment block stands a young man, flanked by two 'heavies'. They exchange a small package for a sum of money. Few words are said, the less the better. Then they disappear in their various directions, and are swallowed up by the shadows of buildings, and the darkness of the night. Finally I reach the door only to find a beggar clawing at me for some money. The change in my pocket sends him on his way.

I turn the key in the lock and step inside. The musty air of the old building fills my lungs, and I start coughing like an old man. I head straight for the armchair and flop into it with a weary sigh. Outside, the rain lashes against the window like an angry beast, furious at my comfort inside. I reach forward and switch on the television. It buzzes to life. No sooner have I sat back than the lights flash and the room is plunged into darkness. The TV whines and goes blank. Above me the storm bellows a roar of thunder mocking my despair. What a wonderful night!

P: 28
C: 28
L: 29
M: 9
Total: 94 **Grade A1**

Comment

The above composition is written in the form of a realistic narrative about the writer's experience of a large city. The description of the busy streets and the isolated situation of the writer are shown vividly. The writer uses some very effective similes: 'getting a seat is something similar to finding a fish in the desert', 'hundreds of people mill around like sewer rats', 'a blustery wind sweeps through the streets like a whetted knife', 'the rain lashes . . . like an angry beast'.

The narrative flows effortlessly along. The writer uses a variety of sentence structures to keep the narrative lively and interesting. Note how the narrative has a distinctive opening and conclusion, which is important for good narrative writing.

Exercises on writing in the language of narration

1. Take a real character that you know. Invent some problem in this person's life. Show how this problem creates a certain conflict between your character and another person. Develop some resolution or solution to this conflict. Write it up in the form of a story.
2. Imagine a person that you know and place them in one of the following situations:
   - losing his or her job
   - having an accident which changes his or her lifestyle
   - winning the lottery
   - being left with an inheritance.

   Write this up in story form.
3. Write a narrative on one of the following topics:
   - The fatal moment.
   - Midnight and we were in the forest . . .
   - Trapped!
   - Watching the sunset.

The language of argument

Argument is the process of making a point and trying to convince other people, using either evidence or facts, that this point is worthy of belief, and of being accepted or adopted in action. It is a way of presenting information so as to convince or persuade the reader about some viewpoint. The language of argument is a type of informative writing, but it also has a certain degree of persuasion at the basis of its structure. It differs from the language of persuasion in that it appeals to reason and to logic, rather than to emotion or feelings.

Uses of the language of argument

- Legal documents.
- Scientific and medical journals.
- Journalistic reports.
- Editorials.

Features of the language of argument

1. A *claim* is a statement that is arguable. In a well-constructed argument, claims must always be supported. Claims can be supported in the following ways:
   - with data or evidence
   - with facts
   - with examples
   - with statistics, where information is presented in the form of numbers.
2. Good argument must be supported by *evidence* that is *valid*. An argument is valid when the conclusion follows logically from the preceding statements. To test the validity of an argument:
   - assess the truth of the statement
   - assess the truth of each argument
   - assess the truth of each sub-argument.
3. Argument is *effective* when evidence and reasoning are both presented in a persuasive manner so as to convince the reader that certain opinions are preferable to others.
4. In understanding the language of argument, it is important to distinguish between a *fact* and an *opinion*. A fact is something that actually exists or occurs: it can be proved by an objective or detached observer. The process of confirming that a statement is true is known as *verification*.

Fact, inference and opinion

A fact differs from an opinion because facts can be *verified*, whereas opinions must be *supported*. An opinion is a judgment or a belief in something that is held by a person. An opinion can be based on a logical *inference* from the facts. For example, the following statements are examples of facts:

> A motor car has a steering wheel.
> Football is a game that is played in Ireland.
> Warsaw is the capital of Poland.

We can add some opinions to these facts, for example:

> Motor cars should all have strong steering wheels.
> I think that football is a game for boys only.
> Warsaw is a magical city.

To test factual statements, we must examine the evidence. To test statements of opinion, we must:
- examine the evidence of fact
- examine the inferences drawn from it.

An inference is an interpretation of a fact; it is a subjective reasoning process. We frequently make inferences about things without realising it. For example, we meet someone we know very well who does not greet us. We may infer that we have done something wrong, or that they are in bad humour. The reality may be quite different; they may simply be distracted or tired.

Faulty generalisations

These occur when we draw the wrong conclusions from certain data. Such generalisations can be unqualified. The statement 'Killing is wrong' can be considered true. However, killing in self-defence may be justifiable, and so this statement could be considered an example of an unqualified generalisation. Hasty generalisations or jumping to conclusions is another example of a faulty generalisation. For example, an article on rock music that claimed that all rock stars commit suicide could be an example of a hasty generalisation.

Glittering generalities

This is a method of obscuring an argument by keeping it deliberately vague. Glittering generalities usually involve making sweeping statements, broad generalisations and extravagant claims about something. The following phrases or expressions are examples of glittering generalities:

> Women all over the globe use this shampoo.
> You cannot live without a mobile.
> The single biggest cause of death is smoking.
> All soaps are candy-coloured caricatures of things.
> For tens of thousands of students, exams are treated with total apprehension.

Such statements are vague and abstract. Examine what the facts are here; what is the writer saying?

Sample compositions in the language of argument

Drugs in sport

It is long past the time when some concerted international effort should have been taken to get to grips with the increasing problem of drugs in sport. It is quite clear that the task of eliminating drug abuse from sport will not be easy. It may not even prove a simple matter to identify the substances that should be banned, and it is obvious that the detection of these substances can be both scientifically and politically difficult. And even when they are detected, the imposition of penalties upon those people who have abused them can prove legally difficult.

There can be no doubt, however, that the problem needs to be addressed. No nation is immune from the problem. The recent Tour de France – dubbed the Tour de Farce when it should more seriously have been described as the Tour de Pharmacie – gave a depressingly vivid picture of the need to rid sport of the menace of drug abuse.

COMMENT

The above extract is taken from an article on the subject of drugs in sport. It is an example of the use of argument in writing.

Question A [Comprehension]
(i) Sum up the main points of argument on the issue of drugs in sport from the above extract.
(ii) Identify the number of facts and opinions used by the writer in the above passage.

Question B [Writing task]
Write a list of suggestions for your school magazine on what you would consider to be the best method of dealing with the problem of drugs in sport.

Depression is a real risk for teenage drinkers

One of the most worrying consequences of teenage drinking is the relationship between it and depression. The psychological effects of bingeing are two-fold; depression secondary to alcohol abuse is a well-established outcome in all age groups. Among the young, however, there appears to be a transient – but real – risk of a suicidal gesture at a point when they are deeply ashamed of their alcoholic excess. This is an acute and temporary phenomenon, but an important finding in the context of increasing suicide in our society.

A simple but crude measurement of whether alcohol is causing a problem in a person's life is to run through the CAGE questionnaire. Have you ever felt you ought to cut down on your drinking? Have you felt annoyed about others criticising your drinking? Have you ever felt guilty about your drinking habits? Have you ever used alcohol as an eye-opener (to overcome a hangover)?

A positive answer to two or more questions suggests you have an alcohol problem. There are no simple answers to teenage drinking. Education undoubtedly is a key.

COMMENT
The above extract is written in the language of argument on the subject of the relationship between teenage drinking and depression.

Question A [Comprehension]
(i) Identify the main points of argument made by the writer above on the subject of teenage drinking.
(ii) Pick out two examples of facts that are valid from the above extract.

Question B [Writing task]
Write a letter to the newspaper on your ideas on teenage drinking. In your letter, suggest some solutions which might be used to help solve the problem of over-indulgence in drink.

How to write in the language of argument
When writing in the language of argument, the focus is on presenting facts and argument on a certain issue or topic and arriving at a conclusion. In this type of writing you are trying to convince your reader that your argument(s) are valid. When writing in the language of argument, it is important to:

- organise facts and ideas correctly
- produce a lucid and persuasive piece of writing.

Method
1. Take a definite stance on the topic. For example, in the topic 'Should television advertisements be censored?' you may decide to agree or disagree. The important thing is to clearly establish, both to yourself and to your reader, exactly what your own position is on this issue.
2. Identify who your audience is, i.e. whether you are writing for a group of young people, educated professionals or a class of schoolboys.
3. Establish what tone or point of view you will use.
4. Draft an outline of the main ideas for each paragraph.
5. Avoid giving a one-sided presentation. Write in a balanced way.
6. Support every fact you make with evidence.

Remember that good argument writing is clear and concise. It is structured on original ideas, organised thought and a balanced and logical presentation of facts. For that reason:
- use language that is formal and precise
- express ideas in a logical manner
- use transitional words to link your ideas
- anticipate the readers' opposing views
- defend your own ideas in a forceful and detailed way
- avoid the use of clichés, repetition and emotional or offensive language.

Sample compositions in the language of argument
The following compositions are written in the language of argument. They are taken from actual students' work and are graded according to the standards required at Ordinary Level. Study them carefully and pay special attention to the commentary that follows.

Write an article for your school magazine, using the language of argument, on the topic 'Where would the world be without sport?'

> Who knows where the world would be without sport? Lost perhaps. The main thing is we have got sport as part of our lives. Not too many people realise it, but the fact remains that sport affects and influences people all over the world. It doesn't matter what race or colour you are, or what step on society's ladder you occupy, sport is a part of everyone's life whether or not you are an athlete.
>
> There is an old saying, 'A healthy mind comes from a healthy body.' Exercise sends oxygen to the brain and helps it to perform at its optimum. It also provides oxygen to the heart, lungs and blood. This helps to keep all the organs in good working order, thus fighting illness and disease. Active people are more likely to eat healthy food and less likely to smoke because exercise creates hormones that makes you feel good, and most people like to maintain that feeling.

Sport and exercise play a vital part for patients suffering from anything like a heart attack to a car crash. Physiotherapy patients are encouraged to walk, jog, cycle and swim as part of their recuperating programmes as well as receiving occupational therapy. Other surgical patients are encouraged to exercise because often the lack of exercise was the cause of their illness. Those who take regular exercise generally maintain a healthy weight and are more likely to live a prolonged and disease-free life.

On a recreational level, exercise helps to break the monotony of daily routines. You can escape from the boredom of everyday life and the hassles and stress of the workspace, even if it is only momentarily. Sport can take your mind off things that may be bothering or upsetting you. Sports such as swimming can be relaxing and therapeutic, while certain types of kickboxing are a good way to relieve anger and tension. In fact, the safest way to vent your anger is to take it out on the bag or the ball. Young people are often encouraged to take their aggression and frustration out through the medium of sports. This can lead to far more positive results.

Another positive aspect of sports is its huge social arena. Whatever activity you do, whether you do it alone or not, there will always be other people who do it too. There are clubs for every sport, and these can be the perfect place to meet someone with similar interests. These clubs and groups, whether it be the local tennis club or the gym, are bound to have social events, fundraising activities or a Christmas party. There are often annual meetings of clubs throughout the country where you can meet new people who enjoy the same hobby as you do.

Sport also influences people who couldn't be bothered to run for a bus. Sport is one of the greatest entertainers worldwide. A football match can be shown anywhere in the world and everyone will understand the game. A race can be run and everyone will know who won it. There is an endless list of sports shown on television – from soccer, to rugby, to tennis or athletics and so on. In Ireland, Gaelic games attract massive live and TV audiences. Every weekend we witness the packed soccer stadiums, the capacity-filled racecourses, and the overflowing GAA stands. Who hasn't seen Dublin packed during rugby internationals or watched people on television camp outside Wimbledon to ensure they get to see their idols? Every four years the Olympics attract the greatest worldwide television audiences, never mind the millions who flock to see them live.

In providing entertainment for us mere mortals, sport creates a livelihood for talented and devoted sport stars and athletes. Gifted youths are often motivated to pursue an education in order to represent a school or college. Prestigious scholarships are awarded to such students who often go on to become professionals and even represent their country. Sport offers a satisfying and comfortable life for professionals, who may not have attained such success with another career choice.

While all of these aspects of sport are so valuable the most important part of sport's wide spectrum for me is the self-development it creates. I believe sport is the greatest education you can receive. You can only be taught the basics in sport, the real skills you must develop yourself. During the game, or the race, or the competition you are forced to think for yourself. You are faced with a real situation where you often have to make split second decisions – and live with the consequences. This kind of experience does not come from studying books, taking exams, or even being coached by someone else. It comes from what you've got inside you and only you can bring it out.

Without sport, people would have no escape from the ordinary and the mundane in life, and their self-development would be light years behind what it should be. Who knows how much less we would have advanced without sport? Thankfully it's been around for as long as we have, and with it we can't go too far wrong!

P: 29
C: 28
L: 28
M: 9
Total: 94 **Grade A1**

Comment

The purpose of this exercise is to write an article for a school magazine. The writer has achieved this purpose very clearly in this task. Every point is coherently linked and clearly supported with evidence and examples. The writer outlines a broad range of advantages associated with sports. The language and style is clear and varied. Note how the writer uses a variety of different types of sentence structure in order to maintain the reader's attention.

Write out the speech for a debate on the topic 'Is science fiction fact or fiction?'

Chairperson, fellow speakers, teacher and pupils, I am here today to propose the motion that science fiction is a fact not a fiction.

Look up the meaning of science fiction in a dictionary and you will read stories about imaginary scientific discoveries or space travel and life on other planets. Science, like fiction begins with imagination. Many people today regard science fiction as a form of escapism and a large proportion of the older generation consider it to be sheer and utter nonsense.

Yet more and more of this so-called nonsense is becoming reality. Since the advent of the technological revolution in this century, science fiction is rapidly becoming science fact. The most popular science fiction section is undoubtedly space travel and exploration. *Star Trek* and *Star Wars* are two modern epics that would immediately spring to mind; yet this fascination began long before these classics. Jules Verne provided the first jolt in 1865 when he described a rocket fired from a cannon that goes to the moon. Sounds familiar? Just over one hundred years later, this became reality when Neil Armstrong and Edwin 'Buzz' Aldrin landed on the moon on July 21 1969. Their spacecraft of course was a Saturn V rocket. Definitely a case of science fiction becoming science fact, Ladies and Gentlemen.

In 1952 artist Chesley Bonestell depicted a space shuttle with wings, astronauts on space walks and an orbiting space station. It wasn't long after this we saw all of this, although the space station took a little longer. In 1968 the science fiction film *2001: A Space Odyssey* created the view of what a space station would look like. At the time the film was released this was considered impossible. This is until December 1999 when we saw the reality of a space docking on the current mission to build the International Space Station. Another case of science fiction becoming reality.

More than a decade before the launch of the first satellite, science fiction writer Arthur C. Clarke predicted how a few communications satellites could link the entire planet. Again he was correct. Not even NASA is untouched by the science fiction phenomenon. A researcher, John Mankins, admitted recently that he thinks like a science fiction writer, imagining new programmes and concepts. His plan for a magnetic launch system, he says, is remarkably similar to one that appeared in the 1951 movie *When Worlds Collide*. A lot of what we do is influenced by what we see in science fiction, Mankins says. And why not? Many science fiction creations have become reality, too many in fact to be ignored.

Science fiction is not simply confined to rockets and spacecraft. The area of medicine is very well portrayed in many science fiction films and programmes. Far-fetched methods of curing patients, usually involving high-tech gadgetry, are normal. This can range from replacing lost limbs with robotic replacements to curing blindness by means of computers. Rapid advances in robotics have seen patients fitted with mechanical prosthetic arms. Even though they may appear to be far from the likes of the robotic arm Arnold Schwarzenegger sported in the *Terminator* films, they are on the right track and are a godsend to patients.

Meanwhile, curing blindness is a much more daunting task. Up until recently there was little hope of a cure for blindness. However, a major breakthrough occurred only this year when doctors successfully fitted a microchip into a patient's eye and connected to the nerve endings. They were relying on nerve impulses to make the chip work and it turned out to be a complete success. Before the operation the patient had been blind from birth, now he can read his name from a piece of paper. This is not unfamiliar to a *Star Trek* character that wears a computerised device over his eyes, to help him see. A similar device has been built in conjunction with the microchip; it's almost as if the device jumped off the silver screen itself.

One of the most popular elements of science fiction movies is the futuristic replacements of our means of transport. Common factors are that the vehicles become faster and can even fly. More often than not, the vehicle incorporates a computer to control it rather than a steering wheel. In the 1977 film *Star Wars*, George Lucas depicted a form of transport called a landspeeder which hovered off the ground and travelled at tremendous speed. This also has now become a reality. An inventor in America has created a hovering vehicle that can travel at speeds of up to 600kmh. What's even more unusual is that the vehicle looks exactly like the landspeeder from *Star Wars*. Hovercraft like this is definitely the way forward. Hovering increases speed, reduces noise and makes journeys shorter.

Whether science fiction is accurate or not, nevertheless it creates a credible vision of the future and the possibilities of space development. It is also a source of inspiration for many designers and scientists, and indeed it is they who will ultimately shape our future.

Chairperson, members of the opposition, fellow students and teachers, I thank you all for taking the time to listen to us here today, and I move to propose the motion.

P: 27
C: 25
L: 27
M: 8
Total: 87 **Grade A1**

Comment

The above composition is clearly researched at a deep level. The writer draws on a number of different examples and current references to films and medical advances to support the various points that are made. All the examples used are rich, varied and relevant. This composition achieves its task, which is to write a speech in a debate. The composition begins and ends as it should, by addressing the audience correctly.

Exercises on writing in the language of argument
1. Write a composition, using the language of argument, for or against the topic 'Drugs should be legalised'.
2. Outline a series of arguments on why you think smoking should be banned in all public places.
3. Compose a number of arguments in which you propose another type of examination besides the Leaving Certificate.

THE LANGUAGE OF INFORMATION

Some objectives of the language of information may be to:
- convey information in a succinct or terse manner
- give instructions or make requests
- persuade or influence the reader to adopt an attitude or act on a certain issue or matter.

Uses of the language of information
- Reports.
- Media (newspaper, television and radio) accounts of certain things or events.
- Instructions.
- Memos and letters.
- Summaries.
- Bulletins.
- Forms and questionnaires.

Each of these has different objectives to achieve. Reports give a factual account of some situation or set of circumstances. Media accounts usually give a report of different events in a clear and factual manner. Instructions offer a clear and terse explanation of the procedure or technique involved in doing something. Memos are short messages written in an informal style. Summaries give a condensed account of information. Bulletins present information in an interesting and dramatic way. Forms and questionnaires request information in a clear, concise manner.

Features of the language of information
- **Clear organisation of information:** Express arguments and information in a logically and coherently.

- **Relevant content:** Do not digress from the main point of what you are writing. Avoid introducing useless or irrelevant information.

- **Style:** Use short sentences and only the necessary number of words. Use factual, not emotive, words in functional writing. For example, do not write 'The company's increase in expenditure this year has been the most disastrous and outrageous example of extravagance and waste.' Instead, write 'This year the company has spent far more than was budgeted.'

- **Avoid the use of slang, commercial jargon and buzzwords:**
    - *Slang* is informal language.
    - *Commercial jargon* is the use of dated or stereotyped formulas. It was once popular in business correspondence but is now out of date. An example of commercial jargon is 'Enclosed herewith' instead of 'I enclose'.
    - *Buzzwords* are more suited for advertising writing or informal conversation.

In addition, good informative writing must be:
- simple, clear and concise
- comprehensive; it must deal with all aspects of the subject
- appropriate to the target audience
- objective in tone.

In this section we examine the different features of reports, instructions, letters, memos, etc., and study how to write them for examination purposes.

Reports
Reports give a factual account of some situation. The main function of a report is to study or analyse material or information and to present it in a clear and standard form.

The layout of a report
Some of the following headings may be used in a report. Not all reports demand such detailed layout; however, it is a good idea to be familiar with the following terms in order to know how to use them:

Terms of reference/title: These are the main issues that the report has to deal with; the instructions that are given to those writing the report about what they have to investigate. A report on the number of school leavers who emigrate and work abroad could have the following terms of reference: 'Report on the number of school leavers who emigrate'.

Introduction: This sets out fully:
- the main details of the report
- the questions under investigation or study
- the time limits
- the material or methods used.

Work carried out: This contains detailed information on what has been done, for example any statistics which have been gathered on the topic.

Findings: Under this heading comes the main body of information gathered in the report. The material in this section must be organised carefully and any irrelevant points must be discarded. Only information relevant to the issue should be included in this section.

Conclusions: The conclusions of the report are based on the terms of reference and the findings. They should flow naturally from all the evidence and findings and should be clear, simple and objective. They may suggest action which could be taken to remedy a situation.

Recommendations: These include your own interpretations of any improvements or points that can be taken into account as a result of your findings during the report. Present these simply and if possible in the form of a list.

Summary: A condensed version of the report, which provides a short, succinct account of both findings and conclusions. A good summary should concentrate on giving an outline of the main points, particularly the conclusions and recommendations.

The following is an example of a report which uses some of the headings described above.

Title
Report on the number of students who work abroad in the summer months.

Introduction
Under instructions from the secretary in the Department of Social Welfare, the following report on the number of students who work abroad in the summer months has been authorised. A list of conclusions and recommendations will be drawn up.

Procedures
A detailed questionnaire was issued nationwide to all houses. This questionnaire was designed to find out how many young people between the ages of 15 and 20 years have succeeded in finding employment abroad during the months of June, July and August.

Findings
On the basis of this questionnaire, it was discovered that most of the students who have sought employment abroad are in third-level colleges, and are aged from 17 years upward.

Conclusions
The majority of students who seek and find employment abroad are studying in third-level colleges. It would seem that the pressure to earn a large amount of money during the summer months is on third-level students, and that employment abroad is the means to achieve this. In addition, third-level students have longer summer holidays, which

> makes it worthwhile to look for employment abroad. Most second-level students manage to stay in the country and find some type of employment.
>
> Sue Hampton
> Department of Social Welfare
> October 2008

COMMENT
A good *title* helps to focus clearly on what the report is about. The *introduction* sums up all aspects of the report, and may include the reasons why the report is being undertaken, the time limits involved, details of those carrying out the report, and who authorised it. The *procedures* section contains detailed information on what has been done to obtain information. In this case, questionnaires were issued. Sometimes surveys and interviews may also be undertaken, and statistics gathered. The *findings* section records details of what has been discovered. The *conclusions* are based on the findings.

How to write a report
The style of report writing must be factual and objective. Avoid the use of emotive or ambiguous language.

Before you begin to write a report, ask yourself the following questions:
- What is the purpose of this report?
- What objectives am I hoping to achieve with this report?

Remember, a report is effective when:
- it is understood without too much effort
- the findings are acknowledged to be valid and are acted upon.

Pre-report writing
It is necessary to spend time preparing the material for a report before actually beginning the process of writing it up. This pre-report writing will determine the quality of the finished product and enable you to structure and organise your material more effectively. As part of the process of gathering material for a report, look at the following points:
1. Establish the purpose or objective of the report – is it to describe or evaluate a situation or set of circumstances? Is the report explaining a procedure or situation?
2. Once you have established the purpose of the report, decide on a title, as this will help you to focus more clearly on what the report is about. You may be asked to write a report on how secondary schoolgirls use their free time at weekends. You could use a title such as the following: 'The use of free time at weekends by schoolgirls aged 14–19.' When you have established a title, it will help you to limit the topic and concentrate on exactly what you must write.
3. Find out who will read the report. This will affect the style of your report. Writing a report for the school committee will demand a different style than writing one for the managing director of a large company.

4. Find out whether the report has a time limit, and if so, what this is.
5. Look at the resources at your disposal. What budget have you been allocated? What equipment have you got? What materials will you need?
6. Study how to structure your report. Will your report be structured in sections with sub-headings? Will the report be a summary?

Checklist for reports
1. Does the title indicate the nature of the report?
2. Are the objectives of the report clearly stated?
3. Are all the terms used in the report clearly defined?
4. Is the report written in the correct tense? Generally, reports are written in the past tense.
5. Is the language of the report clear? Are there obscure phrases, evidence of bias, emotive terms or intemperate language in the report?
6. Are all the claims clearly substantiated by fact?
7. Are the conclusions based on evidence?
8. Are the recommendations feasible?
9. Is the report signed and dated?

Media accounts
A media account of an event usually gives a factual and objective description of what it is reporting. However, this account can often be influenced by a number of things: the type of publication, the readership targeted in the article or the writer's own viewpoint of the event.

Instructions
Instructions can be written on technical or human subjects. Technical subjects involve giving detailed guidelines on following certain procedures, such as changing a light bulb, fixing the plug of a hairdryer or changing the bag of a vacuum cleaner. These types of instructions may use specialised vocabulary and perhaps a series of numbered stages or steps.

On the other hand, instructions can be written on human subjects, such as 'How to increase your self-confidence', 'How to benefit from the points scheme', 'How to cope with exam stress' and so on. In these types of instructions, the use of generalised vocabulary and illustrations helps a great deal. The style is more relaxed and informal.

In writing instructions, as in all writing situations, take into account:
- your subject matter
- your audience
- the best techniques which can be used to communicate that subject matter to that particular audience.

Writing instructions
When you are writing a set of instructions, you must examine the following.
- What is the purpose of the instructions?

- Who are you writing them for?
- How can you write them in the best possible way?

Method

1. Work out exactly what you want to achieve – are you trying to teach children how to cook, or to outline the stages of a game or to operate a machine?
2. Make your statements specific; remember, instructions must be clear.
3. Make sure there is a logical sequence in the stages of your instructions. Each stage should follow on logically from the preceding one.
4. Say one thing in each sentence, and make sure that each stage is manageable.
5. Put the most important item in each sentence at the beginning.
6. Use the imperative form of the verb.
7. Use short sentences and short paragraphs.
8. Avoid jargon.

EXAMPLE 1

How to run

Wear good running shoes.
Run early in the morning as it is better for your health.
Wear comfortable clothing.
Always warm up before you run.
Always run with somebody, never run alone.
Rest every ten minutes or so.
Walk for a few minutes after you finish.
Don't run if you feel tired.
Never drink water while you are running.
Don't run until two hours after eating.
Don't run if you have got a cold.
Don't run fast downhill.
Don't run on roads in fog.

EXAMPLE 2

How to make potato cakes

1. Peel the potatoes and slice them.
2. Put the potatoes in a saucepan with some water and a bit of salt and boil them for 20 minutes.
3. Mash the potatoes.
4. Put the mashed potatoes, the flour and the butter or margarine into a bowl and mix them with a fork.
5. Make 12 potato cakes with the mixture.
6. Fry the potato cakes in a frying pan until they are brown on both sides.
7. Cover the cakes with the grated cheese. Put them in a dish and keep them warm in the oven.

Memos

A memo (or memorandum) may be defined as a letter that is informal and brief in style. The main differences between a letter and a memo are:
- a memo is informal
- the message is immediate
- memos are written within offices or workplaces.

In general, both letters and memos involve
- getting the reader's attention
- making a claim
- supporting the claim by justification or explanation
- calling for action; this may include what you want the reader to do, what you will do or both.

Memos generally explain or outline all details in a short, terse form. Avoid long sentences and pompous words. Use information that is relevant and avoid digressing. Keep a polite and courteous tone.

The following is an example of a memo that has been sent to all Youth Services on behalf of the National Youth Federation.

TO: All member Youth Services
FROM: Martin Walsh
RE: Youth Club Insurance Premium 2010
DATE: 8 September 2010

Since December 2004 the National Youth Federation has succeeded in holding premium costs at the current level, despite escalating changes in the public liability insurance markets. The factors that have enabled the organisation to achieve this have been good standards of administration in the operation of the insurance service and the maintenance of a good track record vis-à-vis claims.

Consequently, I can now confirm that we have managed to keep the increase in insurance rates to 7.5%.

The youth club premium inclusive of registration fee for 2010 is €240.00:
Public Liability Insurance: €180.00
Personal Accident Insurance: €24.00
Total: €204.00
Government Levy: €4.00
NYF Registration Fee: €22.00
Youth Service Registration Fee: €10.00

Letters

There are different kinds of letters.
- **Formal letters:** These include business letters, letters of complaint, letters of application for a job, sales letters, form letters and letters to the newspaper.

- **Personal letters:** These include letters of condolence, letters to a friend or pen pal and letters of sympathy.

When writing any kind of letter:
- know what you want to say
- set out your information logically and in paragraph form
- use the correct layout and tone.

Features of a letter
1. Use correct layout and make it pleasing to the eye.
2. The sender's address is usually written in the top right-hand corner. Often a letter from an organisation or a private individual is on printed letterhead paper that includes the sender's name and address.
3. Write out the date fully, e.g. 23 January 2010. Remember, all letters must be dated. You can lose marks by not putting a date on your letter.
4. Reference numbers are usually written either above or below the recipient's address.
5. Begin the letter by addressing the person by name or simply 'Dear Sir or Madam'.
6. The first sentence should contain the main point of your letter.
7. Conclude your letter with either 'Yours truly' or 'Yours sincerely'. Remember, 'Yours' begins with a capital letter; 'sincerely' has an e; 'truly' has no e.
8. Use the correct tone for the context. Use a formal, tactful and courteous style, especially when you are conveying unwelcome information to someone.
9. Choose appropriate language. Avoid using clichés, verbose or wordy statements and jargon. The language should be clear and simple.

Examinations on the writing of letters and memos are testing:
- the coherent organisation of information
- the use of appropriate expression
- accepted standards of layout.

How to write a letter
1. Decide what you want to say.
2. Set out your information logically and organise it into paragraphs. In a letter, paragraphs are signposts that enable the reader to follow your message more clearly.
3. Choose a suitable tone and vocabulary when writing letters. Remember to be factual and not emotional in letters.
4. Use correct spelling and punctuation.
5. Avoid verbose or long-winded language and clichés. Choose fresh, concise language that is free from jargon.
6. Write the main point of your letter in the first sentence.

Read the following examples of different types of letter and study the commentary carefully.

Letter applying for a job

12 Deansdrive,
Longford.
20 November 2010

The Manager
Duggan Motors
15 Claire Street
Dublin 6

Dear Sir,

I wish to apply for the position of Motor Mechanic that was advertised in the *Evening Herald* on 14 November.

I have had an interest in cars for a number of years. I have been working in the Statoil Service Station in Longford town for the last three summers. I worked as a general assistant and a petrol attendant.

I am very interested in motor mechanics and I feel that I would be ideally suited for this job. I am a member of the Springtide Car Club.

I enclose a copy of my CV together with two current references. I would be available to attend for an interview at any time that is suitable to you.

Yours truly,
Jim Feeney

Letter of complaint to the local newspaper on the topic 'Violence on the Streets'

Dear Sir,

The increase in the number of street brawls has become worrying. Furthermore, I believe that everyone must tackle this serious problem. The gardaí on their own cannot deal effectively with this problem. There is a profound obligation on all of us in politics, in education and in the media to combine our strengths and deal with this issue. Young people themselves have to be challenged to make their own input. I believe young people are the ones who must identify the cultural conditions that have given rise to this appalling situation. More than any other sector in society, I believe that their efforts to find solutions will be the most valuable solution.

Human life has always been held as sacred. I believe that there is an overwhelming need at present to reassess the principles of life and look again at our attitude to the life of another person. I feel that our young people have the right to be brought up in a society that has a clear moral code and a profound respect for the human person. No self-respecting society can turn a blind eye to what is clearly a visible slide into barbarism. Clearly, what happened in Golding's book *Lord of the Flies* is happening on the streets of our cities daily. We must ask ourselves whether we are spreading the problem or working towards some real solution.

Yours sincerely,
Cormac Quinn

Remember, when writing a letter of complaint you must:
- focus clearly on the results you want and not so much on the incompetence of the people involved
- outline your problem clearly without giving way to anger; controlling emotion is essential to get the desired result
- keep a record of all contacts and transactions made
- make sure you are complaining to the right person
- keep letters of complaint short.

Notices and bulletins
Bulletins concentrate on layout and attracting the attention of the reader with short, catchy phrases and words. The aim of notices and bulletins is to attract the attention of a number of different people. For that reason, they must be:
- well positioned on a notice board for all to see
- big and attractively laid out
- up to date.

Notices are effective only if they produce the results that were intended. For that reason, the language should be vigorous and direct. The presentation should be simple and bold and the message comprehensible to everyone. Keep messages brief and terse. The opening or heading should be eye-catching, for example:

> **NOTICE**
> Floor of corridor to Sales Department is
> **Wet**
> **BE CAREFUL!**

Writer's Association
Main Street
Tralee
Ref: 410/2010
Date: 3 August 2010

Dear Member,
The next meeting of our Writer's Association will be held on Tuesday, 24 August at the Teachers' Community Arts Centre, Main Street, Tralee.

Yours sincerely,
Douglas Madden
Secretary

COMMENT
The information in the above notice is reduced to a minimum. The vocabulary is simple, and sentences and paragraphs are short. The layout makes it easy and eye-

catching. Note how two devices from advertising are used:
- the headline, which aims at catching attention
- the appeal to action at the conclusion.

Forms and questionnaires
Forms
1. Read the instructions carefully and follow them.
2. Leave no part of the form unanswered.
3. Supply all details fully, such as first names, dates of attendance on courses or at colleges.
4. Where sections do not apply to you, draw a line through them or simply write 'not applicable'.

Questionnaires
A questionnaire is a document that is circulated in order to obtain information by means of a series of carefully designed questions. This information is then collated and deductions are made about the issues involved.

Sample compositions in the language of information
The following compositions are written in the language of information. They are taken from actual students' work and graded according to the standards required at Ordinary Level. Study them carefully and pay particular attention to the commentary that follows.

Write an informative article for the newspaper on your views about some of the problems experienced in a modern city with which you are familiar. Propose some solutions to these problems and include a title for your article.

> **Horrors of the modern city**
>
> In the past, city inhabitants have had to put up with numerous horrors. These range from living in cramped slums in the inner city to surviving without efficient public transport from the outskirts into the city itself. Today, however, the present horrors of the city, while not being as atrocious as living in one room with ten other people, are almost more infuriating and stress-inducing than any others which a city has encountered before.
>
> At the moment the word on the street is 'traffic'. People don't seem to understand why there are so many delays, and why it takes an hour to make a ten-minute journey. There are a couple of reasons for this, the main one being the huge amount of traffic on the roads. Newspaper reports show photos of lines upon lines of traffic, bumper to bumper, at junctions. What they fail to mention is that it is almost certain that there is only one person in each car. When you think about this, and then think about the fact that there are over 400,000 cars owned by Dubliners, that makes a lot of cars on the road every day. The fact that the number of Dublin registered cars has doubled since 1996 makes for a bleak future on the road if things are to continue in the same pattern.
>
> Another problem our numerous motorists encounter are delays due to roadworks. It is incomprehensible that Dublin City Council go to such lengths to painfully re-lay and

resurface the roads to such a high standard, only to dig them up and lay down wires or cables or pipes within about three months of surfacing the road. These road horrors lead to mayhem both morning and evening at least five days a week. The dreadful accidents occurring daily are a reminder to us of the epidemic of aggression on the roads. As one contributor to the *Irish Times* newspaper noted, it has not reached full-scale road-rage, but there is simply a general 'bloody-minded attitude'.

Many people claim that they wouldn't use their cars, if public transport were more reliable. The DART provides an excellent service to southsiders and a similar service is an absolute necessity throughout the rest of the city. To encourage the use of public transport, laws could be enforced to reduce the cars on the roads in certain areas at certain times. One option that would certainly convince drivers that public transport is worthwhile would be to increase the price of petrol and diesel. Whichever solutions are deemed most suitable, it is vital that something is done to expel this daily nightmare from our city.

A smaller but perhaps more important side effect stemming from the abundance of cars on our roads is pollution. The mass emission of carbon dioxide fumes from exhaust pipes, combined with fumes given out by factories and plants such as the ESB plant on the East Wall, as well as Fuels burnt by private homes are disastrous to the ozone layer. Not only this, but they also pollute the city air. Pollution in the sea, and in Dublin Bay especially, causes our beaches to be dirty, smelly and generally unhealthy. In fact, the Irish Sea has become the most radioactive sea in the world.

Dumping also occurs in the city and on its outskirts. City streets and parks are particularly bad for litter and Dublin's reputation as a clean and beautiful city is rapidly slipping away. A simple solution would be to enforce fines for littering, or better still to place more bins throughout the city for public use. Serious surveillance must also be kept on the outskirts of the city where many people have found it convenient to dump their unwanted goods on farmers' property.

Unfortunately, dumping seems to be one of the lesser horrors our city has to bear. Drugs have ceased to preoccupy the press and the media simply because people have become bored of hearing about this problem. But the stark reality is that drugs continue to devastate families. Now research has also concluded that the problem won't go away too soon. Addiction has been proven to be genetic. The University of Pittsburgh claims that 80% of drug addicts they tested had a particular genetic sequence linked with cocaine addiction. The crime and violence associated with drug addiction remains and poses a gloomy outlook for future generations.

Clearly there are plenty of problems to be addressed in the modern city. Many of these have quite straightforward solutions, others are more complex. Despite this the present government should be concerning themselves more with the here and now instead of wasting time and money on investigations into who paid how much to what ex-politician. The horrors of our city need to be dealt with immediately, or we will be leaving a city that is unbearable to live in for the generations to come.

P: 28 C: 28
L: 27 M: 9
Total: 92 **Grade A1**

Comment

The above composition is an example of the informative use of language. The writer has clearly researched the subject matter and clearly outlines some of the major problems confronting the modern city. There are abundant opinions and suggestions for areas of improvement within the modern city. The language and imagery used are both clear and varied. The writer makes use of relevant and current examples to inform the reader about the current situation. The composition is structured into a clear opening and conclusion.

Write an article for a serious journal, using the language of information, on the topic 'The entertainment industry'.

The entertainment industry is comprised of four different areas – music, film, theatre and television. Since the 1920s, when Hollywood was established in the USA, the entertainment industry was largely associated with America. Now it has branched out all over the world.

Up until the nineties, Ireland had a very small entertainment industry worldwide. Most of the entertainment was contained on a nationwide scale and there was little output on the international front. In the last decade, an unprecedented surge in the growth of Irish entertainment has occurred. This type of entertainment includes music, dance, film, books, and poetry. Music groups such as U2, Boyzone, Enya have achieved huge success abroad. These groups together with the many Eurovision awards have helped to put Ireland on the map. Shows such as Michael Flatley's *Lord of the Dance* and *Riverdance* have revolutionised Irish dancing throughout the world. In the world of film, we have experienced success in movies such as *The Commitments*, *The General* and *Angela's Ashes*.

The entertainment industry thrives on its many famous stars such as Arnold Schwarzenegger, Bruce Willis, Tom Cruise, Jack Nicholson. The Oscars has become one of the most prestigious events in the entertainment world. Awards for various films, film directors and actors form the highlight of this popular event.

Current fashions and trends are heavily influenced by the entertainment industry. Teenagers worship celebrities from all over the world and view them as role models. Unfortunately, some of these celebrities overindulge in both drink and drugs and sadly can cause a good deal of problems for teenagers.

Ireland has seen an influx of celebrities and filmmakers in the country. Many film stars and famous musicians have come to settle down in Ireland. They have a lot more privacy here as both the press and fans tend to leave them in peace. In addition, more and more films are being made in Ireland because of tax exemptions. Recent films include *Saving Private Ryan*, *Angela's Ashes*, *The Blockbuster*.

Theatre has also been a rich source of entertainment for years. Shows such as *Cats* and *Jesus Christ Superstar* have been running for years in London's West End and on Broadway. Theatre is a huge source of income for the economy each year. Many Irish shows have won acclaim throughout the world.

The entertainment industry has contributed to the richness and enjoyment of people's lives for centuries now. In addition, it has contributed to increasing the economy of countries by providing employment, and through its various styles of production. It is an industry that can only continue to flourish.

P: 28
C: 29
L: 28
M: 8
Total: 93 **Grade A2**

COMMENT

This is an original piece of informative writing on the subject of 'The entertainment industry'. The writer has taken examples from a broad field of entertainment: film, theatre, dance and music. The writer has organised the points into different paragraphs each of which outlines a different aspect of the entertainment industry. The writer is clear and concise in the use of language.

Perhaps for that higher mark, the writer could develop some of the points made in a bit more detail.

Exercises on writing in the language of information
1. Write an informative report on the subject of third-level educational opportunities for students from the inner cities.
2. Compose an informative article for your school magazine on your proposals on how to get rid of waste products.
3. Write an account of some area of technology with which you are familiar. In your account, outline the advantages of the system you are writing about.

PERSUASIVE WRITING

Persuasive writing is used by writers to try to convince you about something. It is the type of writing that forms the framework of political speeches, advertising writing and marketing.

Persuasion can be carried out by:
- manipulation
- appealing to the emotions
- argument.

The language of argument and that of persuasion are quite similar; however, the techniques used in each are distinctive. Because the aim of the persuasive writer is to manipulate feeling and emotion, there is a heavy reliance on emotive vocabulary, using feeling and emotion to elicit agreement or acquiescence.

Uses of persuasive writing
- Letters.

- Political speeches.
- Film reviews.
- Some newspaper reports.
- Advertising writing.
- Marketing journals.

Features of persuasive writing

Because persuasive writing aims to convince you about something, most of the techniques used are directed at the emotions and senses rather than at the intellect. The language of persuasion relies on emotive argument in order to communicate its message more forcibly to the reader.

All types of persuasive writing use the same tactics. It is important to examine the following features of persuasive writing, which are used by writers to persuade or convince. The language of advertising in particular makes use of many of these features:

- slogans
- repetition
- statistics
- imperatives and commands
- rhyming words
- rhetorical questions
- buzzwords
- tones
- humour
- irony and satire
- instructive writing.

Slogans

A slogan may be defined as a short, punchy phrase that sums up an idea. Headlines or advertisements usually contain slogans. A slogan is a point made without any support, for example:

> Colour with confidence.
> Only the sweetest young peas pass the bird's eye.
> Keeps colour fabulous, not faded.
> Cherry Crush – get a new crush on colour.
> A fragrance to seduce the senses.

The purpose of a slogan is to fix an image in your head, so the writer uses graphic images, and perhaps a play on words wherever possible.

Repetition

Repetition is a hallmark of persuasive writing, particularly of the language of advertising. Look at the following examples of effective word repetition taken from an advertisement:

It takes an entire year to build a Rolex. Every single one of those parts will have been tested. Every single part inspected and cleaned over and over again. The case will have been sculpted from solid metal. The case back will have been screwed shut. No wonder it takes a year to build a Rolex. No wonder it can take a lifetime to appreciate it.

Look at the following lines taken from an advertisement on olive oil:

Use it as we do – in cooking, in baking, in dressing every kind of salad. Good for the heart. Good for the health. Good for the taste buds too!

Statistics

Statistics are another device used by persuasive writers in order to win a reader over to accepting another viewpoint. The use of statistics lends an air of authority to an otherwise dubious piece of writing. Look at the following example of statistics taken from advertisements:

99% of migraine sufferers find relief from Dynoc.
85% of school kids fight the flu with vitamin C.
80% of businesses now use Sprint.
Now 82% of people in the country have chosen to opt for a Baxi central heating system.

Imperatives and commands

Imperatives and commands are also a feature of persuasive writing. Imperatives demand immediate action:

Buy now . . .
Send in this form and you will receive . . .
Order today . . .
Pay in the next ten days and you will receive . . .
All you have to do is . . .
Use this coupon to send for our free brochure . . .

The use of such language in persuading somebody creates a sense of urgency in the reader or audience.

Rhyming words

Persuasive writing often uses words that rhyme, as this can create a sense of movement in the article or piece of writing. For example, look at the following sets of words and analyse their effect:

Penetrates to the point of pain.
The weed killer that really kills weeds.
The outcome is income.
Get the fruit zing and a tonic spring.

Rhetorical questions

A rhetorical question may be defined as one that is used to emphasise a point. The question usually contains the answer within itself and is used merely as a device to persuade.

> How can something that's so good taste so great?
> How can a 9-LB vacuum be so powerful?
> Just how fast is fast?
> Do you have enough RAM to make a splash?
> How about a tasty tonic to help you get up and go?
> Feeling housebound instead of outward bound?

Buzzwords

Buzzwords may be defined as words that are popular and familiar to the general reader. They are used to attract and sway a reader over to adopting another side, for example:

> Technology so affordable you can extend the virtual office to virtually everyone.
> Fashion Flash: Update that cool look with fashion's best buys.
> Chill out in a relaxing room that's rich with eastern promise.
> Desirable Denim makes the perfect cover-up on a breezy summer day.

Tone

Tone is the relationship that a writer establishes with the reader. Tone is a very important ingredient of effective persuasive writing. A writer wishing to persuade can adopt any number of tones, including:
- humour
- irony or satire
- instruction.

Humour

A writer can also use humour to illustrate a point, as in the following paragraph about computers.

> Of all the bits and pieces connected to computers, floppy disks cause us the most pain. An American company lost many man-hours trying to track down a fault in their chief executive's brand new personal computer. He would work away happily but the next day there would be gaps in the reports and tables he had compiled. The machine and the software were tested, the walls were checked for possible radiation leaks, the secretary grilled for possible sabotage. But the specialists could find nothing wrong.
>
> After a week of checks and head scratching the data processing manager was called in to explain herself. Only then did she notice that the boss stored his floppy disks by sticking them to the sides of his steel desk with magnets.

Irony and satire

Both irony and satire can by used by a writer for purposes of ridicule or mockery. Irony can also be used to hammer home a point more effectively. In the following paragraph, the writer makes clever use of irony to mock the ability of humankind to deceive themselves.

> If humankind could take unto itself one of the gifts given to the simpler creatures, it would surely be the power of flight. Somehow a bird in flight seems to represent for us the essence of the human spirit, to symbolise our longing for freedom. We have even imported the notion of flight into our everyday speech as a source of our most common metaphors. It is not surprising, then, that we have laboured ceaselessly and in a variety of ways to master the art of personal flight. And we have been utterly confounded in our ambitions. The truth of the matter is that we were never intended to fly. Our bodies are not streamlined; our skeletons are not hollow. Nevertheless, we continue to delude ourselves. We announce that we intend 'to fly', as though somehow we were doing it all by ourselves! Come to think of it, this is our attitude to everything, isn't it?

COMMENT
The above passage is an excellent example of a writer's use of irony and satire. The writer wishes to point out how humans delude or fool themselves about their ability to fly. The writer mocks this blindness in humankind and then goes on to satirise the fact that we are like this (we fool ourselves) about everything.

Instructive writing
This type of writing instructs or teaches the reader about something. A writer uses the imperative *must* or *have to* and a dogmatic tone in this type of writing. Look at the following example of dogmatic or instructive writing.

> As man proceeds towards his announced goal of the conquest of nature, he has written a depressing record of destruction, directed not only against the earth he inhabits but against the life that shares it with him. The history of the recent centuries has its black passages – the slaughter of the buffalo on the western plains, the massacre of the shore birds by the market gunners, the near-extermination of the egrets for their plumage. Now, to these and others like them, we are adding a new chapter, and a new kind of havoc – the direct killing of birds, mammals, fishes, and indeed practically every form of wildlife by chemical insecticides indiscriminately sprayed on the land.
>
> (Rachel Carson, *Silent Spring*)

Writing in the language of persuasion
As a good persuasive writer you must be able to:
- express your views clearly and logically
- foresee all possible angles of opposition and be able to tackle them effectively.

How to construct or write a persuasive composition
Before you begin to engage in any type of persuasive composition, whether it involves writing an article for a youth magazine or a serious journal or constructing an advertisement, be aware of the following points:

- know your audience or reader
- know your subject
- establish the correct tone with your audience or reader
- state your purpose clearly
- use persuasive techniques.

Know your audience

Have a good knowledge of who the reader or audience is. A striking talk on drug dependence is hardly likely to stimulate a group of old-age pensioners. Similarly, an excellent article outlining the advantages of pension schemes will not attract the attention of a group of teenagers. Identify as clearly as possible your audience/reader's level of knowledge, their motivations and interest in reading the article.

The following headlines are all taken from different magazines and are written in a persuasive style. Identify the particular target audience in each case.

> Meet the Kellogg's family
> Relief for Knee Pain
> New help for an old problem
> For a great night's sleep you really need a Sealy
> First Rule in Business: Watch your back

Know your subject

It makes no sense to start writing about something that you know nothing about, particularly when you are trying to persuade somebody to adopt your viewpoint. Consider the following paragraph on the subject of women and the fashion industry.

> Does the fashion industry contribute anything to our society? We must ask ourselves this question. Fashion designers take advantage of women and they simply use them in order to make more money. Women are different than men because they depend more on how they look and it affects them more.

COMMENT

There is nothing in the above sentences on the subject of women and the fashion industry that will help you to adopt any viewpoint on this subject. The ideas are weak and repetitive.

REWRITTEN VERSION

> **Women and the fashion industry**
> It has to be admitted that the fashion industry really contributes little to society. Fashion designers are rarely concerned with vital things like warmth, comfort and durability. They are only interested in outward appearance and they take advantage of the fact that women will put up with any amount of discomfort, provided they look right.

> There can hardly be a man who hasn't at some time in his life smiled at the sight of a woman shivering in a flimsy dress on a wintry day, or delicately picking her way through deep snow in dainty shoes. When comparing men and women in the matter of fashion, the conclusions to be drawn are obvious. Men are too sensible to let themselves be bullied by fashion designers.

COMMENT
In the above extract on the same topic, the writer gives examples to support the points made. These examples are clearly stated and relevant. Remember to research your subject well before beginning to write on it.

Establish the correct tone with your audience
Once you have identified your target audience, adapt your message and tone accordingly. You cannot use a lofty or philosophical tone with a group of schoolchildren; neither can you use a colloquial tone of address in a speech to the governors of your school, for example. Do not use informal language or slang if you are addressing a group of academics or the Minister for Education. Similarly, do not use formal language if you are writing on pop music for a teenage magazine.

It can sometimes help to introduce a note of humour or irony into your writing in order to gain the attention of your readers more readily.

State your purpose clearly and confidently
Outline your intention clearly in your opening paragraph.

Use persuasive techniques
Some examples of persuasive techniques can be the use of effective images or anecdotes in order to support your viewpoint. These can also serve the functions of arousing certain emotions about your topic in readers and of getting them on your side.

The following paragraphs are an excellent example of how humour and the anecdote work together to communicate the fact that this generation defines itself by the shoes it wears.

> There's a defining moment in *Saturday Night Fever* that puts you right inside the head of the main characters. It's not the tragedy on Brooklyn Bridge, or the great, final dancing sequence. It's the scene where John Travolta's character Tony and his friend are having a heart-to-heart. It's a poignant moment as Tony's friend tells him he can't fit in with Tony's gang, no matter how hard he tries. Tony attempts in vain to console him as they stand face to face. His friend won't listen any more; he turns and walks away in tears. The camera pulls out, and what are *they*? The poor guy is walking on huge, 12-inch platform shoes. You want to laugh (in fact you do), but he's wearing them because he's too small and he wants to be as tall and as cool as the gang. It's at that point you know what chasing the disco fans of 1970s Brooklyn felt like. It was all about the shoes. Just like Dublin these days, really.

> One by-product of our booming economy is that young people have more money to spend on big shoes. 'You are your shoes!' the magazine ads seem to shriek as groups of youths in three-tier gold trainers glare out of the page at you. You should be wearing shoes a children's TV presenter wouldn't wear, in an array of zany colours that beggars belief. Shoe-gaze next time you're out at the weekend. They're everywhere, overbalancing at bars and stumbling after taxis every Friday and Saturday night. And that's just the guys.

Bear in mind the following guidelines when writing a persuasive composition or article:
1. Avoid the use of sweeping statements or vague, broad generalisations such as the following:
   All students suffer from extreme examination pressure.
   All Irish people are alcoholics.
   Refugees are untidy.
   All teenagers take drugs.
   All students study.
   Teachers are strict.
2. Do not make unsupported statements. Back up each point you make with sufficient evidence or effective illustrations.
3. Avoid using an aggressive or a bitter tone, as it will only alienate your reader.
4. Do not distort the truth. While a certain amount of hyperbole or exaggeration is permissible in persuasive writing, it is never acceptable to distort or pervert the truth or to tell a lie in your writing.

Sample compositions in the language of persuasion

The following compositions are written in the language of persuasion. They are taken from actual students' work and graded according to the standards required at Ordinary Level. Study them carefully and pay particular attention to the commentary that follows.

Compose a persuasive speech for your class on your ideas on the topic 'Is it now time for male liberation?'

> Dear fellow students, I would like to address you today on the topic of male liberation.
>
> It is true that women's liberation has come a long way, especially over the last thirty years. Feminists worldwide have sought for equality of rights quite successfully. Women now enjoy the right to a career and the right to vote, thanks to their hard-working predecessors. However, it is certainly not time for women to give up their fight, or, worse still, for men to seek male liberation. Women may have been awarded equal rights, but that doesn't mean that prejudices don't exist.
>
> These days it is common to see almost as many women as there are men in the workplace and this is a significant achievement for women's liberation. Unfortunately, the workplace is a typical atmosphere in which women suffer abuse, degradation and even assault. You merely need to read the daily papers and weekly magazines for proof. Over

60% of females starting a new job are harassed by male employers, 70% of women beginning work feel pressure to have a close relationship with their boss and would be afraid to refuse the offer of a drink after work. These are not circumstances that suggest that male liberation is necessary.

Furthermore, women are subjected to bias where promotion is concerned. In America a man has a 27% better chance of being promoted than a woman. Women may be physically weaker than men, but they are stronger emotionally. A woman is less likely to crumble under severe pressure. Men under serious mental pressure are more likely to react aggressively.

Another prejudice in the workplace concerns pregnancy and maternity leave. Maternity leave is granted to women for a period before the birth and for a period after the child is born. Obviously a mother needs to care for her newborn child. But doesn't the child belong to the father as well? Is it not deemed necessary for a man to care for his baby? Men are not expected to care for a child in the same way as a woman and this is wrong. Fathers should have to take 'paternity leave' to support their wives and to share the work of bringing up the child.

The media is a living proof that women have not reached the same level as men in modern life. Advertising is one of the single most prejudiced areas of the nineties. The recent 'Wonderbra' campaign is a mockery to women's liberation. It uses a beautiful blonde with a voluptuous cleavage to advertise what is supposed to be a woman's product, to men. The first slogan was 'Hello Boys!'. This has since been followed by such sexist remarks as 'I can't cook, but who cares?'. These advertisements imply that as long as a girl is 'well endowed' physically, then she doesn't need anything else to be attractive. A second campaign is the Fiat Punto car. This advertisement uses a naked Claudia Schiffer to promote its sale. Are women not expected to buy this car, or are they supposed to be attracted to a blonde woman wearing no clothes?

What about the atrocious conditions of women in Middle Eastern, Asian and South American countries? When girls are born under Taliban rules they are considered useless. They are slaves of their father and brothers until they are married. Then they become the 'property' of their husband. They must cover every part of their body, and are not allowed outside in daylight. If a woman commits adultery, she is imprisoned or even stoned. Yet, a man may have as many wives as he chooses.

These conditions are even more unacceptable than those in the western world. It seems totally insane that women who make up half the population of the world, are subjected to such intolerable lives. I ask you ladies and gentlemen, surely, before men seek male liberation, women must first be able to enjoy equal status within the world, without bias or prejudice? I think you will agree that it is not yet time for male liberation.

Chairperson, fellow speakers, teachers and pupils, thank you for listening.

P: 28
C: 29
L: 29
M: 9
Total: 95 **Grade A1**

Comment

This is a good example of persuasive writing on a challenging topic. The writer uses many different techniques of persuasion, for example the use of relevant examples such as women in the workplace and the pressures they experience. The writer also makes reference to the media and the advertising strategies that are used there. The writer takes both sides and foresees all possible opposition.

Compose a persuasive article on the topic 'Television is the opium of the people'. Target your writing at young teenagers.

> It's been a long hard stressful day at school. A student trudges solemnly home, under a weight of work still to be done. After labouring for a few minutes with the front door lock, she hurls her schoolbag to the floor with the usual feeling of revulsion. Enter mother with the customary line, 'How was your day?' She receives a grunt in reply. Right now the student simply does not want to engage in conversation, in fact the only activity she desires is one that requires absolutely no brain power – switch on the TV.
>
> In a house not too far from this scene an over-tired teacher decides he has had enough of corrections for one day. He wades through a vast array of assignments and tests, to the safe haven of the living room, to relax in front of the telly for a few minutes . . .
>
> It's been many a long year since the television cast its nets over the world, and there's no denying the effect and significance of the catch. Like a snake charmer, she plays her haunting melodies and we all submit to her sorcery.
>
> The box entertains us, informs us, relaxes us and intrigues us. We are collectively captivated. It is my belief that the underlying reason for our enthralment is the simple fact that we have to put nothing back into it.
>
> A hugely popular song released this year is entitled 'You get what you give', meaning that what you get out of life is a result of the effort you make. The small screen is the one glorified exception – all of the magic is ours in return for nothing.
>
> I am a self-confessed TV addict. I quiver with delight at the opening titles of my favourite shows or movies. I covet the lives and figures of my favourite characters. I anxiously wait for the utterly obvious to happen. I've tried to ignore my little habit; persuade myself I could cut down to one or two hours at the weekend, but there are times when I'm tired, stressed and depressed, and I am sure I see a celestial light shining down on that wonderful feat of science. It is times like those when I know I must surrender myself to that temptation with complete abandon.
>
> I'm going in to rehabilitation. Though there are few amenities for the TV addict, and support groups are hard to come by, I have developed a treatment, which I'm sure many other people around the globe could reap the benefits from. The moment I feel myself reaching for that remote control, I start to think of how I could otherwise be spending my time – how I could achieve something, and perhaps have something to show at the end of the day.
>
> There's a great poem in my old Junior Cert. textbook. It's by Roald Dahl and it's called 'Just suppose there was no TV'. It suggests that our minds and imaginations would be a

lot healthier and I would probably be forced to agree, despite my affection for the thing. Life after all, is supposed to be something interactive, not something you watch other people experience.

When I look back on the years I spent at a height of less than five feet, I remember all the ridiculous things I got up to with my sister and my friends. In the years to come, when I reminisce about my teenage years, I don't want them to be punctuated by the latest series of *Friends*, or any other programme.

According to John Locke, 'No man's knowledge here can go beyond his experience.' That goes to show that it is our duty to have a taste of everything we can. Therefore, we can't afford to waste valuable time in front of the box, can we?

P: 28
C: 28
L: 27
M: 9
Total: 92 **Grade A1**

Comment

The above composition on television is a good example of effective persuasive writing. The writer uses an anecdote in the opening paragraph in order to introduce the topic and establish certain attitudes towards the subject. The language and style used is lively and energetic. All of the examples and references are relevant and appropriate.

Exercises on writing in the language of persuasion

1. Write a short persuasive article for your local newspaper on the value of having sport as a compulsory part of the curriculum. Target your article at a general readership.
2. Write a newspaper review of any film or play you have seen. In your review, point out the main merits of the film or play and the reasons why you would recommend it.
3. Compose a persuasive composition for a teenage magazine that seeks to establish the need for a greater degree of selectivity in the viewing of television programmes.
4. Write an advertisement for your favourite make-up, targeting it at your own class. In the advertisement, include price and special offers, and make use of imperatives.
5. Write a persuasive article for a popular magazine on your view of working mothers.

Descriptive writing: The aesthetic use of language

This section deals with the way descriptive language can be used to create an aesthetic effect in writing. The emphasis is on how adjectives and other words can be used to create an idea of beauty and harmony. When a writer uses language in an aesthetic manner, there is a focus on painting vivid pictures or images.

Uses of the language of aesthetics
- Fiction.
- Drama.
- Film.
- Poetry.

Features of the aesthetic use of language
1. The use of imagery, i.e. the capacity of words to create pictures. Imagery can also be defined as word pictures; it is the way a writer uses words to conjure up a picture or image about something. Imagery is at the basis of all writing but is particularly important in poetry, drama and certain types of fiction and, in a different way, in film.
2. A stress on how language can be used in an artistic way.
3. The different ways in which words can be used to create concepts of beauty and harmony.

Sample passages that demonstrate the aesthetic use of language

> Then at dawn we came down to a temperate valley,
> Wet, below the snow line, smelling of vegetation;
> With a running stream and a water-mill beating the darkness,
> And three trees on the low sky,
> And an old white horse galloped away in the meadow.
> Then we came to a tavern with vine-leaves over the lintel,
> Six hands at an open door dicing for pieces of silver,
> And feet kicking the empty wine-skins.
>
> (T. S. Eliot, 'Journey of the Magi')

COMMENT
The above extract, from the poem 'Journey of the Magi' by T. S. Eliot, is an example of the use of clear descriptive language.

Question A [Comprehension]
(i) Pick out three different images that you like. Write a short note on why they appeal to you.
(ii) What type of atmosphere is created in the above lines? Support your answer by reference to the extract.

Question B: [Writing task]
Imagine you are one of the characters in the above extract. Write an imaginative account of what happens to you.

> And so it happened that on a warm windy evening I drove over to East Egg to see two old friends whom I scarcely knew at all. Their house was even more elaborate than I expected, a cheerful red-and-white Georgian Colonial mansion, overlooking the bay. The lawn

started at the beach and ran towards the front door for a quarter of a mile, jumping over sundials and brick walls and burning gardens – finally when it reached the house drifting up the side in bright vines as though from the momentum of its run. The front was broken by a line of French windows, glowing now with reflected gold, and wide open to the warm windy afternoon, and Tom Buchanan in riding clothes was standing with his legs apart on the front porch.

We walked through a high hallway into a bright rosy-coloured space, fragilely bound into the house by French windows at either end. The windows were ajar and gleaming white against the fresh grass outside that seemed to grow a little way into the house. A breeze blew through the room, blew curtains in at one end and out the other like pale flags, twisting them up towards the frosted wedding cake of the ceiling, and then rippled over the wine-coloured rug, making a shadow on it as wind does on the sea.

(F. Scott Fitzgerald, *The Great Gatsby*)

COMMENT
The above description is a vivid example of how language can be used to please the senses, or, in other words, aesthetically.

Question A [Comprehension]
(i) Describe the features of the characters represented in the above extract.
(ii) Pick out two examples of the writer's use of vivid images and explain what they represent to you.

Question B [Writing task]
Write a conclusion to the above passage.

How to write in the language of aesthetics
The ability to write in a way that demonstrates the aesthetic quality of language involves a capacity to use images. Language that is aesthetic is rich in beautiful imagery and description. Learn the art of writing description well. Good descriptive writing concentrates on giving a clear, vivid picture. Conrad has described descriptive writing in the following way: 'By the power of the written word, makes you hear, makes you feel; above all makes you see.' Good description, therefore, concentrates on involving all of the senses.

Method for writing descriptive composition
1. Select details of what you are describing with great care, and concentrate on registering a few small details.
2. Be selective in what you write about when describing. Do not include every feature, but concentrate on one or two.
3. Refer to time in some way. This can be the geographical context, the country, county, the landscape, or the time, season or historical period.
4. Remember effective imagery is created:
   - through association of words

- by means of similes, metaphors or rhythm
- by direct description.
5. Use images and language that appeal to the different senses. Visual images can include features of colour, shape and size. The use of images that appeal to the ear, or to the senses of taste and touch, create a deep and lasting impression on your reader. Look at the following description, which draws on all the senses to gain the maximum effect.

> The scullery was water, where the old pump stood. And it had everything else that was related to water: thick steam of Mondays edgy with starch; soapsuds boiling, bellying and popping, creaking and whispering, rainbowed with light and winking with a million windows. Bubble bubble toil and grumble, rinsing and slapping of sheets and shirts, and panting mother rowing her red arms like oars in the steaming waves. Then the linen came up out of the pot like pastry or woven suds or sheets of moulded snow.
>
> (Laurie Lee, *Cider With Rosie*)

COMMENT

The effect of the description is to conjure up a highly vivid picture of the scullery and how the washing was done. The writer draws on all the senses: the sense of smell through the starch and the soapsuds, the sense of touch in the references to 'slapping the sheets' and 'rowing her red arms like oars in the steaming waves'.

Describing people

The ability to draw an effective description of a character requires the following:
- drawing an image of their inner character, motivations, moods, situation
- painting a picture of their background, age, professional situation, emotional state.

Sometimes a writer uses the actions of a character or their particular environment to show how they feel inside. For example, look at the following description.

> She turned and went back into the bedroom, sitting at her triptych mirror to begin the nightly brushing of her hair. As she picked up the brush she leaned forward and angrily plucked out a long strand, bright as a silver wire, examining it as though it were infected. Her blue cotton nightgown was cut in a deep V exposing her long white back, the vertebrae like knuckles down her spine. She took up the brush again and began to comb her hair forward over her face with a jerking movement which brought back to him the sight of her kneeling at the toilet bowl, her finger in her mouth, retching as she vomited up half a box of chocolates or part of a cream cake, eaten less than an hour before.
>
> (Brian Moore, *Lies of Silence*)

COMMENT

The above description highlights the fact that this woman is angry and dissatisfied with life. We also learn from the description that she obviously has an eating disorder.

Remember, when you use language to register the deeply aesthetic dimension, you need to use your imagination in a powerful and creative way. All styles of poetry, drama and film and some styles of fiction are examples of where language can be used in an aesthetic manner. Plays and drama depend on the ability to write effective dialogue for their effect. Good dialogue must highlight the interactions between the different characters in a terse, punchy and effective way.

Sample compositions demonstrating the aesthetic use of language

The following compositions show how language can be used in an aesthetic way. They are taken from actual students' work and graded according to the standards required at Ordinary Level. Study them carefully and pay particular attention to the commentary that follows.

Write an imaginative composition with the title 'The Concert'.

> The shrill chatter of excited ticket holders was abandoned in the lobby, and only the odd tentative whisper was heard as the congregation made their way to their seats, in a most reverential fashion. They waited, to receive that minute piece of perfection, which they had paid dearly for, but where was the bearer of this most precious gift?
>
> The air was taut with expectation, but still nothing happened. Ladies shuffled in their seats, making sure they were safely established to get a full view of the piano. Men cleared their throats and squinted once more at the programme in the dim light. The orchestra flicked through their music once more, having long since finished tuning up. The hall was in an uneasy slumber, yet anticipation tainted the air – its colours growing darker by the minute. The slowness of time was reflected in the soft fluidity of every small, gradual movement made and the sad silence provided the backdrop for all of this.
>
> The soul of the place was irretrievably altered with one swift movement as the stage door was glided back with startling speed. A short, stocky man, with flyaway hair and an ill-fitting tuxedo was outlined in the doorway. His face was creased with concentration. Each line that extended over his unforgettable features told a story of a lifetime spent in striving for perfection, that every note he dared to touch in his career had been organised, that the ardour he felt for the music increased his talent tenfold. He gave strength to Wallace Stevens' belief that 'Music is feeling, then, not sound'. All this was to be seen in those crevasses on the small man's face, his genius was on display for all, but only if they knew how to look.
>
> They did not know how. The overwhelming relief spread through the crowd like a mighty wave, and was carefully channelled in to thunderous applause, which flooded towards the stage. They were not here to understand, just to appreciate. One was not required to fathom the bare truth or naked motivation – the raw passion for the art. It wasn't expected.
>
> Dutifully, the pianist stepped to the front of the stage and was consequently drowned in more applause.
>
> He drew nearer to the piano with short, languid steps, as the last trickles of applause faded away. The anticipation was almost unbearable.

It appeared he was finally going to sit at the instrument, but he moved carefully past the stool. He caressed the smooth, pleasing, black side of the piano with a tenderness usually reserved for the tiniest and frailest of babies. Suddenly, the piano no longer seemed like an inanimate object. This masterly artist had breathed a spirit, a life into it that was previously inconceivable. They were to work together. The onlookers were captivated, enchanted, and collectively held their breath.

With the slightest dint of a smile, he moved back towards the stool. He sat down slowly, and arranged himself as well as he could. He surveyed the inviting keys, inhaling their magical power. He was overcome by their seduction, unable to look away, but still not ready to play.

In limbo, time is no significance. Those delicate, porcelain hands, unusually long and elegant, hovered over the keyboard. It was time.

Nobody can remember the first note, nor can they remember the last, but a great force had entered that auditorium and left an indelible imprint on the soul of the listener, and altered their views and definitions of music. Each note spoke so much more than any words; each bar brought many emotions.

This short, stocky man, with flyaway hair and an ill-fitting tuxedo had brought his sorcery to his audience, cast his spell over them. As his fingers moved deftly across the keys, he seemed to be in control, yet also it was as if the music consumed him. He was the music – it came from a dark place within him.

To describe the music would be an impossible task. How would you define music to a deaf person? There are no words adequate enough and no accurate definitions to be found. The applause swelled and hung in the air for eternity.

P: 29
C: 29
L: 28
M: 9
Total: 95 **Grade A1**

Comment

The writer here makes use of description in a very effective manner. Images such as 'the shrill chatter of excited ticket holders', 'the air was taut with expectation', 'a short stocky man with flyaway hair and an ill-fitting tuxedo was outlined in the doorway' give the reader a very clear picture of the whole scene. The writer cleverly shows the whole atmosphere of the place and this is clearly sustained throughout. There is a strong sense of unity in the storyline – the writer links the opening and concluding paragraphs very effectively.

Compose a short descriptive account of some scene in nature that impressed you. In your account concentrate on using small details in your descriptions.

A sharp and bitter east wind blows in across the meadows stirring the clumps of withered grass that rises above the patches of soft crisp snow. It whistles through the tall gaunt trees at the top of the valley and shakes the feathers of the blackbird that is perched on a high branch. One single robin turns towards the biting wind and bares his red breast before flying swiftly across the stormy sky. Clouds loom up from the horizon.

Beyond the valley lay the sea like a mighty animal lifting the spray from the waves and bursting into white spume on the cliffs. Gannets move in from the bay, their wings flashing like light against the sky as they glide effortlessly across the silver grey sea. Strips of sunlight catch the breakers on the rocks.

Up in the hills the wind continues to curl through the dead leaves impaling itself on a scraggy hawthorn branch or on a strand of barbed wire. A yellowhammer flits through a gorse bush lending a flash of colour to a nearby bush. The holly and ash trees hiss amid the quivering of the wind, while the boughs of the large beech tree rustle loudly.

On the rim of the quarry a vixen lies looking out across the valley. Above the meadow, a heron circles slowly on its big grey wings. The vixen's ears twitch to the sound of machines below in the valley. Much more pleasant however, is the sound of the water flowing from the mountain stream filling the entire valley with a sense of freshness and fertility. The dark silhouette of a rook can be seen winging its way across the green, lush fields to the long row of beech trees that stretch up from the meadows.

As the sun begins to set, it spills a gold light across the low western hills. Streaks of light radiate from golden-edged clouds. A cow stands at the edge of the reedy lake. The wind begins to ruffle the calm waters of the lake and fan the reeds so that they look like great goose quills lodged in the mud. A flock of gulls lying on the short grass near the lake rise up languidly and drift like blown snowflakes over the rim of the cliff.

The vixen eases herself up as she hears whimpering in the den. She makes her way through the dock leaves and under the brambles beneath the overhanging rocks where her cubs wait to be fed. As she curls her bush around them and gives them warmth, there is a contented silence in the quarry. The evening smoke begins to drift low from the chimneys of the valley. Night has settled in.

P: 27
C: 27
L: 28
M: 9
Total: 91 **Grade A1**

COMMENT

The above piece of writing is an example of how language can be used in an aesthetic way. The writer concentrates on drawing some vivid and clear pictures of nature and natural scenes. Note the emphasis on colour: 'red breast', 'white spume', 'grey sea', 'dark silhouette', 'sun spills a gold light'.

The writing here is characterised by its sharp emphasis on drawing clear description through a series of small but significant details, such as 'the sea like a mighty animal', 'gannets move in from the bay', ' the dark silhouette of a rook wings its way across the green, lush fields', 'streaks of light radiate from golden-edged clouds'.

Exercises on writing in the language of aesthetics

1. Write a descriptive article for a holiday magazine on a city scene preparing for a new millennium.
2. Compose a sketch or dramatic scene for a play on any topic you are interested in. Focus on drawing out specific features of the characters you are presenting.
3. Write a poem or short story on some scene from city life that has impressed you. In your story, concentrate on using small details in your descriptions.

ANSWERING QUESTION B, PAPER I

This section will deal with the short writing exercises that are asked in Question B in Paper I. In this section, there will be samples on how to write:

- interviews
- reviews
- diary entries
- a speech
- a radio talk
- text for a property page of a newspaper
- writing on a photo/picture.

Interview

You may be asked to write an interview with someone who is famous or a popular TV personality.

Start by giving your reader a clear picture of who you are representing (a radio or TV show) and who exactly you are interviewing.

You are a disc jockey in a popular radio show. Write out an interview you had with a famous model or actor.

> Hi! Roddy Stewart here from Radio Dublin. This is your early morning show and here with me today is the beautiful Kate Moss on a short trip to Dublin.
>
> Roddy: Hi Kate, welcome to Dublin and especially to our show this morning. It's great you managed to make it to our studios. We know you're here for a big fashion show in the RDS. How are things going?
>
> Kate: Great, Rod. And thanks for inviting me on your show. We launched the show last night, so things were pretty busy.
>
> Roddy: I notice you're bringing your baby with you now everywhere. It's so cute. You and Pete must be delighted.
>
> Kate: Yes, things are definitely looking up. Myself and Pete are moving on in spite of all the media talk and hype, which certainly can get you down.

COMMENT
This is just a short extract of an interview. The important thing to note is to give each speaker a new line for their conversation. Write the name each time and follow this with a colon, as is done above.

It can help to know something about the person and to use this as material in your interview.

Review
You may be asked to write a review of a restaurant, CD, film, book or popular soap.

Reviews at Leaving Cert level do not need strict, formal headings. However, it can help to follow the usual format of a review without the headings.

> I recently took it upon myself to visit the new gastro pub off Fletcher Street. Sarnium can be found next to the AIB. Upon entering, one is exposed to black leather chaise lounges, diamond-encrusted tabletops and dim lighting. These hints of post-Celtic Tiger materialism can seem daunting and intimidating. However, I managed to convince my somewhat uneasy partner to scan the menu.
>
> I gingerly opened the leather-bound menu while cradling a glass of house wine in my hand. I opted for the feta cheese salad drizzled with an opulent brandy sauce and served on a bed of crisply tossed lettuce. Don opted for the safe fillet steak with pepper sauce.
>
> Our meal arrived forty minutes later. Both dishes were superbly presented and Don's steak looked scrumptious. Both meals were very pleasant, even if the salad had a slightly settled air to it.
>
> Dessert consisted of a wide choice of death by chocolate, baked pears in red wine and Bailey's homemade ice cream. I chose the Bailey's while Don decided on the pears. Both were very good.
>
> The damage came to €64, not bad, really, considering we had a bottle of fairly decent house wine. Service was quite slow and the background music was a bit too loud. All in all, Sarnium did live up to its reputation of being a good restaurant with quite good food.

COMMENT
- Start a review by naming the book, restaurant or CD you are reviewing.
- Give a short description of the place, plot or content of what you are reviewing.
- Write a short paragraph evaluating or weighing up the merits/demerits of what you are reviewing.
- Conclude by recommending (or not) the suitability, price or age of what you are reviewing.
- Write up your review in a series of short paragraphs.

Diary entries
- You may be asked to write a series of diary entries or simply one diary entry.
- Diary entries are short and personal.
- Generally, the sentence and paragraph structure of diary entries are quite short.

- List a date and a time when you start the diary.
- It is not necessary to write 'Dear Diary' each time.

The following is an example of three diary entries written by a famous celebrity on a very special day.

> Thursday, 4 June, 5 p.m.
> Am really tired after that photo shoot, and certainly will be exhausted when today is over. I was delighted with the premiere of the film this evening. I could not believe that we won the top prize in the Cannes festival for our film.
>
> Friday, 5 June, 3 p.m.
> Am looking forward to the banquet, which is taking place in Powerscourt Castle. It is going to be crowded, with lots of exciting people. I am really looking forward to meeting Pierce Brosnan, who is here on holidays for a few days.
>
> Monday, 8 June, 2 p.m.
> Everything is going great. I have just had a phone call offering me another job in a big film starting in November. I am so excited. It means working with Richard Gere and Sandra Bullock. I think I may take it even though I had been intending to take a break that month. Life is so exciting.

COMMENT
The main point to note about diary entries is that they should give the reader an insight into the type of person who is writing them.

Speech
You might be asked to write a speech to your class or a more formal speech about a topic.

Begin by addressing your audience and introducing yourself to them, e.g. 'Fellow classmates, I would like to speak to you today about a fund-raising event which we hope to orgnanise at senior level in the school.'

Write your speech in paragraphs. Conclude by going back to your audience and thanking them, e.g. 'Thank you all for listening and I hope that together we can manage to achieve something really worthwhile in the area of raising money for our beloved school.'

Script for a radio talk
You might be asked to write a short talk as part of a radio programme. Make sure to mention the name of the radio show and who exactly you are, your name and function.

The Types of Language

> Good morning, listeners, Heidi Smith here in 67 FM studios. In today's programme we'll consider a key emotion in our society today, and that is anger. Is anger a destructive emotion? Though it pains me to admit it, yes it is. Why else are we hearing countless reports of rape, murder and violence on our streets? There seems to be an uncontrollable amount of rage out there, between angry drivers on the roads, irate teenagers on Saturday night binges or housewives getting beaten up.
>
> This morning we have here in our studio Professor Good from the University of Toronto, who is an expert on anger and the disorders it causes. Good morning, Professor Good, we're delighted to have you here with us today.

Comment

As you can see, this is only an extract from a radio talk. The opening begins by establishing the context and the name of the presenter. The rest of the talk can be structured into short, clear paragraphs. Use language that is accessible to a general audience when writing a script for radio.

Text for the property pages of a newspaper

Sometimes you may be asked to write an advertisement for selling a house or a piece of property. In this case, use persuasive language.

> **'Something extra nice in Nice.'**
>
> Stretching across the Cote D'Azur of the Mediterranean, Nice is one of the most illustrious and captivating cities in France. Miles and miles of golden coastline span the city, where sandy beaches and aquamarine waters play host to millions of sun worshippers annually.
>
> Located about 500 metres from Nice's most popular beach, La Langue Plage, this new apartment development, Apartments Du Soleil, offers top-range facilities in an idyllic location. The development consists of 214 three-bedroom apartments, all en suite and all facing the sunny south. Each apartment has a stunning view of the sparkling Mediterranean and each comes complete with modern facilities and furnishings.
>
> Some of the attractive selling features of these apartments are the large swimming pools which adjoin the complex. In addition, there are two restaurants and a pool-side café.
>
> Families with small children would find these apartments ideal. There is a club for kids running from May to August, where children from as young as six months can be entertained by responsible carers.
>
> Apartments Du Soleil will be completed in May of this year. They will range in price from €280,000 to €350,000, depending on size and facilities.
>
> These apartments are ideal for a family who would like a second home in sunny France and for all those people yearning for an idyllic pied-à-terre.
>
> All those familiar with the literary works of Gerard Didier will remember his words on Nice: 'Nice has taught me to love, to laugh and to live.'
>
> Details can be obtained from Hynes Ltd or by e-mail at niceapart@goodmove.com

Comment

The text of a property advertisement is written in language designed to persuade. The above extract mentions the special features of these apartments as well as prices and contact details.

Structure your answer into short paragraphs. Adding a small homely detail about the place can also increase the appeal of the advertisement. Even if you are not asked to write a title, it is helpful to make up an appealing or catchy title or headline to market your property better.

Writing on a photograph or a picture

- Begin by summing up the subject matter of the photo or picture, e.g. 'This is a photograph of a rural landscape in winter' or 'This is a picture of an abandoned orphan in Africa.'
- Write on the background, foreground and middle ground of the photo/picture.
- Concentrate on small details, either in the person or place in the photo/picture.
- Look at unusual camera angles or positioning in the photo/picture.
- Look for any examples of contrast in the photo/picture and explain why this is used.
- Write on what you think may be the purpose of the picture/photo.

6
Samples of Paper I with Model Answers

STRUCTURE OF PAPER I

Study the following samples of Paper I. They all follow the same layout as the examination at Ordinary Level. In each paper there are four different comprehension texts. Some of these texts may include a photograph or an advertisement. Each text is followed by a number of questions that correspond to the type of questions that will be asked in the examination.

Model answers are included with the questions on each text. The purpose of these answers is to provide a method of approaching a particular question. None of these answers is definitive; a variety of different approaches may be adopted.

To improve your technique in answering comprehension-type questions, it is recommended that you try answering the questions yourself first, and then compare your answers with the sample answers provided here.

Comprehending and composing
Time: Two hours and fifty minutes. Total marks: 200.
This paper is divided into two sections:
1. Comprehending.
2. Composing.

Section 1: Comprehending (100 marks)
This section contains four texts on a certain theme. These texts will vary in style. There may be a piece of prose fiction, or a photograph or advertisement. In this paper you are required to answer *two* questions, question A and question B. Question A and question B must be taken from two different texts. Question A will test your ability to understand the passage, while question B is a specific writing task, such as constructing an advertisement or writing a letter or list of instructions.

Section 2: Composing (100 marks)

In this section you will be required to write a composition, from a choice of topics that can be written in a different language type. These topics may be linked to some of the ideas in the written passages. There will be a wide choice of writing styles, so that you may answer in whatever language type or style you like. Some of the exercises in the composition section below are related to some of the preceding passages.

FIRST SAMPLE PAPER: HOLIDAYS AND PLEASURE

Theme: This paper contains three different texts on the general theme of 'Holidays and pleasure'.

Section 1: Comprehending
(100 marks)

Text 1

Paradise at Balmy Prices

No one who has any style would be seen dead in the Caribbean in summer. It's where we escape to in the depths of winter, isn't it? Not necessarily. For the cognoscenti, who make the islands their second home, summer is a favourite season.

Patrick Lichfield spends every summer with his family at his holiday home in Mustique. Like other canny travellers, he has realised that going 'out of season' can work to his advantage.

Deserted beaches – Mustique apart – are still hard to find, but the Caribbean summer does guarantee the holiday essentials of sun, sea and sand at lower prices than in winter. High-spending Americans and Canadians are in short supply, so when the demand for rooms falls, most wise hoteliers cut their rates.

Some of the world's most luxurious hotels, catering to the titled rich and famous, are to be found in the Caribbean. They, too, cut their rates in summer and many offer not only babysitting but children's clubs with supervised play. Glitter Bay on Barbados's fashionable west ('platinum') coast is a good example. A week there including flights for two adults and two children costs €5,958 next January, €3,942 next month with Caribbean Connection.

Don't assume that the Caribbean summer is just about beach life. There is much to leave the sunbed for. Most of the yacht races are staged during summer. There are also craft, sport and music festivals, including Jamaica's Reggae Sun Fest (this year's starts tomorrow), which attracts an international crowd. St Lucia has just switched its carnival from February to July and Grenada holds its family-friendly carnival in August (6–10). Both events are unashamedly pitched at tourists, but none the worse for that.

Question A

(i) Who is the target audience for this article? Make reference to the article for support in your answer.

(ii) Identify what the writer's purpose is in the above article. Do you think he/she achieves that purpose?

Question B

Write out a short advertisement that could accompany this article for a holiday magazine. Include a caption and some persuasive techniques.

SAMPLE ANSWER TO QUESTION A

(i) The target audience for this article is families or people who will enjoy a holiday in the Caribbean. The writer of the article mentions a man called Patrick Lichfield who spends every summer with his family at his holiday home in Mustique. The article makes reference to 'deserted beaches', and hotels that offer babysitting and 'children's clubs with supervised play'. Honeymooners can also take advantage of a holiday of this type to relax and enjoy the various sights.

(ii) The main purpose of this article is to outline the advantages of taking a holiday at a reasonable price somewhere such as the Caribbean.
I believe the writer achieves this purpose very well, for the following reasons:
The title of the article, 'Paradise at Balmy Prices', and the accompanying photograph are both very appealing and attractive. In addition, the writer gives an example of a package tour that is reasonably priced.
The writer also gives a list of exciting activities that are available. These include yacht races, crafts, sports, music festivals and carnivals.

Sample answer to Question B

Why not escape from those troubles to a
PERFECT PARADISE IN THE SUN?
Book now for that holiday of a lifetime
Airtour Operators now offer you a unique two-week Caribbean holiday
Yachting, Water-skiing, Windsurfing, Music Fest are all yours
Simply phone: 01909832541
Fax: 01927767560

Text 2

Holidays in the sun: Tips to take with you
Before booking a holiday, read the brochure and booking conditions carefully.
- When booking, pay some of the fee by credit card. Then you will have rights against the credit card company if something goes wrong, provided the holiday costs at least €100.
- Always take your travel insurance policy with you, so if anything goes wrong you can read and comply with the conditions.
- Keep a diary of events while you are on holiday. Make sure your complaints are recorded and that operators are aware of this.
- When you arrive at the resort, if you find your hotel is overbooked or any other important element of your holiday isn't provided, the tour operator must make alternative arrangements. If this isn't possible or you have grounds to refuse the alternative, you are entitled to be brought home. Take pictures if it is going to help your case.
- If anything is stolen, you must get a police report at the resort.
- Most booking conditions have clauses limiting the amount of compensation to which you are entitled. Make sure you read these carefully to be fully aware of your entitlements.

Question A
(i) Comment briefly on the effect of the layout in the above set of instructions. Do you consider this layout to be effective? Give reasons why.
(ii) In your opinion what type of person do you imagine the writer of the above instructions to be?

Question B
Write a list of hints for a magazine that has a general readership on how to take care of your health during the holiday period.

Sample answer to Question A
(i) The layout of this article is short and snappy. The main points are set out in bullet format. The writer uses the minimum amount of words and this makes the effect more striking and much clearer. Sentences are short and to the point and they convey only the

necessary information.

(ii) The writer of this article seems to be a practical and experienced person. He/she is clearly aware of his/her rights when travelling abroad. All information about the possibility of things going wrong is covered in the above article and clear solutions are proposed in each case. It is clear, therefore, that he/she has considerable experience of any disasters or accidents that may occur on holiday. The writer also has the knowledge and expertise to suggest solutions for the problems in each case.

SAMPLE ANSWER TO QUESTION B

Holiday health

Whether you are holidaying abroad or at home, the following advice will help you stay fit and healthy this summer:

- Take out travel insurance to cover you in case you become sick when you are away from home.
- Make an appointment with your GP at least two months before going away to make sure that all your vaccinations are up to date.
- Phone the Health Literature Line on 22009878 to obtain your free leaflet, 'Health Advice for Travellers'.
- Don't forget your insect repellent together with a remedy for bites and stings.
- Remember to pack a sunscreen suitable for your skin type.

Have a happy holiday!

Text 3

> I landed at Calais with £10 in my money-belt – enough to take me to the Hilckmanns, in Mainz. There I could be sure of a warm welcome; they had stayed with us for six weeks during the previous summer while Anton was being taught Irish – his twenty-second language – by my father. I slept in my fleabag each night — the weather was almost too hot for long-distance cycling – and had unwound considerably by the time I reached Mainz. There I relaxed for a week before getting work as a farm hand in the village of Ober Saulheim, some fourteen miles further down the Rhine. I spent the next six weeks hoeing vines, scouring churns, harvesting straw, mucking out cow byres, grading eggs and corking wine. My working hours were not much shorter than at home – 5.00 a.m. to 11.00 p.m. with a half day on Sundays – but I welcomed being (by Irish standards) slave-driven. It was exactly what I needed at that time. Ceaseless labour, with only four half-hour breaks for meals – two of them picnic-style, eaten on the job-site – left me without the energy to fret. At the centre of me a hard little knot of guilty misery remained untied and I dared not think about the future. But meanwhile constant exertion in the open air, good food, few cigarettes and unbroken nights of deep sleep were rapidly restoring my health.
>
> (Dervla Murphy, *Wheels Within Wheels*)

Question A

(i) Point out three features of narrative writing from the above extract.

(ii) What particular impression do you get about the writer of this passage? Give reasons for your answer.

Question B
Write a short narrative account of some experience in your life that you considered to be very productive and satisfying.

Sample answer to Question A
(i) One of the main features of narrative writing is a clear beginning, middle and conclusion. The writer begins the article by telling us how she arrived in Calais. She then goes on to tell us how she slept in a fleabag each night. We learn that she got work as a farm hand in the village of Ober Saulheim fourteen miles down the Rhine. The writer goes on to give us an account of the type of work she did – scouring churns, mucking out cow byres, corking wine. She concludes by telling us how this type of work in the open air together with good sleep helped to restore her health.

(ii) One of the impressions that I get about the writer of this passage is that she is an adventurous type of person. She tells us that she travelled on her own to Calais with only £10 in her money belt. She also enjoys cycling and life in the open air. She is an adaptable person. She has no problem about sleeping rough. She takes work as a farm hand in a strange country. We can see also that she is a determined person as she mentions the fact that she throws herself into a lot of hard work. She is obviously suffering from some experience in her past, as she mentions that 'a hard knot of guilty misery remained untied'.

Sample answer to Question B
I sat upright in my bed and nursed my black cup of steaming coffee. The weather outside my window contrasted greatly with how I felt. The mature golden leaves of the trees were luminous and the intense blueness of the sky drowned any signs of dreariness or gloom. I decided that it was time to start my painting, which had been commissioned by the museum. My composition would be entitled *Youth, Change and Old Age*. This painting was going to absorb my whole attention and portray all my talents to the full. I would explore textures, tones and shapes in all their brilliance!

I began by gathering my equipment together. I placed my paint-box, easel and palette on my workbench. Slowly I began to sketch, adding brainstorm to brainstorm, trying to produce some original product. But to no avail. I wiped the perspiration from my frustrated brow. My search for inspiration had become desperate. I walked out onto the street. Rain clouds had gathered and very soon I was soaked. I was strangely oblivious to the feeling of dampness. My whole being was numb.

Suddenly, the solution came to me. It was like a magnificent giant lightbulb. It lit up my whole world. The words of Jean Anouilh came to me: 'The object of art is to give life a shape.' Yes, I thought, art speaks not only to us, but also for us.

Armed once more with my paintbrush and paint I declared war on the enemy. I began by chipping my paintbrush into a concoction of yellow and white paint. Next I chose a green colour mixed with a sliver of gold to bring out a bright hue. Finally I finished with a brownish golden line across the bottom of the canvas. Triumphantly I observed the finished product, the end result. Three lines of different textures, tones and hues spelled out to me the different transitions of life, Youth, Change and Old Age. My work was complete. I was fully satisfied.

Section 2: Composing
(100 marks)

Write a composition on any one of the following:
1. 'I came across a sandy bay secluded from the world.' Write an imaginative short story on your experience of being marooned on a desert island.
2. Compose a short paragraph for a holiday brochure on an ideal family holiday.
3. Write a letter for a popular magazine outlining some tips on how to use summer holidays to their fullest advantage.
4. Write out some points for a debate on the topic: 'Nowadays people need to be taught how to enjoy themselves.'
5. Write a short narrative account of your experiences of getting lost in a foreign city.

SECOND SAMPLE PAPER: STRONG CHARACTERS

Theme: This paper contains three different texts on the general theme of 'Strong characters'.

Section 1: Comprehending
(100 marks)

Text 1

> **Where Anne Frank lives**
> This long, narrow room shared by Anne and Margot was next to their parents' bedroom; the Van Pels were in the two rooms above. A specially made revolving bookcase concealed the only entrance to the secret annexe, and there were blackout curtains on every window.
>
> Inside this sealed-off little universe, the most extreme cautions were in force with regard to cooking, rubbish disposal and use of the single lavatory. Everyone whispered during the workday for fear of being overheard by the warehousemen, who knew nothing of the fugitives living over their heads. They moved about – in stockinged feet – only when it was absolutely necessary.
>
> The summer of 1942 passed in a procession of tedious days. In November Miep told them that their dentist, Fritz Pfeiffer, was desperate for a place to hide. Margot moved in with her parents, and soon Anne was sharing her room with the newcomer.
>
> Once, when burglars broke into the warehouse, police came and searched the building while the eight huddled in the secret annexe – the fake bookcase was all that stood between them and the terrors of deportation. One day Anne heard footsteps on the staircase, then a rattling at the bookcase. 'Now we're done for!' she thought. Then the footsteps receded. 'We were out of danger so far!'
>
> When Anne had filled every page of the diary, Miep brought her loose sheets and blank

ledgers from the office, and the writing went on. The diary was her best friend, she wrote, and she let her imagination run free, as she herself could not. 'I feel like a songbird whose wings have been ripped off and who keeps hurling itself against the bars of its dark cage.' Cooped up under the constant scrutiny of five elders, she wondered if anyone would understand that she was just a teenager badly in need of some good plain fun.

Question A
(i) The above article is written in an autobiographical and narrative style. Identify two features of autobiographical style from the passage.
(ii) What impressions of Anne Frank's character do you gain from the above extract? Give reasons for your answer.

Question B
Imagine you have been taken prisoner on board a hijacked plane. Compose an entry for your diary about your reaction to the incident.

SAMPLE ANSWER TO QUESTION A
(i) A striking feature of autobiographical style is when the writer uses personal reference to themselves. In this extract, Anne refers to the fact that the neighbours made room for one more.

She also mentions that when she heard footsteps on the staircase her immediate reaction was 'Now we're done for'. Later on, she describes her imprisonment in the following way: 'I feel like a songbird whose wings have been ripped off and who keeps hurling itself against the bars of its dark cage.'

(ii) The impression that I get of Anne's character is that she is selfless. She always thinks of others, for example she states 'We are done for' when she suspects that their place of hiding has been discovered. She also has a rich and vibrant imagination as she mentions the fact that she feels free to express herself in her diary.

SAMPLE ANSWER TO QUESTION B
Thursday, 31 May, 3 a.m.

It is stifling on board. At present all the passengers around me seem to be asleep or at least dozing. There is a small boy behind me who keeps crying and moaning all the time. He is obviously hungry. The initial terror of everyone on board has now been changed to exhaustion. There is little air and the smell is appalling. Everyone seems to be exhausted and paralysed with fear. The plane is still travelling in the air, to God knows where. From my seat in the centre aisle, I am catching a glimpse of the two armed terrorists who boarded the place in Geneva and who now hold guns at everyone. I imagine the other two are somewhere in the cockpit trying to terrorise the pilots. This is my worst nightmare, cooped up here with 159 frightened passengers. Who knows how this will end?

Text 2

From pride to dignity

For years director David Lynch was exclusively associated with the eccentric and the surreal. However, this film, based on a true story, is his greatest surprise yet. All layers, complications and plot twists are set aside to focus single-mindedly on a single-minded old man and his amazing journey.

Richard Farnsworth brilliantly portrays Alvin Straight, a 73-year-old widower from Iowa. Having not spoken to his brother, Lyle, in over a decade after a bitter falling-out, the true importance of family over everything else becomes clear to him. Receiving word that Lyle has suffered a stroke, Alvin resolutely decides to set out on his own to visit his estranged brother and make peace. With failing hips, and without a driver's licence, Alvin sets off on the 375-mile trip to Wisconsin on his motorised lawnmower.

Encounters: Travelling at a snail's pace for over six weeks, Alvin encounters a variety of individuals, from a runaway teenager to war veteran. Amid endless cornfields and golden

> sunsets we come to know more about this proud, stubborn man, the pleasures and pain of being old, and his steadfast belief in the family bond.
>
> By the time Alvin finally crosses the Mississippi River and makes the final push to his once-beloved brother's home, it's impossible not to succumb to the emotional poignancy of this long-overdue meeting.
>
> *The Straight Story* is a beautiful film. With its sensitivity and studied pace it reveals that Alvin's simple views of life and subtle wisdom will reward all of us with an insight into the irrelevancies of complicated modern living.
>
> To sit back and become part of this old man's laboured journey to rebuild a broken relationship at this late stage in his life is a humbling lesson in the difference between pride and dignity.

Question A
(i) From your reading of the above film review, what do you think was the main purpose in making the film *The Straight Story*?
(ii) Pick out three features of the main character of the film.

Question B
Write a short review of a film that impressed you. Give reasons about why you were impressed.

Sample answer to Question A
(i) In my opinion, the main purpose of making this film has been to show how heroic this man Alvin is. The director of this film wishes to show the audience how one man can fight against all the odds in order to rebuild a friendship. It also shows us that both the family and human relationships are still very important in modern life.

(ii) The main features of the central character, Alvin, are the following.

He is an old widower who is stubborn and proud. We learn that he has not spoken to his brother for over a decade because of a row.

He is a determined character. He travels 375 miles on a lawnmower to visit his estranged brother and make peace with him.

He has a strong belief in the importance of the family bond. We get glimpses of this through his powerful determination to become reconciled with his brother again.

Sample answer to Question B

A film review

One film that greatly impressed me was *Schindler's List*. This film, which was directed by Stephen Spielberg, deals with a real event that occurred – the Holocaust. The film centres around a Nazi businessman called Oscar Schindler. The film shows the changes that occurred in his character during World War Two. In the beginning Schindler looks on the war as a way of becoming rich and making a good future for himself. However, as events develop, Schindler's attitude towards the war and in particular towards the Jews begins to change. As a result of his efforts, thousands of Jews are saved from death.

The film really is a story of deliverance. The main character is played by the Irish actor Liam Neeson, who plays the part excellently.

Part of the power of this film comes from the photography, which is black and white for most of the story, and which adds to the realistic effect. In this film Spielberg succeeds in bringing to life what exactly happened in the war – the gas chamber, the roundups, the daily life in the camp and even more, the courage of one man to stand out against an evil and corrupt system. This film is truly worth watching.

Text 3
Advertisement

Question A
(i) What is the significance of the illustration in relation to this advertisement?
(ii) Identify two different techniques used in this advertisement and comment on their effectiveness.

Question B

Write an informative article for a teenage magazine about what you consider to be the value of working during the summer holidays.

SAMPLE ANSWER TO QUESTION A

(i) The illustration gives us an image of a man who appears to be confused. He is surrounded by a number of different coloured socks. On his right side is a small, neat box of Persil Tablets. The idea in this advertisement is that by using the box of Persil Tablets, all your problems with sorting out different types of socks will be solved.

(ii) The advertisement opens on an anecdotal approach: 'I once heard a story about Frank Sinatra.' This is a clever and effective device in order to arrest the reader's attention. In the case of this advertisement, the writer wants to reinforce the idea that Frank Sinatra used a different pair of socks every day, but that by using Persil Performance Tablets your clothes will look newer.

The writer also uses an illustration of a man surrounded by a vast number of different types of socks. This is an effective device to show us his confusion. The picture of the box showing Persil and the small tablets highlights the fact that this may be the solution to all the mess in this man's life.

SAMPLE ANSWER TO QUESTION B

I would like to inform you about what I consider to be the advantages of working during school/term holidays. I have been working for five summers now in various jobs around the country. This summer I travelled to Germany and worked for the first time in a hospital. My job involved carrying trays to some of the wards, cleaning floors and doing washing-up. I spent three and a half months doing this.

In addition to the fact that working during the summer months helps to earn income that can be useful later on in student life, I also think there are many other advantages. Some of these advantages may not be immediately obvious and may not be recognised in our world of speed and instant results, but in my opinion, I feel that these advantages far outweigh many of the monetary ones.

One clear effect of working during the summer is that it teaches you some good habits, such as making valuable use of your time. When you have to follow a timetable which involves rising early and going to bed early, this can help you appreciate and value more the time you have free for yourself.

Furthermore, working helps you relate and collaborate better with people. It opens the way for new friendships and different ways of being. When you have to earn your own money for things, it helps you to be more careful at managing and saving, especially as you begin to realise how much it has cost you to earn it!

Working also helps to train you in how to do jobs properly. Many times, you will be asked to do something better because it was carelessly done. This can help later on in life when you find yourself in an area of professional life that really attracts you. Finishing off jobs properly helps you to acquire that clear professional status which is so necessary and useful in this life.

Finally, working during the summer months helps you to understand people and to appreciate what you have got yourself. Many times we can be dissatisfied with our lives. But when we find ourselves working in a summer job we begin to realise that while this is a summer job it would not suit us for life and yet we see how many other people are contented to stay in it.

So it can truly be seen that working during the summer months has a great deal of advantages and especially in the whole area of building our character.

Section 2: Composing
(100 marks)

Write a composition on any one of the following:
1. Write a short narrative account on your experience of meeting someone whom you admire greatly. In your account, concentrate on giving a descriptive account of what features of this character impressed you.
2. Imagine that you have been imprisoned along with Anne Frank. Compose a series of diary entries containing your account of the imprisonment and in particular of the people you were living with.
3. 'This film, based on a true story, is his greatest surprise yet.'
   Write a review of a film which impressed you greatly and which is based on reality. Outline the reasons why you enjoyed it so much.
4. Write an article for a popular teenage magazine on what you consider to be the main features of a strong character today.
5. 'Footsteps on the staircase, then a rattling at the bookcase. "Now we're done for!" I said. Then the footsteps receded. "We were out of danger so far!"' Taking these lines as your opening paragraph, compose an imaginative short story.

THIRD SAMPLE PAPER: FASHIONABLE TRENDS

Theme: This paper contains three different texts on the general theme of 'Fashionable trends'.

Section 1: Comprehending
(100 marks)

Text 1

> **Diet traps . . . and how to avoid them**
> You've dieted faithfully for a month but have lost only one pound. Or maybe the stone you lost last summer is creeping back. Or perhaps you count calories for a mere two days before you 'must' wolf down a chocolate biscuit.
>
> If any of these scenarios sounds familiar, some factor you haven't even considered may be undermining your diet. But once you recognise these six major diet traps, you will be able to break free of them.

Medicine
Did your diet plateau soon after you started a new medication?

Some simply stimulate appetite; others may alter metabolism. Some of the older antidepressants, known as tricyclics, are among the worst offenders, causing weight gain in a significant number of patients.

Break-free strategy:
Before blaming prescription drugs for your weight woes, check you're not inadvertently eating more or exercising less. Then ask your doctor about changing drugs. Don't forget that drug reactions differ greatly from one person to the next.

Anger
Do you stifle your anger? Or do you let it explode? In either case, anger may be your hidden dieting problem.

If you smile when a colleague steals your ideas – then spend the evening digging into a bag of crisps – you're not really fat and happy. You're secretly angry.

Break-free strategy:
Anger needs to be evaluated. If the cause of your anger is relatively unimportant and there is nothing you can do to change the circumstances or the outcome, let it go. It may just save you a few unwanted pounds.

Take a ten-minute break when you feel ravenous. Review what has happened in the past ten to twelve hours to upset you. Did your spouse hurt your feelings? Were you playing martyr again? Could you deal with your rage in less fattening ways – by exercising, perhaps, or discussing the situation with a friend?

Express your needs directly. If you want sympathy or an hour alone, say so. Don't get angry when people can't read your mind.

Learn to say no. Don't let others ask too much of you. Practise letting anger go by pedalling an exercise bike rapidly or taking a long walk, for instance.

Alcohol
Since white wine is fat-free and has only about 100 calories a glass, it's tempting to have a glass or two with a low-fat dinner. But according to a Swiss study reported in the *New England Journal of Medicine*, if about a quarter of your daily calorie intake comes from wine, beer or spirits, the alcohol can slow your fat metabolism by about 30 per cent. In other words, while your body is burning alcohol, it's not burning fat.

Break-free strategy:
If your rate of weight loss has stalled, eliminating all alcohol could jump-start it again.

Depression
Some of this may be due to decreased exercise in bad weather. But if you find it hard to wake up, feel generally tired, and struggle to concentrate, you may be one of the 1.5 million people who suffer from SAD (seasonal affective disorder).

Break-free strategy:
Spend more time outside, even on a cloudy day. An early morning or lunchtime walk is ideal. About 75 per cent of SAD sufferers get fast relief from special light boxes, which are five to twenty times brighter than typical home lighting.

Boost your mood with exercise. Try a few laps round the block, dance to your favourite music or skip.

Stress
Feeling in a constant state of red alert without having the skills to cope can also trigger overeating. Worse, stress may cause fat to be preferentially deposited around the abdomen, where it can do the most harm. Abdominal fat has been linked to higher rates of heart disease, diabetes, stroke and breast cancer.

What is uncontrollable stress? Feeling you're bound to fail, no matter how hard you try. Dreading a situation because you're unsure what will happen, and believing you won't measure up. Overeating at such times provides comfort, but it deadens the anxiety only temporarily.

Break-free strategy:
Learn to meditate. It not only calms you, but according to Dr Williams from Duke University, 'In some studies, transcendental meditation lowered cortisol levels.'

Identify your stress triggers. Does being alone, having a thousand things to do or fretting over money cause you to freak out – and eat? If so, find other ways to save money.

No matter how insidious diet traps may seem, they're not permanent. It's never too late to break free. And when all else fails, remember the final way to escape: more exercise.

Question A
(i) The above article on diet traps is an example of informative writing. Give three examples of factual information from the above passage.
(ii) Do you agree with the ideas in this article? Give reasons for your answer.

Question B
Write out a series of instructions or guidelines for a health food magazine on the reasons why one should eat more fruit and vegetables.

SAMPLE ANSWER TO QUESTION A
(i) The article opens by addressing the reader directly. It uses language and examples that are relevant and familiar to an ordinary reader who may be worried about their weight. The opening sentences paint a picture of problems that are typically associated with weight, such as the fact that you only lose one pound after dieting faithfully for a month. Then the article goes on to point out some simple and basic tips on how to diet.
The article sets out certain problems that may cause a person to become over-weight. These are clearly laid out in sub-headings – 'Medicine', 'Anger', 'Alcohol', 'Depression' and 'Stress'. Then the writer goes on to give a clear explanation on how these different factors can cause a gain in weight. A solution to each of these problems is proposed in each case. This is done by means of another sub-heading: 'Break-free strategy'.
(ii) Yes, I agree with the ideas in this article. I certainly understand the idea in the opening sentences about the fact that many times you must count the calories before eating a biscuit. The paragraphs which are headed 'Break-free strategy' are very helpful in my opinion. They are practical and realistic and I find that I can agree with them. In particular, the ideas on stress are very relevant. The language used by the writer is clear and informative.

Sample answer to Question B

Good reasons why we should eat more fruit and veg

Helps prevent cancer
Eating vegetables and fruit can prevent up to 20 per cent of all cancers. This is because they are rich in antioxidants that protect against free radicals that cause cell damage and initiate cancer.

Helps keep you slim
Because they are low in fat and calories, hearty servings of veg and fruit can help keep you slim, while at the same time satisfy your appetite.

Helps prevent heart disease
Increase your intake of fruit and veg for a healthier heart. The antioxidants, phytochemicals and B vitamin folate help to maintain low cholesterol.

Helps lower blood pressure
Greens contain high levels of potassium and magnesium and so they help to lower blood pressure.

Helps prevent strokes
Studies show that diets high in vegetables and fruits can decrease the risk of a stroke by up to 25 per cent due to the potassium, antioxidants and phytochemicals.

Helps protect eyes
Fruit and veg contain vitamin C and carotenoids. Both of these can help prevent the risk of acquiring cataracts and macular degeneration.

Helps prevent intestinal disorders
Fruits and especially vegetables are major sources of the type of fibre considered to be most helpful in preventing digestive problems.

Helps prevent diabetes
Fruits and vegetables raise blood sugar less quickly than other foods that contain carbohydrates.

Satisfies a sweet tooth
Fruits and vegetables are a healthy way to satisfy a sweet tooth. You will also get an added nutrition boost that works more effectively than the 'empty' calories found in sweets like candy bars and soft drinks.

Fruit and veg can zip up any dish
The diversity of textures and tastes will add interest and flavour to any dish.

Text 2

Espresso – it's the hot new drink

'I'll bring you our list,' says Milva Crini, owner of the Salotto del Chianti, a charming little restaurant in the hills not far from Florence. I have just finished a marvellous meal and I'm ready to round it off with a good cup of coffee. Signora Crini returns with an elegant list of six different varieties of locally roasted coffee. I can choose between Santos, Jamaica, Puerto Rico, Haiti, Hawaii and Guatemala. I go for Puerto Rico. 'My husband Marcello will get it ready for you,' says the signora with a smile.

It is not unusual to be presented with a list of different types of coffee in an Italian restaurant.

We are also becoming more discerning about the quality of the coffee we drink. Forget about a cup of instant; espresso is the hippest hot drink around.

Espresso is the Italian method of passing almost-boiling water through a 'cake' of ground coffee at high pressure, while cappuccino is espresso with steamed, foamed milk and perhaps a light sprinkling of chocolate.

The Italians are masters of coffee-bean roasting, which is the most delicate part of the whole coffee-making process and an essential element in a good espresso.

The great Neapolitan playwright Eduardo De Filippo recalled how, when he was a boy in the early years of the century, it was the senior members of the family who roasted coffee on the balconies. The smell, De Filippo said, was so strong it came in through the closed windows of his bedroom and woke him up.

'Preparing a cup of coffee is both a science and an art,' says Luigi Odello, secretary of the International Coffee Tasters' Institute, who was the first to devise a method for the tasting of espresso coffee. 'The best results depend on getting five things right: the blend, the grinding, the quantity, the equipment – and the personal touch. But only the espresso method brings out the full intensity of the aroma.' It is the fatty substances in the crema, the creamy froth on top of an espresso, that contain all the volatile – or aromatic – elements in the blend.

It takes 35 million granules of coffee ranging in size from one millimetre down to one micron to make one cup of espresso.

The next important stage is the equipment used. The equipment must be clean and in perfect working order. But much still depends on the barista who prepares the coffee. It is he who grinds it, ensures that the right 'dose' of coffee – ideally 7 g – is tamped down so that the water flows evenly at the ideal rate of one millilitre per second and that the crema is about 3 mm thick and evenly spread.

Espresso coffee makers vary in price from about €10 for a stovetop bubble-through model to hundreds of euro for more elaborate hydro-compression machines.

Question A
(i) What is the relationship between the title of the article and the points made by the writer?
(ii) Give three examples of information from the above extract.

Question B
You are on holiday abroad. Write a letter to your best friend in which you give an account of how you spend your time.

SAMPLE ANSWER TO QUESTION A
(i) The whole article gives the reader a series of different points of information on espresso coffee. The article shows us how this is the 'hippest hot drink around'. The article goes on to explain how espresso originated in Italy and the particular techniques which are required to make it the unique drink that it is.

(ii) The following points are examples of information given in the article:

Milva Crini is the owner of the Salotta del Chianti, a restaurant in the hills not far from Florence.

In this restaurant there are six different varieties of locally roasted coffee. These are Santos, Jamaica, Puerto Rico, Haiti, Hawaii and Guatemala.

The best results in preparing a cup of coffee depend on getting five things right: the blend, the grinding, the quantity, the equipment – and the personal touch.

Sample answer to Question B

Hotel LeSport
Malabar Beach
St Lucia
West Indies

7 July 2010

Dear Naoife,

Hope you are well. We are having a brilliant time here in St Lucia. The place is exotic. Our hotel overlooks the beach and in addition, it has its own vast swimming pool.

Every afternoon there is volleyball beside the pool, and when you need to cool down the smart bar at the side will serve you iced drinks. So as you can imagine we are having a marvellous time as we sit on our shaded loungers, either beside the beach or at the pool. The staff here are very friendly and generally good-humoured considering how difficult it must be to keep everyone happy in such hot weather.

I have spent one morning browsing around the local marketplace. I found it a fascinating place with its rich woodcarvings and pottery and all the colourful displays of vegetables and different spices.

Our whole family went out for a meal one night and we enjoyed a delicious feast of fresh fish, which was beautifully cooked and even more delightfully presented. Our night entertainment is varied. Sometimes in the hotel there is a singsong or some music and dances typical of this area.

Generally at the weekend there is a discotheque, which attracts many of the young people around.

It certainly will be difficult to settle down to ordinary life after having such a splendid time here. Looking forward to seeing you when I return.

Grace

Text 3
Advertisement

Question A
(i) Give your impressions of the following advertisement.
(ii) Identify three effective persuasive techniques used in this advertisement.

SAMPLES OF PAPER I WITH MODEL ANSWERS   101

Question B
You have been asked to represent your school in the award ceremony for Environmental Awareness. Compose an imaginative account (150–200 words) of your impressions of the experience. In your account, give a brief explanation of the project done by your school.

SAMPLE ANSWER TO QUESTION A
(i) My first impression of this advertisement is one of wonder and query. For me the advertisement is unusual because I do not expect to see primary schoolchildren flying in the sky on what seems to be pollen and all dressed in different types of clothes. Initially, the advertisement did not make sense to me. I had to study the photograph and words in order to understand what is being said in the end. For that reason, I find it an interesting and unusual approach.
(ii) The advertisement uses a caption that is based on the imperative form: Be inspired, be involved, be aware. This is an effective device to address the reader directly.

   The accompanying photograph is filled with pictures of happy, energetic and lively young people who are flying on clouds in the sky. This serves the function of showing how all the young people are involved in the same activity.

   The advertisement uses clear, factual language to inform the reader at the conclusion, for example 'Tenth year of ESB', '450 schools', 'Finals taking place in Munster'.

SAMPLE ANSWER TO QUESTION B
   I was so excited I could not sleep the night before. The principal of my school had just announced that I had been chosen to represent my school in the Environmental Award for schools nationwide. They were to be held in the Point Theatre in Dublin. Our school had come first in Ireland. I was to be accompanied by the Civics teacher, Mr

Greene. We were staying overnight in a large hotel on the outskirts of Dublin.

The ceremony took place on Friday evening at 8 p.m. sharp. Representatives from schools all over the country were gathered there. I recognised one boy from a school in Waterford whom I had met the previous summer at Irish College.

Our topic had been on the subject of waste disposal. We had constructed the idea of an eco-industrial park. Within this park we placed a mini oil refinery, a chemical plant and a power company. We organised the park in such as way that all of these shared in the use of steam, gas and water. Any excess heat was used to warm nearby homes and greenhouses. Our aim, in other words, was to show how one company's waste could become another's resource. For example, we suggested that the power plant would sell the sulphur dioxide to the Wallboard Company, which uses this compound as a raw material.

As a result of this project our school got first place in Ireland. The President of Ireland and all the RTÉ cameras were there. I was very nervous. The room erupted when my name was called out. I felt honoured to be the representative of my school. It was a truly marvellous experience.

Section 2: Composing
(100 marks)

Write a composition on any one of the following:
1. Write out a list of instructions on what you consider to be the best way to maintain one's weight.
2. Write an informative article for a popular newspaper on the different types of transport today. In your article, outline which type you consider to be the most advantageous and give your reasons why.
3. Write out a series of arguments which you will deliver to your class for or against the subject 'Fashions and trends never really change, they simply reflect what is popular for a time.'
4. Imagine you are a journalist working in the features section of a popular magazine for young people. Write out the interview that you recorded with a famous fashion designer.
5. Compose an imaginative account of your experience of attending a large fashion show in Paris.

FOURTH SAMPLE PAPER: HEALTHY LIVING

Theme: This paper contains three different texts on the general theme of 'Healthy living'.

Section 1: Comprehending
(100 marks)

Text 1

The legalisation of drugs

Sir – I am dismayed by the recent spate of heroin-related deaths because, more than anything else, the deaths have been caused by hypocrisy. We live in a society where the peddling of death through alcohol and tobacco are carefully regulated and highly taxed. However, vast sums of money are spent in this country, as well as in the rest of the world, on trying to eradicate the drugs trade. Has there been any success? The answer is an emphatic no. Not even death sentences have succeeded in denting the volume or profitability of drug dealing.

In Ireland we are building more and more prison spaces and drug lords have been targeted. Yet illegal drugs are still easily available. Isn't it time to recognise that the market will always demand narcotics? And the mature response is to tax it, regulate it and so, finally, defeat the drug lords who will never be beaten by the gardaí.
Yours etc.

Question A
(i) What do you consider to be the main purpose of this letter?
(ii) From your reading of the letter, what type of person would you say the writer is?

Question B
Write the text for an informative brochure on details of one particular drug.

SAMPLE ANSWER TO QUESTION A
(i) The main purpose of this letter is to draw attention to the fact that drugs should be legalised. The writer is angry about the deaths caused by heroin. However, he believes that alcohol and tobacco are as dangerous since they also cause death. His main argument is that in the same way as these are legalised and heavily taxed, so should drugs be made legal. According to the writer, it is hypocritical to legalise alcohol and tobacco and make drugs illegal.

(ii) The writer of this letter is clearly aware of the dangers of drugs. He opens the letter by stating that he 'is dismayed by the recent spate of heroin-related deaths'.

He is angry at the fact that drugs are not legalised and yet alcohol and tobacco are legal. He considers this type of behaviour to be hypocritical.

He is obviously a good citizen who is worried about the state of our society and he feels moved to do something about things.

SAMPLE ANSWER TO QUESTION B
Ecstasy: the facts
The 'E' scene
Originally ecstasy was created as a 'feel good' drug in the US. It is closely associated with 'rave' dance parties and the music that goes with them. Endurance dancing which can last all night has been facilitated by the use of ecstasy. The hot atmosphere of a dance floor raises the temperature of the body. Ravers start to dehydrate, i.e. lose fluid. They need to take a pint of fluid per hour in order to avoid heat stroke, which has killed ecstasy users.

What is ecstasy?
Ecstasy is a hallucinogenic amphetamine, which can by taken in the form of a capsule or tablet. However, many 'E' tablets are cut with other stimulant drugs such as amphetamine sulphate, or LSD, or perhaps a mixture of both. So any 'E' tablet may be an experiment with the unknown.

Why is 'E' taken?
Ecstasy is usually taken at 'raves' or discos to produce a feeling of relaxation with increased energy, happiness and flexibility. Someone using ecstasy usually feels less inhibited and experiences everything with a great deal of intensity. Ecstasy takes effect in twenty to sixty minutes. It is usually at its peak for about two hours and may last several hours after that.

Ecstasy – the effects
Some of the short-term effects can include sweating, increase in heart rate, blood pressure and nausea. This pressure on the heart and respiratory system can kill after a single dose.

Long-term effects can include insomnia, lethargy, anorexia and weight loss. Other effects may include depression, anxiety and panic attacks. Users may become psychologically dependent on the drug.

To sum up
When ecstasy was introduced to the United Kingdom and Ireland, it was originally sold as a party stimulant. However, because other substances have been added to it, the danger of death and other serious consequences has increased.

Further help
Further help is available from:
- your family doctor
- Community Addiction Counsellor
- Health Board
- Garda Síochána
- The Drug Treatment Centre Board.

Text 2

1. Stretch Yourself with Yoga
If you are fed up with step classes, have had enough of aerobics and can't stand the thought of lifting weights, but still want a toned body, consider yoga. No longer associated with a group of people sitting in circles humming strange mantras, modern yoga comes in a variety of forms to suit every body and every need.

And now that yoga has become so popular – it's thought to be second only to walking as the chosen form of exercise for most women – different forms of the discipline have become available through classes up and down the country.

And it's not just your body that can reap the benefits, but your health too. Recent clinical trials have shown that yoga can help with the management of anxiety, asthma, heart disease, mild forms of diabetes and back pain. At the same time, people are discovering through personal experience that yoga can sometimes help period pains, migraine and ME. If you want to combat fatigue through yoga, track down *Beat Fatigue with Yoga* (Element, €8.99) by Fiona Agombar, who suffered from ME for four years until she discovered yoga.

But if you are looking for a form of exercise that you can simply switch off and do, yoga may not suit you, because it requires mental as well as physical concentration. 'An essential part of yoga is how you breathe. Breathing affects everything – the mind, stomach, concentration, energy levels, consciousness and state of mind,' explains Catriona. The correct way to breathe is deeply and at the back of the throat, something that is not easy to do at first, but which concentrates the mind and, in the long term, helps to release stress and daily worries.

'Although yoga takes a lot of physical and mental concentration, it is also ultimately stress-relieving because you focus on yourself, not the other people in the class, your problems or the world around you,' explains Catriona.

2. Yoga with Tears

Yoga is not something that appeals much to those of us who are adrenaline junkies – people whose idea of a stretch is reaching into our handbags for the mobile. It's not that we aren't health conscious: many street addicts have already succumbed to personal trainers, juicers and vitamin supplements. It's just that yoga comes with all that other stuff attached. It looks fine in the Far East but, over here, it looks pretentious, bordering on the ridiculous.

So it was in the spirit of curiosity that I recently attended Faustomaria's two-hour yoga class at the Innergy Centre on Kensal Road, northwest London.

I arrived at the spacious Acorn Hall in a terrible mood, having just rowed with my child's nanny. I was seething with negative energy and the last thing I felt like was ten minutes of quiet breathing. Glancing around the room, I couldn't help wondering what kind of work these people did to be able to afford two hours off at lunchtime.

You really notice the inner machinations of your mind when you're lying on your back staring at a pastel blue ceiling, with mood music playing gently in the background. Every time Faustomaria said the words 'rrrrelease yourrr miiiind' in his charming Romanian accent, everyone let out a sigh – except for me. I needed a kickboxing session more than an internal communion.

Faustomaria practises hatha yoga, a classical form based largely on breathing and postures. Yoga – which means uniting – aims to bring together mind and body. Through mental and physical discipline, one is meant to find peace of mind and, ultimately, contentment. Those who pursue it further – yogis – become enlightened.

Faustomaria introduced each position by its proper name and a short explanation. I was the only one needing direction; the others were all in a kind of trance, moving from one position to the other effortlessly. I thought the famous 'warrior posture' (front leg bent with arms extended parallel to the floor) was a doddle until several minutes had passed and we were still lunging. My legs were shaking violently; no one else so much as twitched.

> With every new stretch, I noticed my mind drifting farther afield. Two hours is a long time to stay still. 'I used to have a one-hour lunchtime class, but it was overrun with stress,' says Faustomaria. 'I work very little with the body. I work on a psychic level, through breathing.' Another hour and I felt I would have had an out-of-body experience.

Question A
(i) Both of these articles deal with the same subject – yoga. Which one do you consider to be the most effective? Outline your reasons.
(ii) Identify two points of information used by the writer in each article.

Question B
Write a short imaginative account of an adventure you had while engaging in some sporting activity. In your account, focus on some valuable lesson or lessons you learned from the experience.

SAMPLE ANSWER TO QUESTION A
(i) The purpose of the first article, entitled 'Stretch Yourself with Yoga', is to inform the reader about yoga and what exactly it consists of. The article gives a number of general points, all of which are aimed at informing a general readership about the advantages of yoga. The article is clearly laid out and expressed well.

The purpose of article two, 'Yoga with Tears', is primarily to entertain and divert the reader. The whole article is developed on the basis of a clear storyline. The writer of the article seems to have doubts about the benefits and this is expressed in an amusing and realistic way.

(ii) The following are examples of two points of information used by the writer in each article:

'Yoga has become second only to walking as the chosen form of exercise for most women.' (Article 1)

'Recent clinical trials have shown that yoga can help the management of anxiety, asthma, heart disease and back pain.' (Article 1)

'Hatha yoga is a classical form based largely on breathing and postures.' (Article 2)

'Yoga – which means unity – aims to bring together the mind and the body.' (Article 2)

SAMPLE ANSWER TO QUESTION B
The place was a forest deep in the heart of Kerry. It was a late August evening. I had gone for a jog wearing only a light cotton T-shirt and a pair of shorts. Three miles into the forest I realised I was utterly lost. In addition, I was completely dehydrated, beginning to get cold and the dark was descending rapidly. Panic began to rise within me. I knew that somewhere inside my rucksack I had a map and compass. I was so weak and confused I couldn't get my mind to read the map clearly. I began to trudge forward slowly. After about ten minutes I came across a lake. I took some water and began to feel better. Slowly, I began to locate the position of the lake on the map and to find out exactly where I was.

One hour later I was standing in a hot shower. At that stage I had learned a number

of valuable lessons:
- Always tell someone where you are going.
- Pay attention to the weather.
- Do not wear cotton as it can turn into a freezing sheath when you sweat.

The main lesson I had learned that day was that as we become more proficient in sports and outdoor life, the more we begin to become aware of certain things such as the weather, the environment, how much food to take. In other words, we begin to learn respect for Nature!

Text 3
Advertisement

Question A
(i) What do you consider to be the main purpose of this advertisement? Make reference to the advertisement to support your answer.
(ii) Do you consider this to be an effective advertisement? Give reasons for your answer.

Question B
Compose a short advertisement on either your favourite food or make-up. Include three effective persuasive techniques, e.g. a slogan, a caption, the use of repetition, buzzwords, etc.

Sample answer to Question A
(i) The main purpose of this advertisement is to advertise tea and show how it is beneficial to your health. The advertisement outlines a number of different things that are contained in tea and explains how these are beneficial to one's health.

(ii) I believe that this is an effective advertisement for the following reasons:
The opening of the advertisement is anecdotal. It speaks about an emperor and shows how his pains disappeared when he began to take tea. This type of approach is interesting and serves the function of arresting the attention of the ordinary reader.
All the benefits of tea are laid out clearly in the section headed 'Properties of tea'.
The company's telephone number is shown clearly on the left-hand corner, thus making it easy to establish contact.
The photograph of the girl gives us an image of someone who is relaxed and healthy looking. This contributes to the whole impact of the message contained in the advertisement.

Sample answer to Question B
MAKE-UP – FOR THAT MAGIC FACE-LIFT!
If you haven't turned over a new leaf for the millennium, you can at least get yourself a new face, as bright as a new penny.
It's always party time, so don't try to hide your light under a bushel – or under too-heavy old-fashioned make-up! Go out and outshine them all. Paint on a party face.
YOU DON'T NEED TO SPEND A FORTUNE ON EXPENSIVE COSMETICS
The cheaper lines are just as glamorous.
Collection 2000 has an out-of-this-world selection of shades for eyes and nails in their Planet Party Range.
Go for the Glitter with Max Factor Gold Dust Collection, which includes all things shimmering and shiny.
Focus on a 24-carat smile with GOLD LIPS in bronze-shot Gold Dust make-up.
CORN SILK Translucent Powder is PERFECT For all Skin Tones ranging from milky white to rich dark black.
Available from Chemists and Department Stores Nationwide.
FACE UP TO THE FUTURE WITH COLLECTION 2000

Section 2: Composing
(100 marks)

Write a composition on any one of the following:
1. 'Most of us take tea with milk that contains a range of vitamins and minerals and can be an excellent addition to your diet.' Write an informative article for a popular

newspaper on your ideas on the subject of 'Healthy eating'.
2. Write out a series of arguments on what you consider to be the advantages of taking physical exercise.
3. Write a letter in response to the letter above entitled 'The legalisation of drugs'.
4. 'You really notice the inner machinations of your mind when you're lying on your back staring at a pastel blue ceiling, with mood music playing gently in the background.' Compose an imaginative account of your experience of teaching yoga.
5. Write a narrative account of meeting a famous sports personality.

Examination Techniques in Paper II

Prescribed texts for examination 2010

Students are required to study:
1. One text on its own from the following texts (texts marked with an asterisk are discussed in this book):

   BRONTË, Emily   *Wuthering Heights**
   FRIEL, Brian   *Dancing at Lughnasa**
   KEANE, John B.   *Sive**
   MACLAVERTY, Bernard   *Lamb**
   MOORE, Brian   *Lies of Silence**
   OZ, Amos   *Panther in the Basement**
   SHAKESPEARE, William   *King Lear*
   STEINBECK, John   *The Grapes of Wrath**
   TÓIBÍN, Colm   *The Blackwater Lightship**

2. Three other texts from the list below, in a comparative manner, according to the comparative modes prescribed for this course.

   Any texts from the list below, other than the one already chosen for study on its own, may be selected for the comparative study.

   A film may be studied as one of the three texts in a comparative study. The comparative models for examination in 2010 at Ordinary Level are:
   (i)   Hero/heroine/villain.
   (ii) Theme.
   (iii) Social setting.

Texts prescribed for comparative study for examination in 2010 (texts marked with an asterisk are discussed in this book):

AUSTEN, Jane	*Pride and Prejudice*
BANVILLE, John	*Kepler*
BARNES, Julian	*Arthur & George*
BECKETT, Samuel	*Waiting for Godot*
BINCHY, Maeve	*Circle of Friends**
BOWEN, Elizabeth	*The Last September*
BRONTË, Emily	*Wuthering Heights**
CHATWIN, Bruce	*In Patagonia*
CHEVALIER, Tracy	*Girl with a Pearl Earring*
CURTIZ, Michael (dir.)	*Casablanca* (film)*
DALDRY, Stephen (dir.)	*Billy Elliott* (film)*
DICKENS, Charles	*Hard Times*
FRIEL, Brian	*Dancing at Lughnasa**
GAGE, Eleni	*North of Ithaka*
HARRIS, Robert	*Pompeii*
IBSEN, Henrik	*A Doll's House*
KEANE, John B.	*Sive**
LONCRAINE, Richard (dir.)	*Richard III* (film)*
MACKEN, Walter	*The Silent People*
MACLAVERTY, Bernard	*Lamb**
MALOUF, David	*Fly Away Peter*
McDONAGH, Martin	*The Lonesome West*
MOORE, Brian	*Lies of Silence**
MURPHY, Tom	*A Whistle in the Dark**
NGOZI ADICHIE, Chimamanda	*Purple Hibiscus*
O'DONNELL, Damien (dir.)	*Inside I'm Dancing* (film)*
OZ, Amos	*Panther in the Basement**
PATCHETT, Ann	*Bel Canto*
RADFORD, Michael (dir.)	*Il Postino* (film)*
SEIERSTAD, Asne	*The Bookseller of Kabul*
SHAKESPEARE, William	*King Lear*
	The Tempest
SOPHOCLES	*Oedipus the King*
STEINBECK, John	*The Grapes of Wrath**
SYNGE, J. M.	*The Playboy of the Western World*
TAYLOR, Mildred	*The Road to Memphis*
TÓIBÍN, Colm	*The Blackwater Lightship**
TREVOR, William	*The Story of Lucy Gault*
WEIR, Peter (dir.)	*The Truman Show* (film)*

Prescribed texts for examination 2011

Students are required to study:
1. One text on its own from the following texts (texts marked with an asterisk are discussed in this book):

BINCHY, Maeve	*Circle of Friends**
BRONTË, Emily	*Wuthering Heights**
IBSEN, Henrik	*A Doll's House*
JOHNSTON, Jennifer	*How Many Miles to Babylon?**
MONK KIDD, Sue	*The Secret Life of Bees**
MURPHY, Tom	*A Whistle in the Dark**
O'CASEY, Sean	*The Plough and the Stars**
SHAKESPEARE, William	*Hamlet*
STEINBECK, John	*The Grapes of Wrath**

2. Three other texts from the list below, in a comparative manner, according to the comparative modes prescribed for this course.

   Any texts from the list below, other than the one already chosen for study on its own, may be selected for the comparative study.

   A film may be studied as one of the three texts in a comparative study. The comparative models for examination in 2011 at Ordinary Level are:
   (i) Relationships.
   (ii) Theme.
   (iii) Social setting.

   Texts prescribed for comparative study for examination in 2011 (texts marked with an asterisk are discussed in this book):

AUSTEN, Jane	*Emma*
BINCHY, Maeve	*Circle of Friends**
BOWEN, Elizabeth	*The Last September*
BRANAGH, Kenneth (dir.)	*As You Like It* (film)*
BRONTË, Emily	*Wuthering Heights**
CHANG, Jung	*Wild Swans*
COETZEE, J. M.	*Boyhood*
CURTIZ, Michael (dir.)	*Casablanca* (film)*
DALDRY, Stephen (dir.)	*Billy Elliot* (film)*
DICKENS, Charles	*Hard Times*
FRIEL, Brian	*Dancing at Lughnasa**
GAGE, Eleni	*North of Ithaka*
HARRIS, Robert	*Pompeii*
HOSSEINI, Khaled	*The Kite Runner*
IBSEN, Henrik	*A Doll's House*
ISHIGURO, Kazuo	*Never Let Me Go*

JOHNSTON, Jennifer	*How Many Miles to Babylon?**
KEANE, John B.	*Sive**
MACLAVERTY, Bernard	*Lamb**
MARTEL, Yann	*Life of Pi*
McDONAGH, Martin	*The Lonesome West*
McEWAN, Ian	*Atonement*
MEIRELLES, Fernando (dir.)	*The Constant Gardener* (film)*
MONK KIDD, Sue	*The Secret Life of Bees**
MOORE, Brian	*Lies of Silence**
MURPHY, Tom	*A Whistle in the Dark**
NGOZI ADICHIE, Chimamanda	*Purple Hibiscus*
O'CASEY, Sean	*The Plough and the Stars**
O'DONNELL, Damien (dir.)	*Inside I'm Dancing* (film)*
PETTERSON, Per	*Out Stealing Horses*
PICOULT, Jodi	*My Sister's Keeper*
RADFORD, Michael (dir.)	*Il Postino* (film)*
ROSOFF, Meg	*How I Live Now*
SHAKESPEARE, William	*Hamlet*
	The Tempest
SHIELDS, Carol	*Unless*
SOPHOCLES	*Oedipus the King*
STEINBECK, John	*The Grapes of Wrath**
TREVOR, William	*The Story of Lucy Gault*

STRUCTURE OF PAPER II

1. The total number of marks for Paper II is 200, which is half the total for the examination.
2. The time allowed for Paper II is three hours.
3. You must answer from four different sections:
    - One question on a single text (total marks: 60)
    - One question on comparative study of texts (total marks: 70)
    - One question on prescribed poetry (total marks: 50)
    - Questions on an unseen poem (total marks: 20).
4. Divide up your time in the following way:
    - The single text: 50 minutes
    - The comparative study of texts: 60 minutes
    - The prescribed poetry: 50 minutes
    - The unseen poem: 15 minutes.
5. Give yourself five minutes to read back over the paper and check your answers against the questions asked. *Do not exceed this time.* Remember, good time-keeping in an examination is essential in order to gain the necessary marks. *You will not receive extra marks by writing beyond the time.*
6. Attempt all sections of the paper. Do not leave out any section of the examination.

Answering literature questions

1. Do the question that you find easiest first. This will cause you to peak; it will boost your confidence and help you with the other sections.
2. Do not rush at answering questions. Spend time working out the implications of the question. Make sure you understand what is being asked in the question. To do this, analyse or decode every aspect of the question.
3. Know the difference between such terms as *justify*, *analyse*, *discuss*, *compare*, *contrast*, *evaluate*, *assess*, *comment* and *paraphrase*.
4. Remember, you do not have to agree with the question that is asked. Show clearly what stance you are taking on the question. Use evidence from your text(s) to back up your particular stance on the question.
5. Rephrase the question in your own words. It can help to formulate it as a direct question. For example, look at the following question: 'The picture we get of Heathcliff in the novel *Wuthering Heights* is of a dark, evil boy whose origins are deeply mysterious. Would you agree with this statement about Heathcliff's character?' Question rephrased: 'Would you agree that the character of Heathcliff is that of a dark and evil boy, and that his origins are deeply mysterious?'
Note that in rephrasing the question you will be able to see more clearly how many *parts* there are in the question. Here there are *two parts* in the question.
6. Draw a circle around the main points of the question, and begin by organising a rough draft.
7. Brainstorm the topic. Use trigger questions: How? Why? Where? When?
8. Begin by *answering* the actual question asked. Your opening paragraph should simply make a *firm* and *clear* statement on the question that is asked.
9. Use the present tense in your answer. Use modern English as much as you can.
10. Give yourself time to look back over the answers. Check your answer for irrelevant statements, incoherent argument and repetition of ideas.
11. Before you construct a paragraph in your answer, consider the following points:
    - What is the topic sentence or main idea of this paragraph?
    - What relationship does this paragraph have to the actual question?
    - Are the ideas in the paragraph given support through evidence or quotation?
    - Does the concluding paragraph tie up all the ideas and refer back to the question?

Remember that it is very important in each paragraph to refer to what is being asked in the question. And remember that each paragraph in your answer has to advance your argument to another stage. Each paragraph is a logical stage in a coherent and developing argument. If the paragraph does not have a bearing or relationship to the question, then discard it.

Features of a good answer on literature

1. A unity of impression, i.e. all paragraphs relate to one another and to the topic in general. The concluding paragraph must synthesise or tie up all the preceding ideas and arguments.

2. Answers that focus exactly on what is asked, that do not beat around the bush, digress or introduce material that is irrelevant.
3. A style that is familiar and clear to your reader. Remember, you are communicating with, not impressing, your reader. Avoid:
   - awkward syntax
   - long-winded sentences
   - repetition
   - the self-conscious 'I think', 'I hope to prove that', 'I feel I have shown that . . .'. These are unnecessary as they weaken your argument. A good literature essay does not need such statements: it should speak for itself.
4. A clear understanding of the question that is asked. The opening paragraph must focus your position on the question and show the direction your answer will take.
5. An individual or personal response. Do not rehash notes or critiques; make the answer your own. Back up what you say with reference to or quotation from the text(s).
6. A maturity of response. Answers in the literature section must show that you have evaluated all sides and are presenting an objective, balanced and coherent answer.
7. A structured and organised argument, with supporting evidence that leads logically to a conclusion. Good essays make progress: they advance an argument, explore an issue and arrive at a conclusion.

Incorporating quotations in answers

Every question on the literature paper requires reference to or quotation from the text itself. Quotations must be positioned in such a way that they play a key role in advancing your argument. The length of quotations must be appropriate to the point being made: give as many words from the text as are strictly relevant to your point – no more and no less. You must explain the relevance of a quotation, i.e. how this particular quotation relates to the point or points being made. To introduce a quotation, use a colon, for example:

> She was much too fond of Heathcliff. The greatest punishment we could invent for her was to keep her separate from him: yet she got chided more than any of us on his account.

The Study of a Single Text 8

The questions in this section will take for granted that you have acquired a deep and thorough knowledge of the novels or plays you have studied. In this section you must:
- Know the main features or characteristics of the central characters well
- Study the plot and how it develops in the text
- Know how language and imagery are used to serve the writer's purpose
- Study key quotes that describe the motivations of the characters and the attitude of the writer to both the characters and the issues that are treated in the text.

How to answer a question on the in-depth study of a text

- Rephrase or rewrite the question. Sometimes it can help to formulate it into a more direct question.
- Take a definite stance or position on the question. Decide clearly whether you agree, disagree or partly agree with the question. You are free to take whatever stance you like, as long as you support it clearly with evidence and quotations or reference to the text.
- Your opening paragraph should outline clearly, in one or two sentences, your position on the question and the direction your essay will take.
- Begin to organise your ideas before you start to write your essay fully. Jot down several points (six or seven) in note form. These will deal with different aspects of the question and will be constructed in paragraphs.

Sample questions and answers

Wuthering Heights
(2010 and 2011 exams)

Question
(a) Describe what happens when Heathcliff first arrives in Wuthering Heights.
(10 marks)
(b) How does Hareton influence the events in the story? (20 marks)
(c) What is Nelly Dean's role in the story? (30 marks)

SAMPLE ANSWER
(a) Heathcliff arrives in Chapter 4 of the novel. Nelly Dean tells us how Earnshaw brought 'it' home and how 'it was as dark as if it came from the devil'. The arrival of Heathcliff throws the Earnshaws into confusion. Mrs Earnshaw wants to fling him out the door, while Nelly leaves him on the landing for the night. He becomes very friendly very quickly with Miss Cathy, while Hindley beats him up regularly. Nelly repeats how he bred a bad feeling in the house from the beginning.

(b) Hareton is the son of Hindley and Frances. Frances dies shortly after giving birth to Hareton. When Heathcliff returns, having been absent for three years, he settles in the Heights with Hindley and Hareton. Hareton becomes strongly attached to Heathcliff, in spite of his rough ways and deep spirit of revenge. Heathcliff plans to avenge himself on Edgar Linton by securing possession of both the Grange and the Heights. He manages to do this through marrying his own son, young Linton, to young Cathy, who is the daughter of Catherine and Edgar. After the death of young Linton, Hareton becomes deeply attached to young Cathy. She teaches him how to read and they begin to fall in love. Heathcliff notices that they are deeply attached and tells Nelly Dean that he can see himself reflected in the figure of Hareton. He also begins to realise how futile his plans for revenge have become. So through the figure of Hareton, order and harmony are restored to the world of the Heights.

(c) Nelly Dean has been the housekeeper for three generations of Earnshaws and later the Linton household. Brontë describes her as 'a specimen of true benevolence and homely fidelity'.

She tells a story of extraordinary, supernatural and incredible events. She exists as a springboard to bring the otherwise incredible, unrealistic events of the novel within our grasp, and to give this amazing story a foothold in the natural world. In this aspect, she largely succeeds – we recognise her limitations and her failures. She is someone we can identify with. She is rooted in our own commonplace, earthly and perhaps mundane world. We believe and accept all she says as the truth, since she is a direct witness to the events taking place in the novel.

Brontë manages to create a truly realistic character in the figure of Nelly. Through her the author is able to continuously shift our vision back and forth between the natural and supernatural worlds. The most incredible events seem to us to be commonplace, recorded as they are by such a sober witness as Nelly Dean. Ironically, Nelly's flaws of character contribute to the dramatic success of the novel.

Lies of Silence
(2010 exam)

Question
(a) Outline clearly some of the dilemmas which Michael Dillon is forced to face in the novel. Do you consider that he deals with these effectively? Give reasons for your answer. (30 marks)
(b) The novel is based on a central conflict between two different types of people. Write a note on this conflict and show how it is resolved at the conclusion.
(30 marks)

Questions rephrased:
(a) Explain clearly some of the predicaments facing Michael Dillon in the novel *Lies of Silence*. Does he handle these problems or predicaments well?
(b) Write a note on the main conflict that takes place in the novel between two different types of character. Show how this conflict is resolved at the end of the novel.

Sample answer
(a) Michael Dillon is faced with a number of dilemmas in the novel *Lies of Silence*. At the beginning of the novel he is married to a woman called Moira, but he is in love with a younger girl called Andrea. He is faced with the dilemma of leaving Moira and settling in London with Andrea. He is unable to confront Moira with the truth about their relationship. This dilemma is further increased and given an added dimension when the IRA force him to plant a bomb in the car park of a large hotel in Belfast. The next dilemma he faces is whether to inform the police about the bomb and endanger the life of Moira, his wife, who is a hostage in the hands of the IRA. He decides to inform the police about the bomb. The police manage to rescue Moira. Michael Dillon has seen the face of one of these young IRA boys. When the IRA discover this, a priest arrives on behalf of the boy to plead with Dillon not to testify. Dillon is then faced with the dilemma of whether to ignore the whole thing, move to London or inform the police about the boy's identity. The remainder of the novel shows us how Dillon hovers between deciding to inform and then changing his mind. Eventually, after changing his mind several times, he decides to ignore the whole thing and not testify. However, his decision is made too late. He is shot by a group of IRA terrorists at the conclusion.

 I believe that Michael Dillon's character is too indecisive. At the beginning of the novel he is clearly not in love with his wife and is in love with this young girl, Andrea, instead. However, he lacks the courage to confront the situation and fails to tell his wife the truth. His wife learns about this herself when she sees the two of them together in a restaurant. Dillon shows courage when he informs the police about the bomb and at the same time he tries his best to protect Moira. Later on in the story, when the priest urges him to remain silent, he wavers too many times. The novel shows him experiencing different emotional states. On the one hand he is angry with the priest and is prepared to inform on the IRA. At another stage, he is prepared to ignore the whole thing. At the conclusion of the novel, when he finally makes up his mind, it is too late. He loses his temper with the priest over the fact that he starts preaching to him about not informing in order to avoid any more killing. However, immediately afterwards he changes his mind. But because he has been so inconsistent in his behaviour for so long, he is shot.

(b) The novel shows the conflict between the IRA and Michael Dillon, who is manager of a hotel in the North of Ireland. The IRA put pressure on Dillon not to inform the police about the fact that he knows the identity of one of their men, who tried to plant a bomb in a hotel car park. Dillon is tired of the Troubles in the North. He is anxious to leave and settle with his mistress in London. He is not interested in politics and wants a peaceful life. He is embroiled in the conflict, however, after the IRA take over his house and force him to plant a bomb. In addition, his wife Moira acts hysterically and speaks out a lot against the IRA through the media. The priest, who is a relation of the young IRA man, is anxious to intervene on his behalf and prevent him from being imprisoned. He is a friend of the family and obviously an IRA sympathiser.

Dillon is angry at the priest's intervention and is unsympathetic towards the position of the IRA. Dillon reacts violently when the priest pleads with him not to reveal the boy's name. At times Dillon appears to be a hostile and determined character. The priest is stubborn, however. He calls to see Dillon several times and warns him. Dillon is firm with him and tells him he will not yield. When he finally changes his mind, however, it is too late. He is shot. The conflict is resolved in the murder of Dillon at the end. He refuses to submit to the IRA demands not to inform. The result is his murder in cold blood.

How Many Miles to Babylon?
(2011 exam)

Question
(a) What type of person was Alec's mother? Make reference to the novel to support your answer. (10 marks)
(b) Outline Alec's attitude at the conclusion of his life. Is he justified in having this type of attitude? Make reference to the novel to support your answer. (20 marks)
(c) Draw a character portrait of Major Glendinning. Do you think he was justified in behaving as he did in the story? Refer to the novel in your answer. (30 marks)

Sample answer
(a) Alec is a young boy who grows up in Ireland in the early years of the twentieth century. He lacks nothing materially as his family are very wealthy landowners. Alec, however, is a lonely child who misses the company of people his own age. Alec's mother is a social snob who insists that he will not mix with the ordinary people who work on their land and who live in their area.

Alec befriends Jerry and as they form a bond of friendship we witness how Alec is truly happy for the first time in his life. When Alec's mother discovers the friendship she soon puts a stop to it. We realise she is a very dominant woman who is used to having her own way. She possesses the capacity to undermine people and make them feel small. Alec describes this when he writes, 'my heart doesn't bleed for her'. Furthermore, Alec's mother always knows how to get her own way. When she realises that Alec is becoming attached to Jerry she decides that it is time for Alec to go travelling 'to broaden his education'. Of course this is a completely selfish act motivated by her desire to dominate him completely.

At another stage in the novel Alec's mother wishes that her son will go to war as she believes that he has 'a moral duty . . . to fight'. Alec is not keen to fight 'for a cause I neither understand nor care about'. And so again Alec's mother decides to thwart him no matter what it costs. Alec tells her that he has no wish to go and fight, and besides 'his father needs him'. Then she tells him that his father is not really his father. She leaves him stunned and shattered in moments and then sweeps away; he is 'dispossessed in a sentence'. This is a totally selfish gesture that only serves to alienate Alec even further from his mother.

It can therefore be seen in conclusion that Alec's mother only thinks about herself and her own image. She uses Alec as a tool to further her own ambitions, which are largely selfish. She manages to alienate her son, as Alec has very little warmth left towards his mother when the story ends.

(b) Alec spends a great deal of time in the trenches. Here he experiences all the bitterness of life and the hypocrisy that is a part of war. He is sustained by his friendship with Jerry. Thoughts of his mother are few, and for the most part they are bitter. Alec has had very little happiness or fulfilment in his life and, as he never believed in war, his first-hand experience in the trenches in France only serves to generate a greater sense of gloom and negativity in his outlook. Alec communicates very little with his mother. At one stage his father writes a letter to him informing him about the situation on the home front and tells Alec that his mother 'is under great strain'.

There is a sense of hopelessness and near-despair in Alec's life as the story draws towards an end. The conclusion is a very dismal and negative one. Alec mentions how 'I have not communicated with either my father or mother'. So Alec's attitude towards his mother is negative and bitter.

To a great extent Alec is justified in having this attitude. His mother never bothered to understand him or consider his interests. She was a snob and simply ordered him to stay away from the only real friend he ever had. In addition, she forces her own will on Alec in order to get him to go and fight in the war. She is interested only in the glory and honour of having a son on the war front serving his country. She is not interested in how the experience will actually affect her son. She alienates her son and is left a lonely and embittered woman at the end.

(c) Major Glendinning is a British officer based in the trenches in France. He has no time for sentiment and instead is a ruthless and cold operator. We can see this fact in all his conversations with Alec and the other men who are forced to fight in the trenches in World War II. Glendinning is quite similar to Alec's mother, Alicia. He possesses the same value system and demonstrates petty snobbery and hypocrisy. We witness many examples of Glendinning's hatred of the Irish and his contempt for their values. He sees them simply as 'bog Irish', incapable of behaving like men, and inept in battle and fighting.

Glendinning is a cold and ruthless operator who sees his men as very much like cattle. Alec challenges Glendinning's way of dealing with people, telling him, 'perhaps if they had regarded us as men in the first place there might have been no war'. This only intensifies Glendinning's hatred and sense of vindictiveness. Glendinning shows himself to be unfeeling and callous when he puts Alec in a situation where he is forced to punish his only friend, Jerry, by heading up the firing squad and shooting him for desertion. Alec's attitude to Glendinning at the end, having worked with him for many months, is summed up in the irony of the line, 'There were moments when I almost admired him'.

Glendinning has no feelings of humanity – he fails to show sympathy or understanding of his officers. He acts in a cold and clinical manner throughout the whole story. He is a hypocrite. At one stage Alec calls on him at night and we see how he is able to drink whiskey and soda, and have a warm fire burning in the grate, while outside his men are dying of cold and starvation. Glendinning does not take the time to understand people and therefore he was not justified in ordering Alec to shoot his best friend. The fact of war and its coldness remains a sad and true reality, but this does not justify in any way the behaviour of Glendinning. In fact his behaviour contributed in many ways to the dismal and negative conclusion of the story and of Alec's attitude to life at the end: 'I am committed to no cause. I love no living person.'

POSSIBLE QUESTIONS ON THE STUDY OF A SINGLE TEXT

1. (a) Discuss the character of Michael Dillon in the novel *Lies of Silence*. In your answer, take into account the particular dilemmas he was confronted with and how he responded to them. (30 marks)
   (b) Do you consider that the opening chapter of the novel *Lies of Silence* sets the scene well? In your answer, take into account the fact that the novel is written as a thriller. (30 marks)
2. (a) Discuss the reaction of Hindley to the arrival of Heathcliff at the beginning of the novel *Wuthering Heights*. How did this reaction contribute to changing Heathcliff's nature/personality? (30 marks)
   (b) Would you consider young Linton to be the real villain of this novel? In your answer, take into account his part in tricking young Cathy into marrying him. (30 marks)
3. (a) Write a short note on the theme of war and its effects in the novel *How Many Miles to Babylon?* (20 marks)
   (b) Did you like the novel *How Many Miles to Babylon?* Write a short response to this question and support your answer with reference or quotation from the novel. (20 marks)
   (c) '*How Many Miles to Babylon?* is a great read.' Write an article for a magazine, in which you support or oppose the above view of the novel. (20 marks)

The Comparative Study of Texts 9

WHAT IS A COMPARATIVE STUDY?

A comparative study of texts (play, novel or film) means the ability to discuss similarities or differences between texts under the following headings.

2010:
- Hero/heroine/villain
- Theme
- Social setting

2011:
- Relationships
- Theme
- Social setting

Hero/heroine/villain
- Be able to identify the main hero, heroine or villain in the texts you have chosen.
- Pinpoint the main features of the hero, heroine or villain in your texts.
- Draw comparisons between the hero, heroine or villain in the different texts you have chosen.

Theme
The theme is the main message in the text which the writer wishes to communicate to the reader. For example, in the novel *Lies of Silence*, one of the main messages or themes is the reality of terrorist violence in the North of Ireland. In the book *The Road to Memphis*, the author's theme is the way in which racism can damage human relationships.

Relationships
- Pick out the relationships that you consider to be important in each of your texts.

- Discuss how these relationships affect the story or plot of that text.
- Compare and contrast different features or aspects of these relationships in your chosen texts.

Social setting
- Be able to identify the type of society or social background shown in each of your texts.
- Examine certain types of customs and traditions in each case.
- Study the position of men and women in this society.
- Know what type of beliefs and values are shown in the texts.
- Examine certain features in this setting, such as power, work, race and class.
- Be able to draw comparisons between the different texts on these points.

ANSWERING A QUESTION ON THE COMPARATIVE STUDY OF TEXTS

1. Know exactly what your three texts for this section are. Take one particular text as your main or anchor text.
2. Spend time choosing your question. Identify clearly what exactly you are asked in the questions: is it a question on hero/heroine/villain, relationships, theme or social setting?
3. Begin by working on a rough draft. Work with the anchor text first. Jot down five or six different points related to the question based on that text. In each point, make sure to have a quotation or reference related to that point.
4. Write out your answer in rough draft form using the anchor text only.
5. Look at the other two texts and draw in the main points of each text to your question, showing how they may compare or contrast. You can do this in two ways: either add on some ideas to each paragraph from the two texts, or simply write a separate paragraph on each text outlining how it is related to the question.
6. All the material from your texts must be included in your answer in a continuous sequence. Do not divide your answer into sub-headings with the title of the texts at the top. The main thing is to link or weave in the texts naturally, and to show how they relate to the question asked, jotting down all points of comparison or contrast between the texts.
7. Organise your points into paragraphs, and make sure that you have used quotations or references from the texts as much as possible.
8. Prioritise and order your points, and make sure that each point refers in some way to the question asked.
9. Start writing the answer, and pause at the end of each paragraph to examine what relevance it has to the question asked.

SAMPLE QUESTIONS AND ANSWERS

Sample question on tension or climax or resolution
(a) 'Tension is an effective ingredient of good storytelling.' Show how this statement is

true of one text on your course.
(b) Compare the use of tension in another text on your comparative course. Which text do you consider to be more effective in conveying tension?

SAMPLE ANSWER
(a) A state of tension is effectively built up throughout the film *Witness,* directed by Peter Weir. In this film, John Book finds himself alone in a corrupt police force. He is forced to go on the run because of the murder of a police officer by another policeman over narcotics and money. Book knows that the head of the police force is involved in shady dealings involving money laundering and illicit drug deals. For that reason, Book seeks refuge in an Amish community.

McFee and Schaeffer, the two police officers involved, discover where he is and hunt him down with guns. Tension is built up when we realise that Book is alone in a barn without any weapons to protect him, while outside the police have the barn surrounded. Book survives because of his ingenuity. He manages to lure one of the men into the barn and drown him with a vast shower of grain. He then shoots McFee with the gun that he has taken from the man he has killed.

(b) In the novel *Wuthering Heights*, tension occurs when Heathcliff tricks Nelly Dean and young Cathy into the Heights. He plans to marry his son, young Linton, to young Cathy and so gain possession of both the Heights and the Grange. Nelly Dean is kept as a prisoner for several days while Heathcliff secures the marriage of his son to young Cathy. Meanwhile, Edgar Linton – Cathy's father – is dying below in the Grange. The tension is increased by the knowledge that young Cathy is a prisoner in the Heights and is unable to be with her dying father. She manages to escape and see her father shortly before he dies.

While both texts contain scenes of tension, in my opinion the film *Witness* is more effective in conveying the tension. The graphic images of Book trapped in a small barn with no weapons to defend him, while all the Amish community are away working in the fields, keep us on the edge of our seats. Furthermore, the images of violence among the armed policemen outside the barn, coupled with the dramatic music, accentuate this atmosphere of tension in the film.

The actual shooting of McFee against the wall of the barn is vivid and bloody. The dialogue at the conclusion is violent, aggressive and loud. All of these factors help create a strong and vivid sense of violence and tension.

Sample question on theme
(a) Choose a text from your comparative course which deals with a theme that is universal. Describe how this theme is developed in the text/film.
(b) Take another text and compare how the same theme is treated. Which text do you find to be more interesting?

SAMPLE ANSWER
(a) The theme that I consider to be universal in the texts that I have studied for my comparative course is memories. In the play *Juno and the Paycock*, memories play a large

part in the life of Boyle, the 'Paycock' of the play. Boyle is unable to face the reality of hard work and responsibility, and instead escapes through fabricating imaginary dreams or memories of another, more heroic person. He reminisces about his days as a gallant captain 'sailin from the gulf o' Mexico to the Antanartic Ocean'.

All of his days are filled with this type of self-indulgent fantasising. These fantasies and false memories are encouraged by his parasite-type friend called Joxer. Right through to the conclusion of the play, Boyle escapes from his responsibilities as father and husband to another world by means of false exaggerated memories. The last image of him in the play is truly tragic. Juno, Boyle's wife, has done everything she can to keep the family together and to get Boyle to face up to his responsibilities. At the end of the play, Boyle comes in from the pub drunk and still indulging in his memories of his fake contribution to the Easter Rising: 'I done . . . me bit . . . in Easther Week. . . . Commandant Kelly died . . . in them . . . arms.' The sad reality is that Juno has now abandoned him to his memories.

(b) In the play *Philadelphia, Here I Come!*, Gar O'Donnell spends a great deal of time remembering his adolescent affair with Kate Doogan. This memory tortures him as he still loves her and now she is married to another man. He is about to embark on a journey to Philadelphia and make a complete break from his life in Ireland in Ballybeg. But the theme of memories haunts him on the night before he goes. He also remembers a beautiful evening when he was alone with his dad on a boat when he was only a young boy. Sadly, his father fails to recall the same memory and this provides Gar with another spur to leave Ballybeg.

The play *Juno*, to my mind, is more effective in portraying the theme of memories. We are given some very vivid pictures of Boyle indulging in absurd and ridiculous fantasising and in false memories about the past. In addition, this type of escapist fantasy, which is set against the reality of a city torn by war, highlights the absurdity and futility of Boyle's attempts to escape reality. It also highlights the type of lazy and irresponsible drunkard Boyle really is. The theme of memories in this play highlights in a truly vivid way the influence of the past upon the present and how memories can play us false as well as true.

Sample question on relationships

The most interesting relationships to read about are the ones that cause unhappiness to the people involved. Give your view of this statement. Support your answer by referring to key moments from two texts you have studied for your comparative course.

Sample answer

The texts which I propose to discuss for this answer are *Philadelphia, Here I Come!* by Brian Friel and *Lies of Silence* by Brian Moore.

The main relationship which causes a great deal of unhappiness is that between Gar and his father in the play *Philadelphia, Here I Come!*. In the novel *Lies of Silence*, the relationship between the central character, Michael Dillon, and his wife, Moira, is one of the most interesting in the novel. In both texts there is undoubtedly a great deal of unhappiness for all characters.

It is the lack of real communication between himself and his father which causes the main problem for Gar O'Donnell in *Philadelphia, Here I Come!*. Gar is determined that all his problems will be solved by going to Philadelphia. There is no communication between himself and his father, and for that reason Gar feels like a failure in Ballybeg and repeatedly condemns the place. This sense of failure and this inability to communicate with his only living parent causes Gar to feel frustrated and deeply unhappy.

Gar's mother died in childbirth and his father has never been able to face this fact. Furthermore, his father has retreated into a dull routine where he fails to engage in even the most basic means of communication. Father and son communicate through the medium of Madge, their housekeeper.

On the other hand, in the novel *Lies of Silence*, Michael Dillon is having an affair with a young girl called Andrea, unknown to his wife, Moira. Early on in the novel, Moira is taken prisoner and her life is endangered when the IRA break into her house and threaten her and her husband. She escapes, but spends her time attempting to revenge herself on the IRA. In reality, she is deeply upset because of her husband's betrayal. She has discovered the truth about his mistress. For most of the novel, we witness Michael caught in a dilemma between deciding to inform on the IRA or forget about the whole thing. Michael is deeply unhappy with this situation. Unfortunately, he delays, and because he is unable to make up his mind, he is murdered at the end of the story.

Sample question on social setting
(a) Take two texts you have studied for your comparative course and compare the different social worlds represented in each text. (40 marks)
(b) In which social world would you prefer to live? Give reasons for your answer.
(30 marks)

Sample answer
(a) The texts I have chosen for this answer are the novel *Circle of Friends* by Maeve Binchy and the film *Cinema Paradiso*, directed by Giuseppe Tornatore.

The social world of the novel is Dublin in the late fifties and early sixties. The novel gives a vivid insight into many different types of family, both rural and urban. The whole story centres on a group of friends who meet in University College Dublin as students. The social world is made up of parties and meeting for coffee and chats. We gain an insight into the middle classes in the background of Benny, one of the main characters. In the figure of Eve, another central character, who was adopted by the nuns and reared in the convent, we see another social level. Jack's family is wealthy, as his father is a doctor, while Nan's parents are working class. There is a strong mixture of different social styles in the novel.

The social world of the film *Cinema Paradiso*, by contrast, is a small village in Sicily at the end of World War Two. The people in this small Sicilian village are simple and unsophisticated. They are enthralled by the cinema, and spend most of their leisure time enjoying a variety of films. Most of them are working class and come from a humble background.

We also see the power of the parish priest, who decides which films are suitable. Poverty is part of life in this village. Young Salvatore's father has obviously left his family, and his wife is bringing up the children on her own.

The social world changes as the story develops and we see the village become more prosperous. This prosperity does not lead to greater happiness, however. The villagers become more discontented with life, and more difficult to please.

(b) The social world which I would prefer to live in would be the one represented in the film *Cinema Paradiso*. I liked the way the people were simple and unsophisticated and how they really enjoyed simple pleasures such as the cinema. There is a special type of charm in the world of this small village, and we can see how Alfredo and Salvatore enjoyed a very important friendship. Truly this world is one I would have enjoyed living in very much.

10 Notes on Some Prescribed Texts

In this section there are notes on some of the texts that are prescribed at Ordinary Level. These notes can be used for answering questions on both the in-depth study of a text and the comparative study.

LIES OF SILENCE
(2010 exam and 2011 comparative study only)

Brian Moore

The story
The novel is set in Belfast and London and deals with the Troubles in the North. Michael Dillon is the manager of a hotel in the north of Ireland who plans to leave his wife because he has fallen in love with a young girl called Andrea. Before Dillon can tell his wife that he is going to leave her, they are invaded by masked men who say they are in the IRA. They force him to deliver a bomb to his hotel while they hold his wife as a hostage. Dillon sees one of the faces of the men. He seizes an opportunity to warn the police about the bomb. After this incident, Dillon is faced with the dilemma of whether to identify the IRA man to the police or simply ignore everything and settle in London with his mistress. He meets a priest who is a friend of the IRA man and who warns him not to testify. Dillon wavers several times between testifying and not testifying. Eventually he decides not to. However, it is too late. Two IRA gunmen burst into his flat and kill him at the conclusion.

Themes
Betrayal
This story shows different examples of the theme of betrayal. Michael Dillon is unfaithful to his wife, Moira, as he is having a secret relationship with a young girl called Andrea. Michael fails to tell Moira that he plans to leave her and settle in London with Andrea. It is only when Moira discovers them both in a restaurant that Michael admits to his wife that he is in another relationship.

The theme of loyalty can be seen in the figure of the priest. Father Connolly knows Kevin's family and wants Kevin to be protected from the police, even though he has been involved in the IRA. Michael believes it is right to inform the police about the IRA and about Kevin's involvement. He changes his mind, but the IRA betray him and have him shot at the conclusion.

Violence

The brutal reality of Northern Ireland and the sinister violence of the IRA form much of the plot of this story. The IRA break into Dillon's home one night with the sole intention of carrying out an act of violence against some British politicians who are staying in the hotel where Michael works as manager. Their intention is to plant a bomb in the car park and kill people. The conclusion of this story is equally violent: Michael is shot by two men while entering his house.

Relationships
Dillon and Moira

Dillon is married to Moira but he is not in love with her. She realises this and is angry. Their relationship is tense and strained, and worsens when she discovers his affair with Andrea. When the IRA hold both of them hostage, Moira reacts in a rebellious and aggressive manner. After their release, she decides to hold interviews with the media and expose the IRA. She is hurt by the way she has been treated, and in some way wants revenge on Dillon.

Dillon and Andrea

They are very much in love with each other. For much of the novel, Dillon is divided between his loyalty towards Andrea and his wish to protect Moira from the IRA. In addition, their relationship suffers after the incident with the IRA. Dillon is clearly confused about what to do – whether to inform or not. This fact creates a good deal of tension between himself and Andrea, yet she stands by him right through to the end.

Dillon and the IRA

Dillon first comes into contact with the IRA when they hold him at gunpoint in his own house one night. He is angry and bitter towards them. Later on, when he meets the priest, he is disgusted at his request and refuses to agree not to inform. However, at the insistence of Andrea and for the sake of peace, he eventually decides to remain silent. His decision comes too late. The IRA shoot him at the conclusion of the novel.

Social setting

The social setting is Belfast in Northern Ireland in the twentieth century. Fear and tension because of the political situation dominate the atmosphere. The tension flowing from the Troubles is evident througout the book. The novel shows us a city which is divided by both religious and political beliefs. Violence and conflict are constant features of life. The novel shows the attempts of the IRA to use civilians to further their campaign.

Hero

Michael Dillon is the hero of this novel. He comes from a middle-class area of Belfast and is manager of the city's Clarence Hotel. He hopes to move to London. He is married to Moira but is in love with another woman, Andrea. He shows courage in informing the police about the bomb in the car. However, he is an indecisive character and spends a lot of time wavering about whether to inform on the IRA boy whom he accidentally saw. Also, he is afraid to tell Moira that he is going to leave her for another woman. It is only when Moira sees the two of them together in a restaurant that he owns up and decides to live with Andrea. His indecisiveness contributes to his death. He is warned not to inform on the boy by the priest. He hesitates and it is this hesitation which causes him to be shot at the conclusion of the novel.

Villain

The villains of the novel are the members of the IRA, who are seen to be a hostile and negative presence. They hold Michael and Moira hostage and force him to plant a bomb in the car park outside the Clarence Hotel. Their representative is a priest who pleads with Dillon to withhold information about one of the IRA members called Kev, who is his nephew. They carry out their revenge on Dillon by shooting him as they are afraid he will testify against Kev.

CIRCLE OF FRIENDS

(2010 comparative study only and 2011 exam)

Maeve Binchy

The story

The title of the novel centres on a circle of friends who all come from various parts of Ireland and who go to college in UCD. It opens in 1949, when Benny Hogan, an only child, is celebrating her tenth birthday. Chapter 2 moves forward to 1957, when Benny is eighteen years old and starting in college. She lives in a small village called Knockglen. Her family owns Hogan's Gentlemen's Outfitters, a large shop in Knockglen. Benny befriends a girl called Eve who lives in the convent with the nuns. Eve's mother died giving birth, and her father went out of his mind and fell over the cliff into the quarry shortly after his wife died. Eve's mother happened to be the daughter of a rich local family called the Westwards. She married the gardener, who was Eve's father, and her family disowned her as a result. Eve is unable to pay the fees to attend university, but she decides to visit Simon Westward and ask him to help her through college. He agrees. Eve owns a cottage near the Westward home, which had been left to her.

We also meet Kit Hegarty, who lives in Dun Laoghaire and keeps students in order to supplement her income, as her husband has abandoned her. Her son, Francis, dies in a motorbike accident. Nan Mahon is another young, beautiful girl who comes from a working-class background and whose father is an alcoholic. She is ambitious and determined to marry well. There is also the good-looking Jack Foley, whom everyone falls for. His father is a doctor.

These characters form a gang when they are studying in Dublin and the story narrates their different adventures. Jack seems to be attracted to Nan, but he begins a relationship with Benny, much to everyone's surprise. Eve begins to go out with a young man called Aiden, who is also part of the gang.

In the meantime, a young man called Sean Walsh starts to work in Hogan's Outfitters and becomes ambitious to marry the only daughter of the business. Benny is not interested in him, as she finds him to be too arrogant and opinionated. Meanwhile, Nan meets Simon Westward, who becomes fascinated with her. They start a relationship and shortly after this she becomes pregnant. Simon abandons her when he hears this. In the meantime, Jack has abandoned Benny and begun to see Nan. Nan tells Jack that she is pregnant with his baby and he feels compelled to marry her. Shortly after this, Eve attacks Nan and Nan's arm is injured. She is taken to hospital and has a miscarriage. She breaks up with Jack, much to his relief.

Benny's father dies suddenly of a heart attack, and it appears that Sean has been taking money and deceiving the Hogans. Sean leaves after this discovery, but remains in Knockglen. He marries a woman called Dorothy Healy.

Benny's mother decides to sell their home, called Lisbeg, and move to a smaller place. Jack is repentant over the situation with Benny and tries to resume the relationship. Benny has changed, however, and has become interested in another boy called Bill Dunne. The story concludes with the gang staying together as friends and Eve and Benny planning to move into a flat the following year.

Themes
Friendship
Friendship between young people who attend college in UCD forms one of the main themes of this book. We meet different types of characters, all from various backgrounds. There is Eve, who has been brought up largely by the nuns in the convent, yet she is one of the most popular girls in the group and a loyal friend to Benny. We see how different characters change as the story develops. The good-looking and popular Jack abandons Benny for Nan. Nan ends up deceiving him by making him believe he is the father of her child. Each of the characters is forced to face some crisis or crises in their lives. Yet the friendship endures between them all, and the last section shows the friends united around a fire.

Women
There are different types of women shown in the novel. There is Kit Hegarty, a very courageous woman forced to face the death of her son from a motorbike accident. In addition, Kit has to keep the house together and sustain herself and her family after having been abandoned by her husband. Benny and Eve are strong women who form a solid friendship. They are loyal people and help the other members of the gang when in trouble. Eve in particular is a valiant woman who is forced to confront Simon

Westward and ask for the fees for college. She is a strong, fearless woman who clearly suffers, but who shows much fortitude and strength in her life and actions.

Benny's mother, Annabel Hogan, is also a courageous woman. She is faced with the death of her husband and the betrayal of Sean Walsh, who had worked for many years in her business.

Loyalty

Loyalty is an important theme in the novel. Benny becomes friends with Eve, who has been abandoned by the Westwards because of the fact that her mother only married a gardener. She is deeply sensitive to how people behave towards her and demands that Simon Westward should pay her fees out of loyalty to her own family. Nan is betrayed later on in the story by Simon Westward, who abandons her as soon as it becomes apparent that she is pregnant. Jack Foley, a young student, is tricked by Nan into believing that she is pregnant with his child, and as a result he abandons his relationship with Benny.

Relationships

Benny and Eve

This is one of the strongest relationships represented in the story. Both characters endure various difficulties and they are still strong and loyal friends at the conclusion of the story.

Nan and Simon

Initially Simon is fascinated by the beautiful and sophisticated Nan. However, when Nan becomes pregnant, Simon abandons her and refuses to face the responsibility of having a child. This relationship disintegrates very soon, as it is based on selfishness.

Social setting

The social background of this novel is Ireland in the mid-1950s. We gain an insight into Ireland, both rural and urban. There are many references to Catholicism and the influence of the nuns in Ireland at that time. The nuns exerted a powerful influence in education and in the social community during this period and carried out a great deal of work through the orphanages. They are shown to be kind, caring people in the story, particularly in the case of Eve, a young girl who has no parents.

College life is seen to be one of constant socialising and gossip. There are insights into different class levels through the various characters represented in the story.

Hero

Jack seems to be one of the main heroes in the story. He is fooled by Nan into believing that the baby she is carrying is his. He acts nobly and loyally in standing by her and deciding to get married.

Heroine

In many ways, Benny is the heroine in the story. She is abandoned by Jack, whom she really loved. She suffers a lot in the story but remains loyal to people. She matures as the story unfolds, and is able to see through Jack's petty vanity at the conclusion of the story.

Villain

Sean Walsh is the villain of the story. He is ambitious to marry Benny so that he can control the business. He shows himself to be a corrupt man when he mishandles the money.

THE PLOUGH AND THE STARS
(2011 exam)

Sean O'Casey

The story

The title of the play *The Plough and the Stars* is taken from a flag. The Covey explains that the flag is a Labour flag and should only be used to build the barricades of a worker's republic.

This story is set in the Dublin tenements in 1916. It centres on a young married couple called Jack and Nora Clitheroe. Jack is a member of the Irish Citizen Army. Nora is ambitious to move out of the tenements. She hates the environment and also the fact that her husband is involved in politics. Mrs Gogan, a charwoman and typical tenement dweller, comments on the negativity of this environment when she tells Fluther Good how the tenements are simply 'Vaults . . . hidin' the dead, instead of homes that are shelterin' the livin'.'

Early on in the play, Jack learns that she has burned a letter which tells him that he has been promoted to Commandant. He has also been ordered to lead a reconnaissance attack on Dublin Castle. Jack is a political fanatic. He delights in putting on his Sam Browne belt and parading with it and his revolver. He is weak. He is described early on as having 'none of the strength of Nora'. He has a row with her and leaves the house in anger.

Mollser is a young girl who also lives in the tenements and is suffering from tuberculosis. This sickness is exacerbated by her surroundings of poverty and squalor. She ironically tells Nora how she envies her health and happy home. At the conclusion of Act II, Clitheroe, Nora's husband, is drinking in a pub with other soldiers in the Irish Citizen Army, chanting how Ireland is greater than a wife and a mother.

Act III takes place in Easter Week 1916. Nora is deeply distraught because she has had no word from Jack. Mollser is dying. Bessie Burgess rushes into the tenements and tells them how everyone is breaking into the shops, and the Volunteers are firing on them. Bessie and the others, including Mrs Gogan, steal a lot of things from the shops.

Shortly after this, Captain Brennan arrives, supporting Lieutenant Langon on his arm. He has been wounded. Clitheroe follows them. They speak about plugging the 'slum lice' (the tenement dwellers) who have been looting goods. Nora enters and causes an emotional scene with Clitheroe. He is ashamed of her behaviour and tells her he does not want 'to be untrue to me comrades'. He asks her, 'What are you more than any other woman?' This scene concludes with Clitheroe leaving Nora lying on the street, while Bessie Burgess goes in search of a doctor.

Act IV takes place in the living room of Bessie Burgess. Mollser's body lies there with Nora's dead child. We learn that Bessie has been looking after Nora for three nights in a row. Captain Brennan arrives in and announces that Clitheroe is dead. His last words were that he was proud to die for Ireland. Nora appears, but she is hallucinating. She screams for her baby and her husband. Bessie tries to calm her down by singing some hymns for her. Nora becomes hysterical and Bessie tries to get her away from the window, as there is shooting on the street. Bessie is hit by a bullet and dies. Mrs Gogan rushes to her assistance.

The play ironically concludes with the image of two British soldiers, Sergeant Tinley and Corporal Stoddart, sitting down in the room drinking tea while they join in singing 'Keep the Home Fires Burning'. Shortly before she died, Bessie had expressed the fact that she was 'no Shinner', but a true advocate of Britain. Yet she dies at the hands of British soldiers, and lies dead while those who killed her sing 'Keep the Home Fires Burning'.

Themes
The futility of violence
The whole play speaks about the total futility of violence. O'Casey shows that many of the people who are Nationalists are also cowards and weaklings. He shows many images of the men as selfish, shallow people. He seems to be highlighting the pointlessness of war and violence in Ireland at this time.

Loyalty
There are different types of loyalty expressed in this play. Nora's loyalty to her husband costs her the life of her child and her sanity. Jack is loyal to politics and believes that Ireland is greater than a woman. He gives his life for Ireland and fails to realise that his domestic happiness has been destroyed as a result of this commitment. His loyalty is shown to be tragic and hollow at the conclusion of this play.

Women
Most of the women in this play experience a great deal of suffering from politics and war. Nora is one of the main women who suffers because of her husband's refusal to dedicate himself to his family. Jack will not renounce his fanatical commitment to politics.

Another woman, Mrs Gogan, who also lives in the tenements, suffers because of her sick child, Mollser, and the poverty of her surroundings.

Bessie Burgess becomes a victim of tragic irony at the play's conclusion. She sacrifices herself to help Nora when she is ill and ends up getting killed by a stray bullet which comes from a British soldier's gun. Bessie ironically spent her life committed to the cause of Britain.

Relationships
Jack and Nora
Initially this seems to be a strong and loving relationship. Nora clings to Jack and wishes for a secure and happy marriage, one that is free from strife and warfare. Jack, however, acts otherwise. His relationship with his wife is secondary to his political commitment.

Nora and Bessie Burgess
This is a relationship based on generosity and self-sacrifice. Initially Bessie Burgess was a rough woman from the tenements. Her concern and care of Nora is sincere and genuine at the play's conclusion. Tragically, she loses her life in this action. Her actions contrast with those of Jack's, whose mindless commitment to politics causes death and tragedy for his family.

Social setting
This play is set in the Dublin tenements during the Easter Rising of 1916. The tragic effects of this rising and its ensuing poverty and destitution are shown in many instances. The women steal from the bombed-out shops, and there is a general atmosphere of hopelessness in the play. The public house plays a large role in social life at that time. It also becomes evident how tuberculosis was a serious sickness in this era.

Hero
Fluther Good, who is a fun figure for much of this play, is one of the heroes in the story. He risks his life by going out to look for Nora and also by settling everything with the undertaker when Mollser dies.

Heroine
Bessie Burgess seems to be the heroine, as she gives her life protecting Nora at the conclusion. She sacrifices herself by staying up several nights to look after Nora.

Villain
Jack renounces his wife and home and commits himself to violence and politics. As a result, his wife loses her child and is left abandoned when he is killed later on in gunfire on the streets.

HOW MANY MILES TO BABYLON?
(2011 exam)

Jennifer Johnston

The story
The story begins in Ireland before the outbreak of war, in 1914. It centres on a young boy called Alec who is born into a wealthy Anglo-Irish family. His parents do not get

on well together, and Alec has a lonely childhood. He becomes friendly with a boy called Jerry, who works as a stablehand for Alec's parents. Alec's mother disapproves of the relationship, and they decide to take him on a trip abroad to Europe to distract him. Alec's mother is very cold, and announces to him that she wishes him to go to the war and fight.

Alec insists on staying to look after his father. She then announces that he is not his real father and that Alec is illegitimate. Alec is devastated. He leaves immediately for France. Jerry has also gone to fight in the trenches. Alec is an officer, and Jerry is called Private Crowe in the war. Major Glendinning is the British officer in charge of the men. He is a tough man who has no time for sentiment or feelings. Alec spends time with Jerry riding horses, even though this is forbidden. Jerry's mother writes to him to find out about his father, who may be dead in the trenches. Jerry leaves to look for his father and shortly afterwards, on his return, he is sentenced to death. Glendinning orders Alec to lead the firing squad on the following day. Alec goes into Jerry's cell on the night before, and shoots him in an act of mercy. Alec is then condemned to be shot for disobedience.

Themes
War
The theme is war and its negative effects. When Alec and Jerry go to fight in the trenches, we get some vivid images of the horror of war. Most of the time Alec is revolted by the sights of bloodshed and violence and is unable to control his hatred for war. Major Glendinning seems to glory in the brutality of war and to see people merely as objects.

Friendship
This is an important theme in the story. During Alec's childhood he experiences deep loneliness and isolation. He finds a true friend in Jerry, but because they belong to different social classes, they are not allowed to express their friendship openly. Their friendship extends to the trenches and causes tragedy at the end. Alec is ordered to shoot his friend Jerry by firing squad. He kills him quietly in an act of mercy and release, and loses his own life as a result.

Relationships
Alec and Jerry
This is the strongest relationship in the story. Alec and Jerry are united from early on in the story. Because of their different social circumstances, however, they are forced to part. Alec remains faithful to Jerry and tries to protect him as much as possible from punishment when they go to fight. Their relationship has tragic consequences. Both characters are forced to die for disobedience during the war.

Alec and his mother
Alec finds his mother very cold and unemotional. He is strongly attached to his father, and is clearly upset when his mother exposes the truth about his background on the

eve of his going to war. He never really forgives her for this, and becomes cold and distanced from her. At the end, he is indifferent to the fact that he will die, as he states that his 'heart does not bleed for her'.

Social setting
There are two different social settings in this story – the Anglo-Irish ascendancy and the military campaign in the trenches during World War I. We also get a glimpse of the lives of the lower-class Catholics in Ireland before 1914. We see how friendship between the two boys is impossible because of the difference in their social backgrounds. There is also a difference when they enlist for war. Alec becomes an officer immediately, while Jerry is made a private. Their duties and lifestyle are quite different when they are sent to France.

Hero
Alec is the hero of this novel. He is forced to leave his family home to fight in the war. He suffers a great deal in his life and he is made to face the dilemma of leading a firing squad to shoot his best friend, Jerry.

Heroine
Alec's mother, Alicia, is the heroine of this novel. She is a selfish and manipulative woman who ends up living a lonely and sterile existence.

Villain
Major Glendinning is a British officer in France. He is cold and unfeeling. He expresses contempt for the Irish and commands Alec to shoot his best friend.

A Whistle in the Dark
(2010 comparative study only and 2011 exam)

Tom Murphy

The story
Act One opens with a picture of three Irishmen called Harry, Hugo and Iggy who are trying to get dressed in a house. Betty is an English girl aged twenty-eight. She is married to Michael and they live in Coventry. His brothers Harry, Hugo and Iggy are staying for a while with them. The family are known as the Carneys and they come from Mayo in Ireland. They take great pride in the fact that they are known as the fighting Carneys. It is evident that Michael does not like this vision of his family. Mush is another character, a friend of the Carneys, who spends his time flattering people.

Betty and Michael have a conversation about the fact that his father, Dada, is arriving with his youngest brother, Des, and that there is little room in the house for everybody. Michael feels responsible for the family as he is the eldest son. Harry begins to tell Michael about how Des had a fight in the pub. Michael is worried about Des as he feels that he will be influenced by the boys and encouraged to fight. Michael tries to convince Harry that Des would be better off staying in Ireland and making something of himself. The Mulryans are another Irish family who challenge the Carneys to fight. The Carneys believe they are all iron men except for Michael and they accept the challenge to fight.

Dada and Des arrive on the scene. Dada is about sixty years old. Des is eager to be accepted by the family and slightly cocky. He has a bruise from a fight in the pub. Michael offers them tea and begins to remember how they planted five trees at the back of the house for each of the five sons. When they speak about the proposed fight with the Mulryans, Michael tries to encourage his father to bring Des home and get him a job. Dada speaks about pride and the fact that he is proud of his fighting sons. As the play unfolds we realise that Michael grew up in a world of violence. His father condemned Michael because he refused to engage in fighting. We also learn that the boys were made to fight one another when they were small in order to get respect from people in Ireland who saw them as boors and violent thugs.

All the boys ally themselves with their father against Michael and Betty, even though they are staying in their house.

The second act begins with Dada and Michael trying to reconcile their differences the following night. This fails, however, as the father is determined that his sons will fight. Michael reminds him of the status of the boys in England – Harry seems to work with prostitutes, while Iggy has a dubious job involving a bit of stealing. We learn that Dada was a policeman. He encourages the boys to go and fight the Mulryans, 'fight for the name and have valour'. Meanwhile, he disappears out the door telling them he has a little surprise arranged for them behind the factory at Rock's Lane where they are supposed to meet the Mulryans. Des decides to join his brothers in the fight.

Michael and Betty argue as she tells him to stand up to his family and how he owes them nothing. We then learn that Michael was attacked when he was younger by a crowd of 'darkies' and his brothers saved him, while he ran away in fear from the fight. From that time on, his brothers have looked on Michael as a coward. Michael is anxious to get away from this background of violence inherent in his family. He is intelligent and knows deep down that his father is a coward and that he spends his time drinking in a pub just shooting his mouth off until the fight is over. Betty urges Michael to fight so that 'they will respect him'.

The third act takes place a few hours later. Dada is drunk and singing a song called 'I hear you calling me'. He begins to speak to Betty about books and education and how he was a policeman once. In his drunken soliloquies we learn that he is very bitter about the fact that while he spent his time trying to flatter the middle classes he was only left with the job of caretaker. He tries to justify and reassure himself by saying that he is proud of his family and by urging them to fight their way through life.

The boys arrive back from the fight and tell their father that they beat the Mulryans. Dada presents them with a silver cup as a reward for 'their courage and bravery in the face of the enemy'. They begin to celebrate and sing 'The boys from the County Mayo'. Betty tells them that Michael had gone to join them in the fight. When Michael returns he is drunk. Harry then begins to dominate the situation and accuses Michael of being ashamed of him and of trying to be better than the family. Dada tries to rescue his position by getting them to fight one another just like they did when they were kids. Michael attacks his father verbally telling him that he has seen through him all the time, and how his father drank with the hob nobs and then came home angry and frustrated because he had made nothing of himself.

Betty comes down the stairs dressed in a coat and carrying a case. She challenges Michael, asking him whether he will come with her or stay with them. Des insults her, calling her 'Whore' and 'English trash'. The boys rally around Michael and Des and challenge them to fight one another. Des begins to attack Michael, who does not respond at first. Des knocks Michael to the ground and Michael picks up a bottle and hits Des. Des is killed. The boys gather around the dead body of Des and leave their father alone in the corner. The play concludes with Dada asking them what else he could have done. He cries out repeatedly, 'I did my best . . . I tried'.

Themes
Pride
This is seen in an ironic light. Dada speaks repeatedly about pride, 'I was always a proud man, everyone will tell you that'. He has failed as the breadwinner of his family because for some reason he lost his job in the police. He is unable to accept this humiliation and instead preaches to his sons about having pride and winning respect from people. Tragically this respect must be won through violence and harassment.

Violence
The play dramatises the violence within an Irish family called the Carneys. The story outlines the tragic consequences of continuous violence and abuse. Michael is the only courageous character who confronts this brutality and takes a stance against it. Tragically he is accused of being a coward by his family and later on by his wife. He is forced to engage in a physical fight with his younger brother whom he wanted to protect. He ends up killing him. The inability of violence to achieve anything positive is dramatised very clearly when the brothers gather around the body of their dead brother and alienate their father who has generated this incessant brutality.

Relationships
The relationships within the Carney family are the main ones shown in this play. Michael, the eldest son, has broken away from their violent ways and managed to establish a life with his wife, Betty, in Coventry, England. Michael is seen by his family as a failure because he will not engage in acts of violence. All relationships are seen negatively as they are shown against the backdrop of violence and repeated abuse.

Michael and Dada
This relationship is governed by bullying on the part of Dada, who believes in encouraging violence within his sons. He sees Michael as a coward and a weakling and humiliates him in front of the whole family. Dada is not sincere, however, as we see when he is drunk that he is like Michael and that he respects education deep down.

Michael and Des
Michael's youngest brother, Des, has been influenced by the others to engage in violence. Des lacks confidence and is insecure, and therefore he is anxious to gain the approval of the members of his family. It is ironic that Michael is the only member who truly cares about Des's welfare and tries to protect him from a violent life. Tragically Michael ends up killing Des when they are urged on by the others to fight each other.

Social setting
The play represents the reality of rural Ireland in the 1960s. Although it is set in Coventry, most of the drama speaks about 1960s Ireland. The themes of snobbery and middle-class culture are important as they are key reasons for Dada's violent attitude to society. Education is important in this play. It becomes evident that Michael differs from his brothers as he thinks more about certain ways of behaviour and about life in general. Their father respects education deep down, even though he is determined to browbeat his children into reacting violently towards life and people in general.

Hero
The hero of this play is undoubtedly Michael. He is the tragic figure who is forced to take a stance against the brutality and violence of his father and his upbringing. In doing this he is forced to fight with his youngest brother, Des, who he wanted to protect from violence. Tragically in this fight Michael kills Des with a bottle.

Heroine
The heroine is Betty, Michael's wife. She is forced to accommodate Michael's brothers and father and is exposed to their violence and constant humiliation of her. She leaves the family unit at the conclusion, challenging her husband to take a stance and join her.

Villain
The villain in this play is the father, or Dada as he is called by his children. He is a truly tragic figure who embodies violence in all its forms. He is unable to face his failures and compensates instead by urging his sons to perform acts of violence in order to gain the respect of the community. In doing this he forces his sons to fight one another, which ends up with the killing of the youngest son, Des. However, even then he will not accept responsibility for the killing.

DANCING AT LUGHNASA
(2010 exam and 2011 comparative study only)

Brian Friel

The story
The play is set in a village called Ballybeg in Donegal, Ireland, in 1936. The Mundy family are at the centre of this story. Kate is the eldest daughter and the only one who

is working outside the home. She is a schoolteacher and feels the responsibility of looking after her four sisters (Maggie, Agnes, Rose and Chris). Their brother, Jack, has just returned from the missions in Uganda after twenty-five years. He is sick with malaria and it seems that he has lost his Catholic religion and engaged in pagan rites while in Africa. This brings a sense of shame to the family as they are living within a small Irish community in the early twentieth century. Furthermore, Chris has a young son called Michael. Michael's father, Gerry, is irresponsible as a father and has abandoned Chris on many occasions. Chris is still in love with him but knows that he will not assume the responsibilities associated with marriage.

As events unfold Kate loses her job because of the situation with Jack. Rose and Agnes spend their time knitting in order to make some money. With the arrival of a new knitting factory to the town their work becomes redundant and they are left without any money. They both leave Ballybeg and disappear to London. Michael, who is the narrator of the play, announces how they were not found until twenty-five years later, at which stage Agnes was dead and Rose was dying in a house for the destitute. Jack also dies, of a heart attack. The play concludes on a grim note. Michael announces that he will be glad to leave the parish. We learn that Kate is tutoring the children of Austen Morgan, who is now married. Kate seemingly always loved Austen Morgan.

Themes
Poverty
The theme of poverty seems to be central in this play. Kate is the only one who is earning money to keep the family together. When the new factory opens in the village Rose and Agnes are compelled to give up their knitting work and they are no longer useful. They end up in England, where they die of poverty and starvation.

Religion
The play is set against the background of a small, Catholic community. Jack, the brother of the Mundy girls, is compelled to return from the missions supposedly because he is sick with malaria. The full truth emerges, however, as the drama unfolds. Jack has abandoned the Catholic religion in favour of pagan rituals and is therefore in disgrace in the eyes of the parish priest. Jack is not allowed to say Mass, and Kate loses her job in the local school because of him. His abandonment of the Catholic religion has brought disgrace on the Mundy family.

Family life
The Mundy girls stick close together throughout the play. Kate is the mother figure and is deeply concerned with holding the family together. Rose has a mild mental disability, she is described as 'simple', and her sister Agnes takes on the special responsibility of looking after her. When things begin to change, and the sisters are no longer able to support themselves, Agnes and Rose are forced to leave and look elsewhere for employment. They end up tragically as both sisters eventually die of hunger and neglect in London.

Change

Another main theme in the play is that of change. We can see this in many instances throughout the play. With the return of Jack from Africa, we see a change in the relationship between the parish priest and the family. Jack is no longer the heroic and self-sacrificing figure that he was imagined to be in this community. In the eyes of the community he has failed as a priest and is therefore a source of shame and humiliation for the Mundy family.

Change also occurs technologically. The Mundy girls have been earning their living for many years by knitting. With the opening of a new factory in the town, their work becomes redundant.

Relationships
Kate and Jack

Kate is a maternal character who tries very hard to keep the family together and to deal with the changes in Jack on his return from Uganda. She suffers when she loses her job in the local school.

Chris and Gerry

Chris clearly loves Gerry even though he has left her and fails to assume responsibility for their child. Gerry is a dreamer who avoids living in the real world and holding down a decent job. He escapes through dreaming and is not able to take on the responsibilities involved in a serious relationship.

Social setting

The play is set in 1936 in a rural part of the north of Ireland around the village of Ballybeg. It is a time when communications have not developed greatly. We learn early on in the play that the Mundys were obsessed with the acquisition of their first radio, which they christened Marconi.

The power of the Catholic religion is evident in this small community. The local parish priest possesses the power to dismiss Kate from her job as a schoolteacher in response to her brother Jack's changed status.

This is also a time when money is scarce and poverty is a striking feature of life. Towards the conclusion of the play we witness how economic change affects the family. The growth of a new factory in the town means that home-produced goods are no longer in demand. Both Agnes and Rose are forced to emigrate to England in search of employment.

Certain customs such as dancing and barn dancing at the festival of Lá Lughnasa are practised in this community. Dance is an integral part of the culture of Ballybeg, and in many ways the celebrations associated with Lá Lughnasa are similar to Jack's dance rituals in Uganda. There are resonances of pagan customs here.

The absence of men in the parish and the unmarried status of the Mundy sisters could highlight the power of emigration within this community. Illegitimacy is frowned upon in this parish.

Hero
The hero of this play is Jack. He suffers because he has been sent home from Uganda in disgrace after becoming involved in some magic rituals there. He is a humble and kind man.

Heroine
Kate, the eldest sister, is the heroine. She struggles to keep the family together in spite of tremendous difficulties in their environment.

Villain
The parish priest, who dismisses Kate, can be seen as the villain. He does not understand the position of the family and refuses to grant permission to Jack to say Mass.

LAMB
(2010 exam and 2011 comparative study only)

Bernard MacLaverty

The story
The novel is based on a man called Michael Lamb who has been a brother in a religious order for many years. His name was Brother Sebastian. His father dies three days before the story begins. Brother Benedict, who runs the Home where Brother Sebastian lives, is a rigid and implacable man. The Home exists for children who have no families. It is run on a very strict basis and Brother Benedict believes in punishing the boys violently. One young boy called Owen Kane has been abandoned in this Home by his mother, who does not want the responsibility of looking after him. Owen is subject to frequent fits and needs to take medicine for them.

Brother Sebastian announces to Brother Benedict that he wants to leave. He was unable to do this before because it would have grieved his father greatly. Brother Benedict refuses to listen to him and announces that he will make it difficult for him to get a job. Michael Lamb/Brother Sebastian leaves the Home with Owen and they run away to London. News filters out through the newspapers that Michael has kidnapped Owen. They spend an enjoyable time in various hotels in London. Michael treats Owen like his father treated him. Michael had a very good relationship with his father, who was a farmer in the north of Ireland.

While in London Michael begins to think of his life in the religious order and sees it as a handful of negatives in his life. He also realises that he cannot continue to wander around London and escape detection. They decide to return to Ireland, as it will be the place where people will least suspect them to be.

Michael gets a plane to Ireland with Owen and they travel to Donegal. Michael knows that there is no hope for either of them sustaining this type of lifestyle. He decides to substitute Owen's tablets for aspirins and they go to a beach in Donegal. Michael wants to protect Owen from returning to the brutality of the Home. Owen has a fit and Michael brings him over to the edge of the water and drowns him there. Michael then walks into the sea with the intention of drowning himself. The water is too shallow and Michael returns to the beach feeling bitter and disillusioned. He has killed Owen to save him, even though he loved him more than anyone in the world.

Theme
Love
The love between Owen and Michael is a strong force in this story. This love is short lived, however. Having experienced some blissful days in London, filled with joy and freedom, they are forced to face reality and return to Ireland. Out of love for the boy Michael drowns him while he is experiencing a fit in order to protect him from further violence in the Home.

Michael's commitment to and love for God have gone cold over the years. He has lost his faith and no longer believes in the vocation he has given his life to. This leads him to abandon the religious order and escape to London.

Relationships
The relationship between Michael and Owen forms the subject matter of this story. Michael abandons his commitment to the religious order and goes to London with Owen. There they both begin to experience life for the first time. This life is one filled with happiness and joy. Their relationship is similar to that between a father and a son. Michael laments at one stage that Owen was not able to experience the type of relationship that Michael had with his own father. The relationship, however, has tragic consequences when Michael kills Owen in order to save him from the trauma of returning to the Home.

Social setting
The novel is set in both Ireland and England. We get a sense of the harshness of religious life in the west of Ireland in the mid-twentieth century, including references to violence and the beating of young boys. Life in London is more stimulating and varied and we get glimpses of Piccadilly and the excitement of the shops and amusements.

Hero
Michael Lamb is the hero of this novel. He has the courage to face the injustices of Brother Benedict and to stand up to him.

Villain
Brother Benedict is the villain in this story. He is cruel and abusive when he is put in charge of children in the Home.

PANTHER IN THE BASEMENT
(2010 exam)

Amos Oz

The story
The novel is written from the viewpoint of a twelve-year-old boy in Jerusalem in 1947. He lives with his mother and father in a small apartment. His father works as an editorial assistant in a small publishing house. The family is Jewish and the father is also writing a book on the history of the Jews in Poland. The narrator's mother is a teacher in an institution for immigrant orphans in the city. The story recounts, in a deeply humorous way, the events that occurred to the narrator and his family in the last year of British rule in Jerusalem.

The narrator speaks about his two friends, Ben Hur and Chita. Through their childish games they organise a secret underground movement and spend their time pretending to rid Jerusalem of the British. Proffy (or Professor) is the nickname of the narrator because he loves looking up big words. Proffy befriends a British sergeant called Dunlop and they become friends. Proffy begins to take classes in English from Sergeant Dunlop. Proffy likes him but is afraid to admit this. In an amusing episode Proffy is summoned by Ben Hur and Chita to a trial in the Tel Arza Woods. Here he is accused of being a traitor because of his friendship with Sergeant Dunlop. He abandons his two friends after this.

The narrator also speaks about how the curfew began to be imposed during the day and tells an anecdote about a particular raid carried out by British soldiers on his home. This incident was the occasion of tension for the narrator because of the fact that his father had hidden his book about the Jews in the library. The whole incident turns out to be very funny as his father begins to show off his books in English to the British soldiers.

After the British move out and Jerusalem is declared a Hebrew state, Proffy's father informs him, in a moving section, about his own childhood in Poland and how he was publicly humiliated by the children in the area because of the fact that he was a Jew. The novel concludes with freedom for Jerusalem together with the narrator's comments about how his story comes from darkness and returns to darkness.

Themes
Imagination
Proffy's imagination is vivid and typical of a young boy. We get some powerful images of his imaginative flights of escapism in fighting against the British forces and trying to oust them from Jerusalem. There is a splendid section where the narrator gets carried away by the enormous burden of having to hide his father's book in the library.

Fear
The fear generated by war and strife emerges in many of the narrator's references to British soldiers and house searches. Proffy's parents are afraid many times for the safety

of their child and reprimand him severely when he stays out after curfew. He articulates much of this fear during the many anecdotes he relates throughout the novel.

Relationships
The story gives us a deep insight into the mentality of a young boy in a war-torn city. It captures in a vivid manner some of the strong bonds of friendship and other relationships that he cultivated during the year preceding British withdrawal from Jerusalem. Proffy's relationships with his two young friends, Ben Hur and Chita, are amusing and graphic insights into the misadventures of adventurous boys. The narrator's relationship with his father is one of obedience and a type of respect. His father is serious and exercises strict control over his son. It is only at the conclusion of the story that we witness the deep humanity and capacity for suffering in his father when he tells his son about his life as a Jew in Poland.

Social setting
The novel is set in Jerusalem in the post-war period of 1947. The references to the curfew outline the restrictions that are associated with a time of war. We gain an insight into the position of the Jews in these years while they are forced to live under British rule.

Hero
Proffy, the narrator, is the hero of this story. We follow his anecdotes and his efforts to make friends as a young Jewish boy growing up in Jerusalem during and after World War II.

Heroine
Proffy's mother is the heroine of this story.

Villain
The British forces that occupied Jerusalem are seen as the villains of this story.

SIVE
(2010 exam and 2011 comparative study only)

John B. Keane

The story
The play centres on a young woman aged eighteen called Sive. She is illegitimate and lives with her brother, Mike, his wife, Mena, and Nanna, who is Mike's mother. There is a matchmaker in the locality called Thomasheen Sean Rua, who decides that Sive should marry an old man called Sean Dota. Sean is rich, but old and ugly looking. Thomasheen convinces Mike and Mena to organise the marriage of Sive to Sean Dota. They will receive a sum of £200 as soon as she marries him.

Sive does not want to marry Sean Dota as she is in love with a young man by the name of Liam Scuab. Liam, however, is not suitable as he is the cousin of the man who abandoned Sive's mother when he realised that she was pregnant. Mike refuses permission for Liam and Sive to marry.

Sive is distraught but is forced to obey her brother and his wife. Nanna does not approve and would prefer her to marry Liam. Two local 'tinkers', Pats and his son Carthalawn, plot together and decide to help Sive escape from Sean Dota and marry Liam. The plot fails, however, as Thomasheen discovers the letter and destroys it. On the night before her marriage Sive disappears and shortly afterwards her body is discovered in a bog hole. Liam finds the body and carries it back to the house, where he announces to Mena and her husband that they are responsible for Sive's death. As Liam cries over the dead body, Sean Dota and Thomasheen leave the room. The play concludes with Pats and his son singing about a maiden who was drowned because of the fact that she would not be a bride.

Themes
Love/marriage
In this play both love and marriage are treated very negatively. Thomasheen, who is supposed to be the local matchmaker bringing together people who love one another in marriage, queries cynically to Mena, 'What business has the likes of us with love?' Love and marriage become synonymous with selfishness and self-interest. Mena and Thomasheen are depicted as two selfish people who see Sive's marriage to Sean Dota in terms of money and expediency and as a matter that will serve themselves.

Women
The women portrayed in this play can be seen in two different ways. On the one hand, women are shown to be strong and filled with a great deal of fortitude. On the other, they are portrayed negatively. Both Mena and Nanna fight and insult one another in an abusive manner and both are seen to be embittered people in different ways. Nanna despises the fact that Mena has no children, while Mena sees the presence of Nanna in the house as a continuous source of irritation. Sive, on the other hand, is seen as a vulnerable target of the self-interest of the people who should be helping her in life. At the conclusion of the play, when her dead body is carried in, we witness the destruction of a beautiful young woman because of the greed of other people.

Money/poverty
The question of money dominates almost every line of this play, which is set against the backdrop of a struggling, rural, Irish economy. We witness the consequences in the community of this deep-seated poverty. Marriage and relationships are seen in terms of money and not merely love. Money is used as a means of exerting control and power over people.

Relationships
Relationships are seen to be largely negative in this play. Sive and Liam have a positive relationship, however, it turns out to be tragic as Sive is forced to marry a man she does not love.

Social setting
The setting of this play is Ireland in the 1950s. It is a time of harsh poverty and people are valued in terms of the land and the crops they possess. There are many references to the fear of the poorhouse and the rough reality of poverty. Marriage and love are both seen in relation to the amount of possessions a person has. It is a time when matchmakers are popular and local trades flourish. The importance of possessing land is stressed frequently in this play.

Hero
The hero of this play is Liam, who loves Sive truly and remains faithful to her up to the end of her life.

Heroine
The heroine is undoubtedly Sive. She becomes a passive victim of the self-interest and selfishness of others.

Villain
The villain is Thomasheen; although Mena can also be seen as a villain. They both collude to exploit the innocence and vulnerability of others and use their power in order to serve their own self-interest.

THE BLACKWATER LIGHTSHIP
(2010 exam)

Colm Tóibín

The story
The novel is written from the third-person viewpoint about Helen and her family. Her husband is Hugh and she has two sons, Manus and Cathal. They live in Dublin in the early 1990s. She is the principal of a comprehensive school. Her husband is from Donegal and they speak some Irish in the family. Manus is very dependent on her, while Cathal, who is two years older, is quieter and more mature. At the beginning of the story Helen and Hugh have a party and there is a lot of singing and people play Irish music.

Shortly after this a man called Paul arrives. He is a friend of Helen's brother, Declan. It turns out that Declan is dying in hospital from AIDS. Paul is his friend and is looking after him; they are both gay. They ask Helen to explain the situation, and the fact that Declan is dying, to her mother.

Helen decides to drive to Wexford to tell her mother. She arrives at Blackwater where her grandmother, Dora Devereux, lives and proceeds to call on her and tell her about Declan's situation. There is an emotional scene between Helen and her granny. Helen goes to the beach near the house and watches all the old buildings that are slowly falling into the sea because of erosion. She stays with her granny that night.

That night she has a flashback to when she was aged eleven and Declan was eight and they learned that their father was sick and had to go to Dublin for tests. Helen begins to recall the time she and Declan went to stay with their granny. While there, Helen acted as a mother figure for Declan. She has memories of them watching the *Late Late Show* with their grandparents and listening to some controversial political people on the television. Their mother stayed with their father and did not visit them. Eventually Helen remembers how she heard indirectly about the fact that her father was seriously ill and dying of cancer. Her granny called her one day to tell her that her father had died. Both she and Declan were devastated.

Larry, another of Declan's friends, arrives in Wexford. Both Larry and Paul decide to stay in Mrs Devereux's house to keep Declan company in his sickness. Dora has a conversation with Helen about how she learned that Declan was homosexual, and how she came to terms with the fact that he is dying of AIDS. Shortly after the arrival of everyone to the house we begin to see how curious neighbours are in the locality. Two neighbours arrive to enquire about who everyone is, and who owns all the cars.

Helen's mother, Lily, arrives and the conflict between them becomes evident. Dora tells Helen about Lily. She went to school in the FCJ in Bunclody. The nuns thought she had a vocation but Dora prevented this by sending her to a family with sons so she could roam the country and go to parties. Dora appears to be a bit of a rebel.

At one stage Helen and her granny get Larry to talk about how he managed to tell his parents that he was gay and how they reacted. Paul also tells Helen about his relationship with a French man and how they were married in a ceremony carried out by an unorthodox Catholic priest.

The novel records the various comings and goings of the different family members and Declan's friends as they accompany him in his illness. There is constant reference to the lightship in the sea, which lies beside the house.

We learn that Helen spent many of her summers working in her granny's house, which was a bed and breakfast. Helen met the man who would become her husband, Hugh, in UCD. They got married quietly in a registry office and her mother has never met Hugh or their two sons. She has been married for seven years. Helen broke away from her family as they wanted her to take up a teaching job in Wexford and stay near them. She refused to work there as she felt she would end up slaving for them. As a result, relations between her mother and granny became strained.

Helen speaks a bit to Paul about her past and about how she missed her father and the difficulty involved in dealing with his loss. She tells him how her mother 'taught her never to trust anyone's love because she was always on the verge of withdrawing her own'. Helen is very bitter about this fact.

As the story progresses, Declan's health steadily worsens and he becomes increasingly dependent on his family and friends. Simultaneously, we witness how the communication between Helen and her mother begins to improve. Lily tells Helen about how she would remember the two lighthouses, Tusker and Blackwater, when she was younger, and how she associated them with the fidelity of a man and a woman. She is thus able to speak about the death of her husband and how bitter she feels because of his sudden death. We begin to realise how much Helen's mother is suffering over the situation of her son, and how she really misses her husband, who would have helped her by sharing the grief. Helen manages to express her bitterness to her mother about the fact that she felt her mother had abandoned her when she was younger.

We see how the family come together in many different ways in Mrs Devereux's house. They decide to go swimming, and recall the past with a great deal of affection.

Eventually Declan must be moved to St James's Hospital when he becomes so sick that none of his family or friends can manage to look after him. Helen drives Declan to Dublin and they leave him in the care of the doctors.

The novel concludes with Helen returning to her home and bringing her mother there for the first time. Hugh is away in Donegal with their two sons. Her mother begins to speak about the future and her hopes that she will get to know the two boys and visit them a lot. They decide they will visit Declan later on in the evening.

Themes
Family life
The novel traces the various relationships between the members of Helen's family. At the centre of the story is Declan, a young man who is dying of AIDS. The story records the efforts on the part of all family members to make his last days comfortable and peaceful. As a result of sickness, the family bonds grow stronger and the various conflicts that governed their relationships are resolved.

Change
A lot of the novel speaks about change, both in people and in Ireland. The story is told using Helen as a filter to express the various reactions to people and events. This ordinary Irish family are forced to come to terms with the fact that Declan is homosexual, and is dying of AIDS. All of this is new, and all of it is tragic to the family. The story also records the changes in the landscape from the time when Helen used to stay with her granny. Houses are larger and people have more money and bigger cars. She notices the dramatic effect of erosion on the land. By the conclusion of the story, there are dramatic changes within the family relationships. Helen returns to Dublin and is beginning to appreciate her husband and family more. Furthermore, her relationship with her mother has improved as a result of Declan's sickness.

Relationships
There are different types of relationship outlined in this novel. We see how Helen, a young married woman, manages to sustain a busy life as a school principal and as a mother of two young boys. Her sons have different relationships with her: Manus is very dependent on her, while Cathal, who is two years older, is independent and aloof.

On the other hand, we read about the relationships of Declan, a young gay man, and his friends. Initially his family are disconcerted by his sexuality and make efforts to understand it.

The theme of relationships is shown in a positive light, as all the relationships involve reaching out to another person because of the fact that Declan is dying. While relationships involve a certain amount of conflict and tension, the novel shows us how love and self-giving transcend these difficulties and manage to bring about a certain degree of reconciliation and peace. We see this particularly at the conclusion of the novel when Helen and her mother are reconciled and their relationship begins again on a positive note.

Social setting
The background of this novel is Ireland in the 1990s. The setting is rural Blackwater in Wexford, and there is a certain amount of affluence in the lifestyle. In addition, through flashback, we gain an insight into 1970s Ireland. Jack Lynch was Taoiseach and we learn that the *Irish Independent* was a Fine Gael newspaper. There are references to the *Late Late Show*, a popular television programme. We see how the family are Catholics as they go to Mass at one stage and decide to pray for Declan. Helen's commitment to her faith is ambiguous as she refuses to pray at certain stages. She also got married in a registry office and not in a Catholic church. This may be due to the fact that she is trying to come to terms with difficult things about her past. The story also deals with urban city life in Dublin. The whole culture of homosexuality is alien to this family and they are forced to face it through Declan.

Hero
Declan, who is the main character around which all the story is drawn, is undoubtedly the hero of this story. His plight – he is dying of AIDS – is tragic, and his suffering is heroic.

Heroine
Helen, who experiences a lot of trauma as a result of her family relationships, is the heroine of the novel. She suffered greatly when her father died. Now she is forced to deal with the fact that her brother is dying of AIDS.

Villain
There is no real villain in this story, unless the virus causing AIDS could be described as a villain.

The Grapes of Wrath
(2010 and 2011 exams)

John Steinbeck

The story
The novel begins with Tom Joad thumbing a lift along a dusty American road. He tells the driver who picks him up that he has done seven years in prison for homicide. He killed a guy in a fight. We are told then about the people in this land who do not own the land they are living on. The 'owner men' came along and evicted all the people as the bank or the company was a 'monster' who needed the money.

Tom meets a preacher called Casey along the road who joins him. He reaches the place where his parents had lived only to discover that the family home has been destroyed by the owner men. Tom meets a fellow called Muley who refuses to leave the land and simply wanders around looking for food. Tom hears that his family have gone to his Uncle John's and that they hope to go to California to get work.

Tom meets his family and they are setting off for California. The family pack up their belongings and head off in old cars. Casey decides to go with them. We hear about the thousands of refugees who are streaming into California in the hope of getting work and food for their children. Along the way Grandpa, who did not want to leave, has a stroke and dies. They bury him in a plot of land but are unable to mark it with a headstone. They meet up with various people who tell them that there is no work in California and that they have been deceived. Just before the Californian border Grandma gets sick.

Ma fights with the guards at the border telling them they cannot refuse them access as they are dying of hunger. Even though the Joad family suffer a great deal in order to undertake this journey, we witness a great spirit of generosity and self-sacrifice from the members of the family. They are generous to the people they meet, sharing the little food they have. The family rally together under the support of Ma, who is a real fighter and they succeed in reaching California.

Tragically, Grandma dies just as they reach the border and they bury her. They find rich and beautiful lands owned by just a few, extremely wealthy, people. These owners are afraid that the migrants will take possession of the land and so rules are strict and harsh. The Joads do not find work. Instead they are insulted and abused; they are called 'Oakies' and told to go home. We find that the more the people are repressed the stronger they knit together as a community. In California the rich landowners have spent their time trying to stem revolts and stop potential leaders emerging from these huge masses of refugees.

All the way through the narrative the people spend their days travelling and change from being refugees to being migrants. The story tells about their attempt to establish some type of community life. Storytelling forms part of their life around the camp fires and they play different musical instruments. For the most part they are intent on finding work and getting money so they will not starve.

At one stage the Joads arrive at a camp that is run very efficiently and has clean toilets and hot water. The people themselves have formed a committee and manage to keep the police away. The police try to break it up by sending in spies to riot at a dance one evening. The whole community are warned, and Tom, who now forms part of this community, helps to avert violence, and thus the police are forced to leave. The Joads have to leave that camp after a while as they are unable to find any work.

They move through a series of different types of camp, all supervised by armed police and all paying very small wages. Ma keeps urging them on and encourages them at every stage. Most of the time they are just working all day for mere food, and they are still living at the side of the road.

Tom meets Casey one night. He has been trying to fight the system and get rights for the people. Some policemen chase him and they kill him. Tom loses his temper and attacks one of the policemen. He is beaten up but manages to escape arrest. Meanwhile, the family have moved on to picking cotton for a while. There are so many people looking for work that the wages are reduced to just two and a half cents per hour. Rose of Sharon gets pneumonia and loses her baby.

Tom is forced to go into hiding and he cannot work. One of the kids tells a neighbour about Tom having killed a man so Ma decides that Tom is safer to leave the area as otherwise he will be killed. He tells his mother that he will work at getting a group together to bring about decent change for the people.

The rains come and the people are forced to huddle in barns as the cars are sinking in mud. They are forced to beg for food from the people who hate them. We learn that their fear turns to wrath as they repeatedly come up against inhumanity from the people with money.

The story concludes with the family taking refuge in a barn from the rains. They meet a stranger and his son who is very sick and needs milk. Rose of Sharon feeds him the milk that she would have given her child who died.

Themes
Family
The story centres on the Joad family who set out for California in a beaten-up truck in the hope of finding work. They meet up with many other families all looking for the same thing. Throughout the whole journey all the families are forced to face adversity and enormous suffering because of the cold and brutal inhumanity of the people who have power at that time. The Joads are a strong united family. The grandparents die on the journey and all the family suffer because they have not enough money to give them a decent burial. The mother of the Joad family is called Ma. She is a strong and generous woman who manages to find food to feed her family and shows no hesitation towards helping anyone in need. The story outlines how these families become stronger and more united as a result of extreme hardship and poverty. The self-sacrifice and generosity shown among the Joads, in spite of the overwhelming difficulties that they encounter, is a striking feature of this story.

Generosity/selfishness
This novel paints a picture of both the generosity and the selfishness inherent in

humankind. The families represented in the story are dispossessed of everything and forced into a situation of absolute deprivation and near-starvation. This situation is sustained for a very long time. Yet there are extraordinary examples shown of how self-sacrificing people can be. Ma is ready at every stage to spend herself in order to feed her family. She never refuses food to a hungry person and is heroic in many ways in her spirit of generosity and self-sacrifice. The last image in the story shows us how Rose of Sharon, her daughter, is prepared to save a boy's life by giving him the milk which would have fed her child.

In dramatic contrast to this theme we are given a chilling insight into the deep inhumanity inherent in humankind. The owners of the land and those who have authority in banking and corporate businesses are seen as monsters and exploiters of people. At no stage will they yield to ordinary human sympathy and show compassion. Instead, filled with a real fear of loss, they are prepared to exercise all manners of tyranny in order to retain control of their money and possessions. These people are seen as depraved and inhumane in a dark contrast to the warmth inherent in the lives of the dispossessed.

Poverty

This novel charts the story of many families who set out for California under the illusion that they will find a new life there that is free from poverty. They are forced to face extreme destitution and hardship. They find that the work and land are in the hands of a few people who are motivated by greed and self-interest. All the families face starvation and disease as they come to terms with the fact that they have been deceived about the promise of work. The novel is a harsh condemnation of poverty and how it destroys people's lives and prevents them from maintaining their dignity.

Relationships
Ma and Tom

Ma is a very strong woman who truly loves her son, Tom. She understands how much of a struggle it is for him to control his temper when he witnesses injustice around him. She helps Tom to become a better character and protects him at the end by advising him to leave the area as the police are looking for him.

Rose of Sharon and Ma

This relationship between mother and daughter is an interesting one. Rose of Sharon is pregnant but her husband, Connie, abandons her as he is unable to deal with the constant frustration of not managing to get work and suitable accommodation. Ma knows that the family must stay together as otherwise their chances of survival are much less. She is a great support to Rose, who becomes depressed throughout the whole ordeal of pregnancy, and especially when she delivers a stillborn child. We can see at the conclusion how much Ma has influenced Rose for the better when Rose is prepared to save the life of a young boy by feeding him with the milk that was really for her baby.

Social setting
The novel is set in the United States, specifically Oklahoma and California, in the 1930s. The story is based on the Great Depression, which occurred as a result of drought and caused a great deal of poverty and suffering.

Much of the story traces the path of migrant farmers who are forced to leave their farms because of large banking corporations who need the land to make more money.

The camps where many of the families settle when they reach California are called 'Hoovervilles'; this name came from President Hoover. They are filthy, cramped and impoverished places.

They manage to get temporary work picking peaches or cotton. There is no sustained work offered to the migrants and control of the economy is kept in the hands of a small number of people. Exploitation is rampant in this society. There are hints that the people will rise up against this injustice and evil. The title of the novel becomes an ironic metaphor for the seeds of hatred and anger growing in people's minds as a result of this unjust situation.

Hero
The hero in this story is Tom. He has spent some time in prison because he murdered a man in a fight. He is a person who is quick tempered. We see how he struggles with his character and keeps control through the help of his family and his mother in particular. He manages to stick by them through all their difficulties and is forced to leave the family unit only because of conflict with the police.

Heroine
Ma, the mother of the Joad family, is undoubtedly the heroine of the novel. She manages to mobilise the whole family at various stages to move on and try to get some work. She is intent on keeping the family together no matter what happens. She is strong and courageous and stands up to injustice fearlessly.

Villain
The owner men who control the land can be seen as the villains in this novel. They manage to maintain control over huge tracts of land and its produce, while thousands of people live in dire poverty and die of starvation.

THE SECRET LIFE OF BEES
(2011 exam)

Sue Monk Kidd

The story
The novel's narrator is a young white girl called Lily, who is living in South Carolina in the 1960s. Her mother died when she was four years old. Lily remembers how her mother and father were fighting on the day she died. Lily was hiding in a closet in the

bedroom and she was discovered by T.Ray, her father. Her father had a gun in his hand and was waving it about. Lily grabbed the gun and believes that she was the one who killed her mother.

Rosaleen is a black woman who works for them and acts as a mother figure for Lily. Lily calls her father T.Ray. He is very violent and punishes her frequently. They grow peaches and Lily is forced to try and sell them by the roadside. Lily loves bees and watching how they work and operate. It is clear that she misses her mother a great deal, and carries the burden of guilt for having killed her.

At one stage Rosaleen announces she is going to vote. When Lily and herself arrive in the small town of Sylvan, Rosaleen is attacked by white men and beaten up. They are both taken to the police station and charged. Some white men come and beat Rosaleen. She is forced to go to hospital. Lily's father is furious at the fact that his daughter is in prison. He tells her angrily that her mother left her and did not love her. He punishes her and is very violent. Lily decides to run away. She goes to the hospital where Rosaleen is recovering from concussion and they escape. They decide to go to a place called Tiburon because Lily has a picture of Our Lady as a black woman, which her mother had kept secretly.

When they arrive in Tiburon Lily goes to buy some food and sees the picture of the black Mary. Then she learns about a lady called August Boatwright who makes honey. They go to her house where they see a picture of the black Mary hanging on the wall. Lily tells August they have run away. They stay there and help with making honey. August lives with her two sisters, May and June. They are Catholics and have a great devotion to the black Mary calling her 'Our Lady in Chains'. They say the Rosary at night. August and her sisters have a group of friends and they call themselves the Daughters of Mary.

Lily is anxious to win the love of August. Lily learns from August that there was another sister in the family called April but she committed suicide. As a result May, who was her twin, did not recover and became mentally disturbed.

Neil is a black man who is in love with June and wants to marry her, but she is afraid of commitment. Lily begins to fall in love with Zach, who is black and wants to study law. At one stage Lily goes to town with Zach and he ends up being intimidated by some white men. He is put into prison. When May hears about this she is unable to deal with the news and decides to go outside to the wall to which she tells all her problems. It is night-time and she does not return. Later on they find her floating in the river. She is dead. They have a wake for her in the house. August finds a note from her telling them that it is her time to die and it is their time to live. As a result June accepts Neil's proposal and decides to marry him.

Shortly after this Zach is released from prison. Lily wants to tell August about her past and her mother but she is unable to find the right opportunity. When she does get round to having a chat with August, Lily learns that August used to look after her mother when she was a child. Lily's mother followed August to Sylvan where she was working then. There she met T.Ray and married him. She only married him because she was pregnant. She had a nervous breakdown and tried to leave him. Then the accident with the gun happened. When Lily hears the story about her mother she has great difficulty in dealing with it and in not becoming bitter against her mother. She becomes a bit obsessed with the fact that her mother left her alone at that time, and that she did not love her. August tells her how Our Lady must become the mother that she never had, and how she must find Our Lady in her heart. August explains to Lily 'how the only purpose is to love and to persist in love'.

Zach tells Lily he is going to study in a white high school, he wants to do law. Rosaleen goes to town and becomes a bona fide registered voter.

T.Ray arrives and begins to beat Lily. He loses control and thinks it is Deborah, his wife. Eventually August and Rosaleen arrive and tell him that Lily wants to stay and go to school. The Daughters of Mary arrive and defend her against her father. He leaves and he tells her that she did kill her mother, but she did not mean to. Lily returns to the house to be greeted by all the women. She is overwhelmed with joy at the love that awaits her in life, and concludes that maybe T.Ray in his own strange way might love her too.

Themes
Family/love
A lot of the story deals with Lily's attempts to come to terms with the death of her mother and with the fact that she feels guilty about killing her accidentally. In addition, her father, T.Ray, is a selfish and violent man who frequently ignores her or beats her up. Lily yearns for love and for her mother. She meets August and her sisters who live together and keep bees. Here she finds all the love and tenderness that she missed in her family life.

Violence
Lily's father, T.Ray, is a violent and brutal man. When he was younger he was deeply in love with his wife, Deborah, but he lacks self-control. He beat his wife and as a result she ran away. She dies while they are having a fight as she picks up a gun to defend herself, but tragically Lily fires it and kills her mother. The novel shows us how destructive violence is and how it only alienates people and destroys family life. At the end T.Ray is left alone with his violent character, having survived the death of his wife and the fact that his daughter refuses to go home with him. There are also instances in the novel of the violence committed against black people as a result of deep-seated prejudice in the United States in the 1960s. Rosaleen and Zach are both brutally beaten at different stages and falsely imprisoned.

Relationships
Lily and her mother
Although Lily's mother is dead when the story begins, this relationship dominates the novel. Lily is tormented by guilt over the accidental killing of her mother by gunshot. She manages to come to terms with difficult facts about her life through her friendship with August, who also cared for her mother. Lily learns a lot of new facts from August and begins to realise how much her mother suffered for marrying the wrong man.

Lily and August
Lily forms a strong relationship with August, a black woman who keeps bees. August is the eldest in her family and has managed to survive many tribulations because of her great strength of character and her strong devotion to Our Lady. August is an intelligent woman who understands all that Lily is suffering. She helps Lily to face up to many important facts about her family, and she shows her a great deal of love and affection. In this relationship between a white girl and a black woman we witness how the bonds of love and friendship can truly go beyond race and colour.

Social setting
Set in South Carolina in the 1960s, the novel depicts a rural community where the people live by growing cotton and selling peaches. The social setting deals with the conflicts that were topical at this time over race and colour. Martin Luther King is mentioned and people are beginning to speak openly about the Civil Rights Act. The white community are coming to terms with the fact that black people are entitled to vote. Rosaleen, a black lady, tries to vote early on in the novel but is beaten up. She manages to become a registered voter at the conclusion of the story.

The story shows us how Lily, a white girl, manages to break a great deal of barriers against black people in this society. She lives with the Boatwright sisters, who are black, and finds real happiness and love in her life. In this environment she learns about the Catholic faith and about Our Lady.

There are other changes in America during this time. For example, we learn that President Kennedy is sending a rocket to the moon.

Hero
Zach, who works for August helping her with beekeeping, could be described as a hero. He stands up against injustice and is forced to face imprisonment because of a deep-seated prejudice against black people in this community. He is a determined character and at the conclusion of the story we see how he is studying in a high school with white people and fixed on becoming a lawyer.

Heroine
Lily is the heroine of this story. The narrative is told through her eyes and we learn about her sufferings in carrying the guilt of having accidentally killed her mother. She is a courageous girl who stands up to the brutality and violence of her father and who manages to find love and happiness. She grows in the story and comes to terms with some difficult truths about her life. She learns to forgive and to find love with the help of August who tells her a lot about Our Lady.

Villain
T.Ray, who is Lily's father, is undoubtedly the villain of this story. He is a man who is completely violent and uncontrolled. He fought with his wife, who had to leave him several times. He spends his time abusing and brutalising his daughter, Lily. He is forced to accept the fact that she stands up to him and leaves him in order to find real love and commitment.

11
Notes on Films

CHARACTERISTICS OF FILMS

There are some points about film in this chapter that may be used in an answer in the comparative study section of the exam. There are also notes on all the films on the prescribed syllabus for Ordinary Level:

As You Like It	2011 exam
Billy Elliott	2010 and 2011 exams
Casablanca	2010 and 2011 exams
The Constant Gardener	2011 exam
Inside I'm Dancing	2010 and 2011 exams
Il Postino	2010 and 2011 exams
Richard III	2010 exam
The Truman Show	2010 exam

A film is about people, places and situations. The way they are shown, and the reason they are shown in a particular way, can vary greatly. A film is a narrative; it tells a story. Being able to say what the film is about is another way of identifying the themes or issues treated.

It is important to understand what particular values or understanding of life are represented in a film. A film can promote or criticise certain issues, depending on the stance taken by the director on the themes or issues being presented.

Examine what values or understanding of life the film emphasises, criticises or prioritises. Ask yourself the following questions:

- Is there a coherent message or moral in the film? If not, why not?
- How does the film leave you at the end? Depressed? Sad? Happy? Why?

The genre (type) of film
A film-maker structures the story or narrative in a particular way. In other words, the particular angle adopted by the film-maker in relation to the subject matter is what constitutes the genre of the film. Film genres can be divided into different categories, e.g. detective/thriller, western, romance, historical, social realism.

Features of the film genre

Films are made up of images that are photographed in a particular frame. Frame means the rectangle that contains the image. Camera frames control what the audience sees and how they see it. According to what the film-maker is trying to say, this camera frame can highlight certain actions and downplay others, or it can point the angle in a particular direction: either towards an object or person or away from them.

Understanding the genre of a film means being able to ask and answer certain questions:

- Is there a pattern of striking camera movements, long shots or abrupt transitions?
- Why does the film conclude on this image?
- Why does the film start in the way it does?
- When was the film made?
- What does the title mean in relation to the story?
- Why are the opening credits presented in this particular way? Why are they presented against a particular background?

Every film uses patterns of repetition that are contrasted with certain important moments. One of the first steps in analysing the meaning of a film involves the ability to recognise these patterns and to understand why they are important.

Note: These discussions of films follow, as far as possible, the same structure as the discussions of the written texts.

INSIDE I'M DANCING
(2010 and 2011 exams)

Directed by Damien O'Donnell

The story

The opening sequence shows two young men in wheelchairs against the backdrop of dance music. The next scene moves inside an institution called Carraigmore Residential Home, where many handicapped people are sitting down in wheelchairs looking at a cartoon on the television screen. The camera focuses on the face of one young man called Michael who has cerebral palsy. A cleaning lady begins to hoover the room and the flex scatters wildly against the wheelchairs. The young man gets upset because he sees the danger of this lead. He is unable to communicate, however, and when the supervisor enters asking everyone if they want Mass, he becomes wild. Immediately after this, one of the attendants in the home falls over the hoover. We realise that this is what Michael was trying to tell her.

Then another young man with spiked hair and a pierced nose arrives at the home. His name is Rory O'Shea. He is suffering from Duchane muscular dystrophy. Rory is only able to move two of his fingers and his head very slightly. It is clear he is very rebellious, as he asks for the key to the door as soon as he arrives at the home. Rory is at odds with the atmosphere of the home from the outset. He plays very loud music as soon as he arrives and uses a lot of bad language. Rory understands Michael immediately and begins to develop a friendship with him. Rory's dad pays him regular visits. Rory is determined to get permission to live independently. He discovers that Michael's father is a very rich man who has dumped him in a home after the death of his wife, and refuses to recognise him as his son because he has cerebral palsy.

At one stage the residents of the home are collecting money on the street for their cause. Rory and Michael are involved in the collection. They collect some money and then go into a pub and meet two girls. They buy them drink with the money, and the girls get drunk. Then the two boys try to get into a club. Initially they are refused entry because they are in wheelchairs but Rory threatens them with the fact that they are discriminating against people who have a disability, and warns them that they will have to pay a €2,000 fine. He pretends that Michael is a barrister. Once inside they use their wheelchairs to join in the fun of dancing. They also notice a young girl whom they learn later is called Siobhan dancing with other young people.

After this incident in the club, they return to the home, soaked and with no money. Eileen, the woman who is in charge of the home, is furious and blames Rory. Rory dresses up the next day in a suit and he and Mark go to meet with the Ability Ireland Board to request independent living for Rory. The Board, however, has heard how Rory mishandled the collection money and so they suggest that he return in six months' time. Rory is very angry after this encounter. It is clear that attaining independent living means a lot to him.

Shortly after this, Michael goes before the Board to look for independent living for himself. Rory accompanies him. The members of the Board are unable to understand Michael's efforts to speak, and so Rory is called upon to translate for him. Michael is granted permission to have what is called independent living, and Rory goes with him as his friend and helper. They are now faced with the prospect of getting enough money together for a suitable flat.

Rory comes up with the idea of appealing to Michael's father for money. Rory behaves in an outrageous manner at the father's office, and when he is refused access to the father, he shouts out how he is reporting 'a case of criminal neglect'. The father is shamed into giving them money. This is a very emotional scene, as Michael is clearly moved by coming face to face with his own father after so many years.

The two boys get a ground-floor flat with wheelchair access and with no rules or interference from anyone. They advertise for a personal assistant and they interview several candidates. None are suitable. Eventually they manage to convince the beautiful young girl Siobhan, who is working in a supermarket, to take the job. They have a wonderful time expressing their freedom and Siobhan manages the job as personal assistant very well.

Michael begins to fall in love with Siobhan. Unfortunately, Siobhan sees her relationship with the two boys as nothing other than a job of taking care of two people who are confined to wheelchairs. Rory watches this relationship developing, and becomes deeply cynical at the futility of Michael's love.

At one stage, in a fit of jollity and rebellion, Rory takes a car and crashes it. Siobhan begins to lose her patience with Rory, who becomes more aggressive and frustrated as he watches Michael falling helplessly in love. She has several verbal arguments. At one stage she walks out as he shouts out, 'I don't want your help, I don't want anyone's help.'

Rory's dad arrives with a birthday card for his twenty-first birthday. Siobhan meets an old friend and he invites them all to a fancy dress. Michael is deeply involved emotionally with Siobhan at this stage. She meets a boy friend at the dance and Michael wants to dance with her. At this stage she tells him that it's just a job. She resigns and brings another man along to replace her.

Michael is deeply upset and cries when she leaves. He goes out in his wheelchair one night and sits brooding on a bridge. Rory joins him and tells him that he is not the only one with a broken heart: 'you have the future, that's what I call a gift. Don't give it up. You can't give it up.' This is a very sad and tender scene. Both boys are crying and the scene is played against the backdrop of some very tender and poignant music. Rory makes a joke about suicide and they return home.

Shortly after this, Rory becomes sick and is taken away at night in an ambulance. He has pneumonia and is in intensive care. This is a very sad scene, with the two boys crying together in the hospital. Rory grabs Michael's fingers and tells him to 'be his own man'. Michael goes back to the Board to plead on Rory's behalf for independent living. He gets permission for him to live independently. He returns to the hospital to meet with Rory's father. Rory is dead. The film concludes with Rory's funeral, attended by his dad, Michael and Siobhan and several people from Carraigmore Home.

The last scene shows us an image of Michael returning to Rory's room and looking reflectively at Rory's wheelchair. He hears Rory's voice saying 'c'mon, are we going out?' The film concludes on a joyful note with an image of Michael in his wheelchair going into a large street on a busy day all on his own.

Themes
Friendship
One of the main themes in this film is the friendship between Rory and Michael. Both are handicapped and physically limited because of their illness. Their physical disability bonds them together from the outset of the film and contributes to enriching their relationship as the film develops. Adversity and suffering only serve the function of consolidating the friendship between the boys even more.

Communication
The film deals with two young boys who are handicapped because of different illnesses. Michael is suffering from cerebral palsy and Rory is suffering from muscular dystrophy. Both boys are able to communicate perfectly with one another. It is interesting that from the beginning of the film, we see how Michael is frustrated as no one is able to understand or communicate with him until Rory arrives. As soon as Rory arrives on the scene, Michael's face brightens up and his whole body becomes animated. There is a strong bond of understanding between them. Rory is the only character in the film that fully understands Michael. He fosters self-confidence within him, and this is evident at the conclusion, when Rory dies. Michael remains living independently and manages to travel into the city alone in his wheelchair.

Love and understanding
The film deals with the fact that even though people may suffer from physical disability, they still retain the capacity to love and be loved. This is particularly evident in the case of Siobhan, the beautiful young girl who spends some time working as a personal assistant for the boys. Michael falls passionately in love with her. Even though he may be suffering from cerebral palsy and is unable to communicate clearly, he still possesses the ability to love and wants to have that love reciprocated. Rory is very clever and quite cynical about this capacity in people who suffer from disability. Rory shows disgust in this part of this film, as he believes that no one can love a person with a disability. For this reason, he has a lot of arguments with Siobhan and eventually she leaves. However, Rory realises that the capacity for life is irreplaceable, and he warns Michael not to take life and the future for granted.

Relationships
Rory and Michael
This relationship is the strongest one in the film and is the basis of the plot. We see the strength between the two boys in overcoming many difficulties. They do this in a light-hearted and jocose way. Their friendship is based on love and loyalty.

Michael and Siobhan
Siobhan is a very caring person who takes her job as personal assistant to the two boys very seriously. However, the relationship changes when Michael falls hopelessly in love with her. Siobhan is very sincere and does not want to lead him on. She is not in love with him and tells him this to his face. He is devastated, as he possesses a strong capacity to love and be loved. Siobhan leaves her job after this.

Social setting
The film is set in modern twentieth-century Dublin. The language used by the characters is rich with the Dublin dialect. All of the scenes are played in an urban area. We are given an insight into a typical Dublin pub in Ireland in the late twentieth century and also the modern disco when the boys insist on gaining admittance. We gain an insight into institutional life at the beginning of the film in Carraigmore Residential Home. This is a typical style of urban institution, with its clean white walls and lack of character or atmosphere. There is one scene when the two boys go to meet Fergus Connolly, who is a senior counsellor in the courts, and they look for money from him. Here we gain an insight into middle-class Dublin.

Hero
Rory and Michael are undoubtedly the two heroes in the film.

Heroine
Siobhan is the heroine. She is a very caring character who understands both boys and yet realises that she cannot offer them the type of love they crave.

Villain
Fergus Connolly, Michael's father, seems to be the villain, since he abandoned Michael when his wife died because he is unable to deal with Michael's illness.

RICHARD III
(2010 exam)

Based on the play by William Shakespeare; directed by Richard Loncraine

The story
In the opening sequence of this film we are told that civil war reigns in England. The king, Henry, is under attack from the rebel York family, who are fighting to put their eldest son, Edward, on the throne. Edward's youngest brother, Richard of Gloucester, leads Edward's army. Their army breaks down the walls of Tewkesbury, and Henry and his father are shot. Edward becomes king of England. He is married to Elizabeth and they have two young sons and a daughter, also called Elizabeth. At Edward's coronation ceremony, Richard gives the welcoming speech. Rivers, Queen Elizabeth's brother, who is an enemy of Richard, arrives for the coronation of Edward. Buckingham, an ally of

Richard's, is a leading statesman who conspires with him at all stages.

Shortly after this Richard seduces Lady Anne, widow of Tewkesbury, whom he has murdered earlier. Richard announces to the audience that since he cannot prove himself to be a lover because of his deformed shape, he is determined to prove himself to be a villain. He frames Clarence, his brother, and has him committed to the Tower of London. Richard then suggests it is Elizabeth who has done this.

Richard then engages a man called Tyrell to murder Clarence, which he does while Clarence is taking a bath, drowning him in his own blood. Richard informs Edward of the death, as Edward is in the process of making peace among the various statesmen. Edward has a stroke on hearing the news and dies shortly afterwards. Richard murders Rivers.

Elizabeth's son is brought to London to be crowned king. Both he and his young brother are kept in the Tower until the coronation ceremony. Hastings is the prime minister. There is a meeting with the archbishop, Hastings, Buckingham and Richard, who is now the Lord Protector. Richard accuses Hastings of treachery; Tyrell executes Hastings. Both Richard and Buckingham then justify this execution to the Lord Mayor by claiming that Hastings plotted to kill them both. Richard also implies that the two princes in the Tower are bastard children, who have no legitimate right to the throne.

The Lord Mayor wishes to crown Richard as king. Richard adopts a false show of piety and reluctance to take on the responsibilities of kingship. Eventually he succumbs, and is crowned king in a ceremony closely resembling a Nazi convention.

After this ceremony Richmond is advised by the archbishop to flee to France for safety. There he mobilises an army to fight Richard. Richard asks Buckingham to murder the two princes in the Tower. Buckingham hesitates and reminds him of his earlier pledge to give him the earldom of Hereford. Richard replies that he is not in a giving mood. Buckingham, knowing his life is in danger, flees to France to join Richmond, and Tyrell murders the two princes in the tower. Richard now plans to get rid of Anne and marry Elizabeth, the sister of the two young princes. Elizabeth's mother flees to England and young Elizabeth is married to Richmond shortly before the battle.

Buckingham is captured by Richard's army, tortured and brutally murdered by Tyrell. Richard's own mother has cursed him and prophesies that his end will be bloody and that she will pray for Richmond's success in battle. Richard is tormented by nightmares on the night before the battle.

The battle takes place at daybreak with tanks and modern military weapons. Richmond drives an army tank through the battlefield, intent on killing Richard. At the conclusion, Richmond and Richard are standing on top of a dilapidated building. Richard challenges Richmond to come to hell with him, and offers him his hand. Before Richmond shoots him, Richard falls backwards into a sea of fire.

Themes
Violence, murder and corruption
Richard's rule is based on violence and fear. His kingship is attained by corrupt and evil means. From the time he becomes king, he commits murder after murder. It is only in the concluding scene, when he has perpetrated an orgy of mass killing, that Richard is finally defeated in a violent and bloody battle.

Betrayal
Richard gains power and kingship through betraying people. He betrays his brother, Clarence, and has him beheaded in the Tower of London. He marries Lady Anne and later on organises her murder. When he realises that his close ally, Buckingham, is wavering in his loyalty to the crown, Richard proceeds to have him tortured and murdered as well.

Relationships
Richard and Buckingham
Buckingham is a close political ally of Richard. Both characters plan and execute many murders. When Buckingham fails to give him his commitment to murder the two young princes, who are Elizabeth's sons, he, too, falls victim to Richard's evil ways.

Richard and his mother
Richard's mother warns him about his wicked ways and forecasts that he will come to grief. After his last encounter with his mother, who leaves England in anger, Richard is struck with guilt and remorse, but refuses to repent and mend his ways.

Social setting
The cultural setting of this film is England in the 1930s. It is a distinctly modern setting for a film based on a king who ruled in England in the fifteenth century. The coronation of Richard is almost Nazi in style. The red flag unfolded behind the grandstand and the red flags waved by the people who are gathered all carry symbols resembling the swastika. There are close associations drawn between the figure of Richard and that of Hitler. The dress is predominantly military-style uniforms, which also resemble those

worn by the Nazis. The surroundings are rich and ornate – magnificent chandeliers, expensive carpets and paintings, large lobbies, elegant photographs and clothes. All are hallmarks of the particular historical setting of this film.

Hero
Richmond is the hero of this film. He fights valiantly against the villainy of Richard and gains the throne of England.

Heroine
Richard's mother is the heroine of this film. She confronts Richard about his evil ways and warns that he will come to no good. Her words turn out to be true.

Villain
The villain of this film is Richard. He is corrupt and evil and murders anyone who happens to get in his way to kingship and power.

IL POSTINO (THE POSTMAN)
(2010 and 2011 exams)

Directed by Michael Radford

The story
Mario is a young man who lives on an island off the coast of Italy. His father tells him to find a job, and he applies for a job as a postman. He discovers that he has to bring the mail every day to a Chilean poet called Pablo Neruda, who has been exiled to Italy because he is a communist. Giorgio is Mario's boss and he has great veneration and respect for Pablo. Pablo writes love poems, and as a result he receives a lot of mail from women. Pablo lives with his wife in a beautiful part of the island called Cala di Sotto. Mario gets one of Pablo's books and asks him to sign it for him. Mario is upset that Pablo has not signed his full name, Mario Ruoppolo. Mario begins to read the poetry book and becomes fascinated with it. Friendship between Mario and Pablo begins to blossom. Mario begins to speak to Pablo about poetry and metaphors. Mario becomes a communist. Mr Di Cosmino is a local politician who spends his time looking for votes from the locals on the island.

After a while Mario falls in love with a beautiful girl called Beatrice. Mario asks Pablo to write him a poem for Beatrice. Beatrice lives with an aunt who opposes her relationship with Mario. Some time later the couple marry, and Mario asks Pablo to be his best man. At the wedding Pablo receives a letter allowing him the freedom to return to Chile. Beatrice becomes pregnant and Mario decides to call the child Pablito. Mario follows all Pablo's movements by reading the newspapers, and hears that he has been to Russia to receive an award. Mario receives a letter one day from Pablo's secretary, asking him to send on some of the objects he left behind in the house. Mario returns to the house and begins to reminisce about all the good times he enjoyed while Pablo was there. Mario decides to tape the different sounds of the sea and the wind on the cliffs for Pablo. He never sends him the tape, however.

Shortly after this, Pablo returns to the island with his wife for a visit. Pablo meets Pablito, Mario's child, and Beatrice tells him that Mario is dead. He died as he was reading a poem he had written, dedicated to Pablo. The crowd at a communist meeting crushed him. The story concludes with the image of Pablo walking along the beach and listening to Mario's words on the tape.

Themes
Friendship
One of the main themes in the film is the strong relationship between Pablo, the Chilean poet, and Mario, the Italian postman. Their relationship begins through Mario's fascination for Pablo's lifestyle and his poems. This friendship grows throughout the film, and Mario becomes a communist in Pablo's footsteps.

Love
Pablo Neruda, the Chilean poet in the film, is known as the poet of love. This theme is shown in a very tender and sympathetic way. The love between Mario and his wife, Beatrice, is deep and strong. This love is not destined to last long, however, as Mario dies when his son is very young.

Relationships
Mario and Pablo
This relationship governs much of the action in the film. It is a strong bond, showing us how strongly each of these two characters feel about life and relationships. Pablo is deeply upset when he discovers that Mario has died at a communist rally. He is also moved greatly when he listens to Mario's poem, which he had written for Pablo.

Mario and Giorgio
The relationship between Mario and Giorgio, his employer in the post office, is amusing and endearing. Giorgio continually reminds Mario how to behave with respect when he is delivering the post to this great poet.

Social setting
The film is set on a small Italian island, where the people live by fishing. It is a simple community, with simple values and a traditional way of life. The people are humble and pleasant, and even though they do not have much money they seem to be contented. We also see some glimpses of the political life of the island. The local politician, who is called Di Cosmino, fails to honour his promises when he becomes elected and the people find they have been betrayed and left without money. On the other hand, the voice of communism is heard through the figure of Pablo, who is a kind person and who shows a deep concern for the ordinary person.

Hero
Mario is the hero of this film. He has a very sensitive nature and gives his life in the service of good.

Heroine
Beatrice is the heroine of this film. She dearly loves her husband, Mario, and is left a young widow with a child when he is killed.

THE TRUMAN SHOW
(2010 exam)

Directed by Peter Weir

The story
The film starts with an image of a man facing the camera and saying, 'We have become bored with phony actors giving us phony emotions while the world we inhabit is in some respects counterfeit. There is nothing fake about Truman himself.' The next scene shows us Truman facing into a camera. He is a middle-class American man married to Meryl, a respectable woman, and living in the suburbs. We are given several images of him travelling to work and greeting the neighbours with a big smile and the words 'Good morning, good evening and good night.' As he meets people he recognises, we begin to realise that he is pictured against the backdrop of various advertisements for different things, such as beer or food.

Truman arrives at work in his office and we see him trying to cut a picture of a girl from a magazine. Later on, there is a flashback where we see that he has a phobia of water because of the fact that his father drowned when Truman was a young boy while they were fishing. It is obvious that Truman blames himself for this experience.

Truman dreams about going to Fiji to experience a different life there. When Truman explains this longing to Meryl, she reminds him about his financial obligations and how she hopes they will have a baby. When Truman is going to bed that night with Meryl, the camera focuses on two men looking at a television, saying, 'You never see anything.' One day, Truman suddenly sees a man who he thinks is his dad, but then two men grab this man and Truman nearly kills himself pursuing them. He goes to his mother and tells her what he saw. It becomes obvious that Truman is being set up for something and everyone else is in on it. He begins to reminisce in the basement looking at old photos of himself and his dad. Meryl comes down to him with a big smile and tells him to 'throw out the mower and get one of the new rotaries'. Then the camera switches to an image of two waitresses looking at Truman on the screen.

Truman meets a beautiful girl called Lauren Garland at a dance and later on in the library. They escape to a beach and she tells him that they have very little time together and how 'everyone knows everything you do'. A man arrives in a car and announces he is her father and that she is mentally unstable. Lauren keeps repeating that it's a fake, a set-up, but she is taken away. She tells him her real name is Sylvia. The two waitresses watching the screen then comment on the fact that he should have taken her to Fiji and how he 'married the other one on the rebound'.

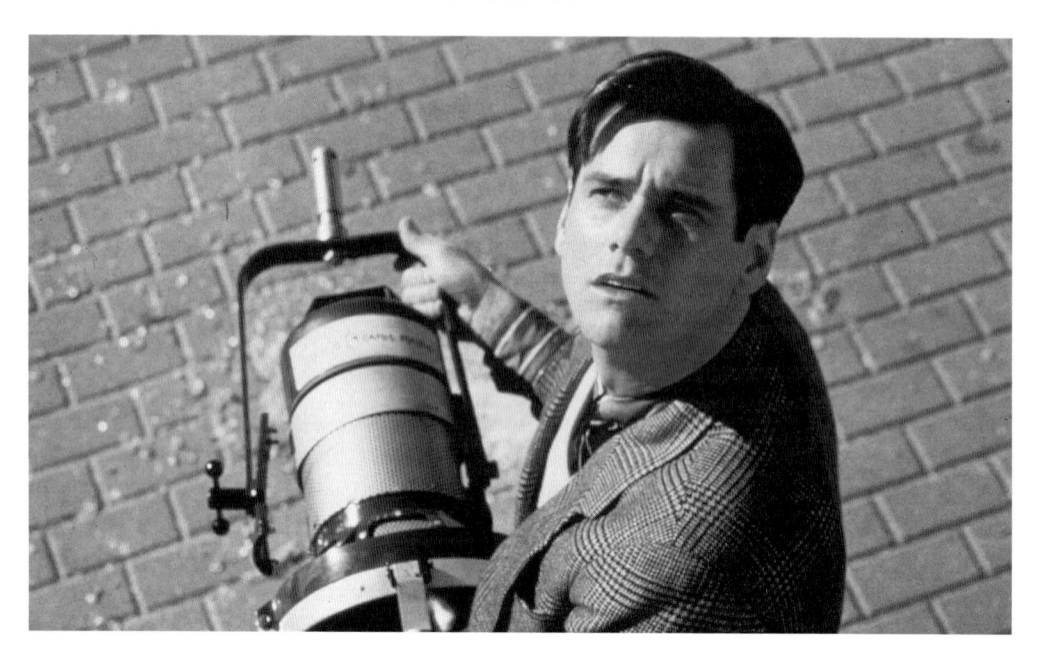

Shortly after this, Truman is driving to work and his radio begins to crackle and he hears a voice saying how he is heading down Lancaster Square. Truman begins to realise that they are talking about him. He becomes suspicious and begins to wonder if he is being followed. He sees a lift in the hotel with food and no backing on the wall. Truman goes to his friend, Marlon, for advice, but Marlon only laughs at him and says it is all nonsense. Truman decides to do something unpredictable, so he arrives at the hospital in his pyjamas one morning and announces that he is going to Fiji. This is a humorous incident, as Meryl is in the operating theatre. It is obvious that Meryl is in on the whole thing. When he tries to book a flight to Fiji, he is told there is nothing for at least a month.

Truman takes Meryl in the car and begins to act madly. He insists on driving to Fiji and she becomes hysterical. When he drives near the water he cannot go over it, as his fear is too great. Back home, he challenges Meryl to tell him what is happening. She hands him cocoa with nuts and he becomes frantic. She shouts out 'do something' and then he knows that something bigger is happening. Marlon arrives with beer. Truman has a long conversation with Marlon, who insists that he would never lie to him, as Truman is the 'closest thing [he] ever had to a brother'.

We learn that the story about Truman is a TV show in its thirtieth year and is a huge success. We are given an interview with the show's creator, Christof, and we learn how they manufactured ways to keep Truman on the island by creating a fear of water and the ocean. Christof explains how he has 5,000 cameras now but started with just one on Truman before he was born. We are shown a picture of Truman with a camera in the cot. We learn that the show is on twenty-four hours a day. Everything on the show is also a way of advertising. Sylvia rings and tells Christof that he is a liar and a manipulator. He answers that he has given Truman a chance to live a normal life.

Truman moves down to his basement and the cameramen are unable to keep contact with him. Marlon goes to the basement, where he discovers that Truman has disappeared. Transmission of the show is cut while everyone goes to search for Truman. Sirens sound all over the city and people are marching in troops, looking for him with torches. Truman's mother, father and Marlon are at the front of the crowd. They find him on the sea, sailing away, and they resume transmission.

Truman comes onto the camera with a sailor's cap and he is looking at the photo of the girl. He is on a boat called the *Santa Maria*. Christof organises a storm over the boat to frighten him and Truman nearly dies. The storm increases in intensity and the boat is smashed. Truman survives, however, and suddenly he hears what seems to be a gunshot. He has reached a wall, which he cannot break through. Truman is broken-hearted. He walks around the edge of this horizon and up some steps marked 'exit'. He opens a door and speaks to Christof, who tells him how his show gives hope and joy to millions, and how he has been watching him all his life. Truman then turns to the camera and says, 'In case I don't see you, good afternoon, good evening and good night.' He then goes up the steps and opens the door at the top. We see Sylvia running joyously down some stairs while Christof takes off his glasses in disgust.

Themes
Reality and illusion
From the outset it is clear that Truman is being used as a pawn in a game. It only becomes clear as the story develops that he is being deceived about the reality of his own life. All his family and friends, with the exception of Sylvia, hide the truth from him that he is the central actor of his own show. His life has a worldwide audience. Everyone believes they are doing a great thing by offering joy to millions of people worldwide. Truman, however, walks away from this world at the conclusion.

Loyalty and betrayal
His friends and family betray Truman by not telling him that he is the chief actor in what is universally known as *The Truman Show*. His whole family deceives him about the truth of his life and all contribute to the show's continuous existence. Furthermore, the show is designed to advertise goods and many of his family and friends are shown against the backdrop of billboards advertising different types of merchandise.

Relationships
Truman and Sylvia
This is the only genuine and sincere relationship in the film. Sylvia tries in vain to warn Truman about the way he is being used, and about the reality of his life. It is only at the film's conclusion that Truman decides to leave the show and live his own life. We can see that Sylvia will be able to have a normal relationship with Truman.

Truman and his family
All relationships in the film, with the exception of Sylvia, are false. Truman's wife was got 'on the rebound', while the relationship with his father is dominated by guilt. But this guilt was another strategy designed by Christof to keep Truman from escaping out of the false world they have created for him. Truman's friend Marlon turns out to be a hypocrite and another traitor who deceives him.

Social setting
The social background of this film is American middle-class suburbia. The film is set in the twentieth century and is a subtle presentation of the reality of media and the manner of its operation. It deals with consumerism and materialism in the twentieth century. The characters' lifestyles are fairly affluent. It is a society where people live in pleasant, organised suburbia and have children. Truman works in an office and travels by car every day. The buildings represented in this small town of Seahaven are modern, and for the most part bright and new. The power of television to generate huge income through reality shows lies at the essence of the film's content. Money is a huge factor motivating Christof, the show's creator, to sustain his deception over Truman, and also seems to govern Truman's family and sly friend. The film exposes the surreptitious and more sinister aspects of media control, and underlines how people can become unconscious pawns in the media game.

Hero
The hero of this film is undoubtedly Truman himself. He is the unwitting agent in a show that he is totally unaware of until the conclusion.

Heroine
Sylvia, the beautiful girl Truman meets and falls in love with, is undoubtedly the heroine in this film. She is the only one who is fully sincere with him about his situation and tells him the whole thing is a fake.

Villain
Christof, the show's creator, is the villain in this film. He manages to manipulate every situation and every person in this small town in order to create his own show.

As You Like It
(2011 exam)

Based on the play by William Shakespeare; directed by Kenneth Branagh

The story
This film opens with some written words across the screen explaining how Japan opened up for trade with the West in the second part of the nineteenth century. Merchant adventurers arrived in Japan from all over the world. They were mainly English. Some traded in silk and rice and lived in enclaves around 'treaty points'. Then they brought their families and followers and created private mini-empires where they tried to embrace Japan's extraordinary culture, its beauties and its dangers. Then we see the image of a Japanese girl wearing a beautiful kimono and dancing while soft music plays in the background.

Meanwhile, some men who are dressed in black are making their way through the castle to attack. Duke Senior is attacked by his brother Duke Frederick and banished to the Forest of Arden with some of his followers. His brother sits on the throne and proceeds to take over the dukedom. The next scene shows us two young girls: Rosalind, who is Duke Senior's daughter, and Celia, who is the daughter of the usurper Duke Frederick. Rosalind is crying over the situation of her father. Celia comforts her by telling her she will return all that she has lost to her.

In the next scene we are shown two men fighting: Orlando, the youngest son of Sir Rowland de Boys, and his brother Oliver. Orlando wants his older brother to give him an education or else give him the money he owes him and let him go. Oliver decides to give him his money. Oliver hates his brother and organises that Charles, a champion wrestler, will fight and defeat Orlando. Oliver is dominated by a lot of internal conflict over his relationship with his brother. He realises that Orlando is gentle, that he was never schooled yet is learned, and that he is considered noble in the heart of the people whereas he, Oliver, is 'misprized'. Oliver decides that the wrestler will sort things out for him by killing Orlando.

Before the wrestling match the girls advise Orlando not to fight as he will be defeated by Charles. He refuses because he feels his life is worthless until he can accept this challenge. It is clear that Rosalind has fallen in love with Orlando at first sight. Orlando fights against Charles and defeats him. Duke Frederick tells Orlando that his father was his enemy and to leave the place immediately. Before Orlando leaves, Rosalind gives him a necklace to wear as a reminder of her.

Meanwhile, Duke Frederick decides to banish Rosalind from the court with the penalty that she will die if she disobeys. Celia then tells her father to pronounce the same sentence on her as she cannot live without Rosalind's company. Duke Frederick is enraged. The girls decide to escape and look for Rosalind's father in the Forest of Arden. They adopt disguises and false names. Rosalind dresses up as a young man and calls herself Ganymede, while Celia takes the name of Aliena. The two girls decide to take the fool, Touchstone, with them.

Adam is the servant of Oliver. He warns Orlando that Oliver intends to burn down the stable where he lives that night. Adam offers Orlando some gold coins and tells him he will serve him in truth and loyalty to the end.

We see Duke Senior in the forest. He is rejoicing in the beauty of the place and in the fact that he is free in the forest, particularly from flattering counsellors. In the forest he is able to find good in everything. One of the Duke's followers is a man called Jacques, who is a melancholy character and spends a lot of his time philosophising.

The girls have reached the forest and have no food. They see two men, one old and one younger, who are shepherds. The younger man is called Silvius. He talks about the love of Phoebe. When Rosalind questions the older man about getting food he tells them his master is 'of a churlish disposition and not likely to do deeds of hospitality'. The two girls offer to buy up his place with gold.

Orlando and Adam are also in the forest but Adam wants to lie down and die as he cannot go on without food. Meanwhile, Duke Senior and all his followers are gathering to eat under a tree. Orlando appears and threatens to kill them all unless they give him food. The Duke tells him that gentleness will have more success than force so to put away his weapons. Orlando leaves to collect Adam while Jacques begins to speak poetically about the different stages in a man's life.

Orlando brings Adam to the group and they feed him. Duke Senior tells Orlando that he knew his father and loved him. Meanwhile, Fernando has tortured Oliver and taken his lands until he can kill Orlando. We see Oliver crying over the burned ruins of the place where Orlando had lived.

Orlando has fallen in love with Rosalind. He cries out to the trees in the forest that he would like to see the face of the fair and chaste Rosalind.

Jacques meets up with Touchstone in the forest and is delighted with this new interest. He returns to the Duke and his men to tell them all about this 'motley fool' he has met and how amazed he is at the fact that the fool is so contemplative. Touchstone meets a woman called Audrey in the forest and they decide to get married. There is a comic interlude where the fool wants to get married quickly so he can have a quick exit from the marriage if necessary. Audrey will have none of it; she wants to be married properly.

Rosalind, who is disguised as a man, meets Orlando in the forest. He has love letters for Rosalind in his hands. She jokes with him telling him he does not know how to love, and that 'love is merely a madness'. She tells him to woo her and pretend it is Rosalind. He agrees. Meanwhile, Phoebe rejects Silvius, the shepherd, and falls for Rosalind, believing she is a beautiful young man. Rosalind rejects her and tries to get her to fall in love with Silvius. Rosalind begins to realise that she cannot live without the love of Orlando.

Orlando discovers his brother lying in the forest wounded. A tiger attacks Orlando and he is wounded. The two brothers are reconciled. Oliver goes to look for help for his brother and meets Celia, who is disguised as Aliena. Immediately they both fall in love. When Oliver returns to his brother he tells him that he loves the beautiful Aliena. He asks Orlando for permission to marry her and he will give him all the revenue from his father, Sir Rowland, and will live in the forest as a shepherd. Oliver decides to get married the following day, and to invite the Duke to the wedding. Orlando is upset as he is fed up of imagining the love of Rosalind. He wants the real thing. Rosalind tells him she can do strange things, she will send Rosalind to him the next day. Frederick hears that his brother Duke Senior is living in an enchanted world where men flock to visit him each day.

On the following day all four couples marry. Rosalind arrives beautifully dressed in a rich sari and is reunited with her father as well as her lover, Orlando. Phoebe marries Silvius, Oliver marries Celia, Touchstone marries Audrey and finally the beautiful Rosalind and Orlando accept one another in marriage. At the conclusion of the ceremony a young man arrives on horseback. He tells them he is the third son of Sir Rowland. He hands Duke Senior some papers and tells him that his lands and dukedom are restored. Duke Frederick had met an old religious man in the forest and been converted. He decided to renounce unlawful possession of the throne and spend his life in contemplation in the forest.

The conclusion of the film is filled with rich music and songs. All the people dance through the forest, filled with joy and delight. Jacques takes his leave, deciding he wants to live in an abandoned cave and contemplate. Shortly after, we see him joining Frederick and sitting in contemplation at a tree. The song 'Sweet lovers love the spring' is heard at the conclusion.

There is a short witty epilogue from Rosalind, who is dressed in the garb of a young boy, telling the audience that a good play needs no epilogue.

Themes
Love
Love is one of the main themes of this play and we see different types of love represented in the film. The love of Rosalind for her cousin Celia is like that of sisters, and they remain loyal to one another throughout. The power of love to heal strife is seen in the conclusion, when four lovers unite in marriage. The love of the brothers Oliver and Orlando destroys their former hatred and animosity. The hatred within Frederick is replaced with repentance and a need to reconcile with his brother. Love is shown as a positive virtue and one that unites people truly.

Rustic life
The rich wonders and joys inherent in the natural world are shown through the colourful scenes set in the Forest of Arden. Here springtime dominates and people are reunited. There is no strife or suffering. Life is rich and filled with sunshine and song. The forest is in continuous contrast to the life at court, which is constantly shrouded in darkness, an image that is suggestive of intrigue and plotting.

Relationships
There are different types of relationships represented in this film. Initially we see how Duke Frederick betrays his brother Duke Senior by taking unlawful possession of his dukedom and outlawing him, and by threatening the life of his daughter Celia. There is a parallel in the relationship between Orlando and his brother Oliver. Like Frederick, Oliver hates his brother and plots to take possession of his lands and kill him. Orlando, like Duke Senior, is forced to flee from the wrath and hatred of his brother.

In contrast, we see the strong bonds of solidarity and kindness shown through the love of Celia and Rosalind. They stay together through every type of difficulty and manage to overcome the evil and treachery that is done to them. The film emphasises the positive quality of relationships and how people can flourish when they love one another and serve one another honestly and faithfully.

Social setting
The film is set in Japan in the second half of the nineteenth century. It depicts a society that has opened its doors to Western trade and shows us wealthy merchants living at coastal trading points. The opening of the film features a typical Japanese kabuki performance. The old Duke enjoys the richness of Japanese culture and its fine arts.

The film reveals a rich contrast between life at court and life in the Forest of Arden. Within the forest, life is magical and pastoral, it is indicative of a life free from anxiety or woe. The rural setting conveys tones of peace and harmony. There is also harmony between people who live a more simple and natural lifestyle. Song and dance form a great part of the world within the forest.

Hero

Orlando is one of the main heroes of this film. He is seen, like Duke Senior (another hero), as courageous and loyal in spite of having suffered the betrayal and treachery of his brother Oliver. He triumphs at the conclusion by gaining the hand of the woman he loves, Rosalind.

Heroine

Rosalind is a heroine in this film. She falls in love with Orlando early on in the film, but is forced to flee to the forest because of the treachery and injustice of her Uncle Frederick. There she meets her lover, Orlando, and is reunited with her father after a series of adventures.

Villain

The villain of this film is Frederick. He betrays his brother and outlaws him to the forest and then does the same with Rosalind and Celia. He rules by violence and tries to force his will over Oliver and get him to take the lands from Orlando. Frederick becomes converted at the end and repents of his evil-doing.

BILLY ELLIOTT

(2010 and 2011 exams)

Directed by Stephen Daldry

The story

The opening sequence of the film shows a hand turning a record on in a machine, and we hear the words of a song 'I was dancing when I was twelve'. Then Billy jumps up and down on the screen. The next scene shows us Billy dressed in sports shorts and preparing breakfast in an untidy kitchen. Billy discovers his granny has gone wandering so we see him leave the house to find her and bring her back.

We next see a group of policemen lining up with armoury for attack and we realise that the miners are on strike and are fighting with the police. Billy's father and brother, Tony, are both miners and are on strike. Billy spends time playing the piano, which was obviously a favourite pastime of his mother, who is dead.

Billy heads off for the boxing club and meets his friend Michael, who clearly has no interest in boxing. It turns out that the hall is shared by a ballet class and a boxing group. Billy does not like boxing and we see he is becoming fascinated by the ballet. When the boxing is over, Billy wanders into the ballet class and is totally captivated. The teacher, Mrs Wilkinson, throws a pair of ballet shoes at him and says, 'I dare you'. Billy slowly puts them on and begins to practise with all the girls. At the end of the class he leaves. Mrs Wilkinson follows him in the car with her young daughter and tells him he has the potential to become a ballet dancer.

Later on we see Billy visiting the grave of his mother, who died at the age of thirty-eight. Billy begins to go to ballet classes all the time, but pretends to his father that he is taking his boxing classes. His father discovers, however, that Billy has not been at the boxing club for ages, and that Billy is taking ballet classes instead. His father is furious and forbids him to attend any more classes. He must stay and mind his grandmother instead.

Meanwhile, Mrs Wilkinson sees the potential in Billy for greatness in dancing and urges him to stand up to his father and continue to dance. Mrs Wilkinson tells Billy that she wants to prepare him for auditions in Newcastle for the Royal Ballet School. She offers to give him private tuition without charging him anything as he cannot afford it.

Michael is Billy's friend but Billy finds him beginning to act strangely as he starts to dress up in girls' clothes. Meanwhile, Tony, Billy's brother, becomes increasingly more violent and aggressive while on strike. He has several confrontations with the police. He gets up one night and takes a hammer from the tool box. His father confronts him but is unable to stop him. It becomes clear that the father is finding it difficult to deal with his two sons on his own and also while there is no money coming into the house because of the strike.

Mrs Wilkinson gives Billy lessons in ballet in secret. They have several rows but she is determined he will be a star.

There are many scenes where the police clash with the miners and use physical violence. At one stage Mrs Wilkinson has a confrontation with Billy's father, Jackie, and brother, Tony. Tony verbally abuses her, telling her Billy is only a 'bairn', a child of eleven years of age. She retorts in a similar manner using verbal violence to both men. Billy is frustrated with everybody and runs out onto the street.

It is Christmas and the situation of the family has deteriorated. They are forced to break up the piano and use it for fuel. The family has a dismal celebration, with Jackie crying about all the pressures in his life. Meanwhile, it becomes clear to Billy that Michael is trying to face up to the fact that he is homosexual. Billy tells him that his own interest in ballet does not make him homosexual. On Christmas night both boys go to the hall and begin to dance ballet, with Michael dressed in a tutu. Jackie discovers the two and is astonished. Billy continues to dance for his father, who looks on in amazement. Jackie leaves without saying a word and the next scene shows us his arrival at Mrs Wilkinson's house. He wants to know how much it will cost to continue Billy's education in ballet. She tells him £2,000 is needed.

Jackie decides to break the picket line and return to work. Tony refuses to let his father return to work against the miners, telling him they will find another way to get the money. Jackie manages to collect the money by pawning some of his wife's precious jewellery and with the help of his friend George.

Jackie accompanies Billy to the Royal Ballet School for his audition and interview. Billy is interviewed by a panel of six judges and forced to dance for them. He is stiff and insecure as they are extremely formal. Billy clashes with a young boy who tries to comfort him and both father and son are reprimanded by the judges for engaging in violence. Before they leave, one lady asks Billy how he feels when he is dancing. He is not sure but tells her that 'I sort of disappear, I feel like a bird . . . like electricity'. Billy is accepted by the ballet school and the family are ecstatic. Shortly after this the union caves in and the miners are forced to return to work.

Before Billy leaves for London he goes to say goodbye to Mrs Wilkinson. There is an emotional scene when he leaves both his father and brother.

The last scene takes place fourteen years later and Billy is performing at the Theatre Royal Haymarket. Jackie and Tony come to the theatre to watch him. They meet with Michael, who is also there to see Billy. Billy appears on the stage. He is an older person now and he dances to the tune of 'Ride a white swan'.

Themes
Change
The whole film dramatises the topic of change. We witness this within society in general, with the English miners agitating for social change. We also confront the theme of change within Billy's family as they come to terms with some harsh realities of life. Billy's mother is dead and his father, Jackie, has to struggle to rear his two sons and look after his own mother as well. In addition, Jackie is forced to come to terms with the fact that his son is different because he wants to have a career in ballet dancing. The film shows us how these changes affect the various relationships that are represented.

Human relationships
There are many different types of relationship represented in the film. Billy has a strong relationship from the beginning with Mrs Wilkinson, who is his ballet teacher. She treats him as an older person and forces him to make difficult choices about his future and his life as a ballet dancer. Many of the relationships in the film are governed by tension and frustration as they show us how different people are forced to face up to challenges and difficulties in their environment. The strong bonds of family and Jackie's ability to be open to his son's ambitions help Billy to further his career and achieve his desires.

Violence
From the outset of this film there is plenty of violence. The miners are on strike and they clash with the police. We see how the police are armed with weapons and shields and are prepared for battle. Furthermore, the film dramatises a good deal of verbal violence, which is characteristic of a culture where poverty and frustration are endemic. Billy's brother is particularly violent, both physically and verbally, as he confronts the police on various occasions.

Relationships
Billy and his father
For much of this film Billy is shown in conflict with his father, Jackie, who is on strike and is completely frustrated at not being able to support his family properly. Furthermore, his wife is dead and he often feels useless. He comes into conflict with Billy, his youngest son, frequently and especially when he learns that Billy is taking ballet classes. This relationship changes when he becomes aware that Billy possesses a talent for dancing and has the possibility of studying in a prestigious ballet school.

Billy and Mrs Wilkinson
Billy meets Mrs Wilkinson early on in the film. She teaches ballet in a large community hall, which is also used for boxing classes. Billy is fascinated from the outset by the ballet class and the music. She immediately encourages him and sees nothing strange about his joining a class of girls and doing ballet. Because of this Billy flourishes and

becomes a brilliant dancer. She is the one to plant the idea in his head about attending ballet school. As a result of this relationship Billy's dreams of being a famous ballet dancer are fulfilled.

Social setting
This film is set in Britain in a working-class mining area. The year is 1984, and Margaret Thatcher is the Prime Minister. The film is based on a real political period when miners were fighting for their rights and were forced to strike for fair wages and working conditions. The issue of poverty and the suffering it causes is dramatised through the miner's strike, which governs the plot.

We see a closely knit community that works together and struggles with the harsh realities of life. Family and family life are important. Within this community there are standard activities such as boxing for boys and ballet for girls. This film dramatises how certain traditional patterns of behaviour are steadily questioned, and how people no longer behave in a predictable manner. Billy becomes an expert ballet dancer, while his friend Michael is shown as a young boy with homosexual leanings. Society is changing and different types of values are emerging as a result.

Hero
Billy is undoubtedly the hero of this film. He is a young boy of eleven who misses his mother, and who loves playing the piano and dancing. He is a compassionate and sensitive boy who tries to understand his friend Michael. He manages to break free from the frustrations of his environment and make a career in ballet dancing.

Heroine
Billy's ballet teacher, Mrs Wilkinson, is the heroine of this film. She acts in a tough manner but underneath she has a heart of gold. She understands Billy's dilemmas and encourages him to achieve his ambitions. She is generous and self-sacrificing and acts as a truly positive force in Billy's life.

Villain
Billy's brother, Tony, acts as a villain at many different stages in this film. He fights repeatedly with Billy and tries to bully him into changing his mind about dancing. He fights with the police and verbally abuses Mrs Wilkinson. Eventually, with the help of his father, Tony changes and improves in his manner towards Billy.

Casablanca
(2010 and 2011 exams)

Directed by Michael Curtiz

The story
The opening of the film shows a large map of Africa while music plays in the background. We hear the French national anthem 'The Marseillaise'. The action of the film takes place in Morocco in North Africa when it was occupied by the French. We hear the voiceover of a man speaking about how, with the coming of World War II, many people were struggling to get from Europe to America. Many refugees were trying to get to Lisbon, which was a gateway to the new world. In Casablanca visas were sold and people came in the hope they could make their way to America.

Then we see a police officer on the telephone. Two German couriers have been murdered on the train from Oran and their documents have been stolen. All suspicious characters are to be rounded up for questioning. The scene moves to an open street with markets and bazaars. Several policemen arrive and begin to arrest different men. One man is shot trying to escape. The police discover literature in his hand about 'Free France'. We then see the words 'Liberty, Equality and Fraternity' on a plaque above him. These are the ideals of the French Revolution. Yet the existing government in Morocco is French/Vichy and is collaborating with the Nazis.

We see a sign with the words 'Rick's Café Américain'. Major Strasser arrives by plane. He represents the Third Reich. He is greeted by the Prefect of Police, Captain Renault. Renault welcomes him to 'unoccupied France'. Strasser is anxious to capture the men who were involved in the murder of the couriers. Renault announces that an arrest will take place that night in Rick's cafe.

That night, inside Rick's, we see every type of person from civilians to police. They all come for different purposes, but mainly to try to obtain visas to exit the country. Sam is the piano player who entertains the guests at night. We hear from Carl, the head waiter, that Rick never drinks with his customers. Rick is shown at a table signing cheques, smoking and playing chess. He is cool and nonchalant, he has no time for fools. He also is not impressed with people who have lots of money. We see him refusing entry to a customer even though he tells him he has gambled in every casino from Honolulu to Berlin.

A man called Ugarte arrives. It turns out he sells visas to people for a profit. He tells Rick he is leaving Casablanca for good and mentions the two couriers. He asks Rick to keep certain letters of transit safely for him for a few hours. Rick takes them and hides them in the piano. A man called Ferrari arrives. He is the proprietor of 'The Blue Parrot', another cafe. He offers to buy the cafe from Rick. Then he offers to buy Sam. Rick refuses. Ferrari would like Rick to work with him on the black market. Again, Rick refuses.

There is a young girl called Yvonne who is in love with Rick. She is at the bar getting drunk and is angry with him. He sends her home under the care of the barman. Rick it seems is not interested in anyone. Rick speaks to Renault outside, who tells him about the arrest that will be made in his cafe in order to impress Major Strasser. We learn that Strasser is in Casablanca to prevent a man called Victor Laszlo from escaping to America. Rick knows the name and is impressed.

Shortly after this Strasser arrives and seats himself at the best table in the cafe. A number of guards arrive and they make an attempt to capture Ugarte. He runs away and pleads with Rick to hide him. Rick refuses and Ugarte is captured. Rick tells everybody, 'I stick my neck out for nobody'. When Rick joins Strasser at his table, Strasser begins to put pressure on him to co-operate in the Laszlo situation. We learn that the Germans have a dossier on Rick, who ran guns to Ethiopia in 1935, and fought in the Spanish Civil War in 1936. Rick tells him he has no interest in politics, he runs a saloon.

Victor Laszlo and his wife, Ilsa, enter the cafe. She recognises Sam, who is disconcerted. A man called Berger approaches their table. He is a member of the Resistance. Strasser comes to the table and tells Laszlo that he requests his presence tomorrow at Renault's office. Laszlo is forced to acquiesce. Later on Laszlo learns from Berger that Ugarte has been imprisoned. He arranges to attend a meeting with the Resistance that night.

Meanwhile, Ilsa speaks with Sam, asking him about Rick. Sam lies that he has gone home and tells her to leave Rick alone, she is bad luck for him. She insists on a song 'for old time's sake' and pleads with him to sing 'As time goes by'. Rick arrives into the room and storms over to the piano when he hears the music. Then he meets Ilsa, who greets him. Sam closes the piano and leaves. Just then Renault arrives and Rick surprises everyone by joining him and Laszlo for a drink. We learn that Rick and Ilsa knew each other in Paris, he tells her he remembers the last place they met, 'La Belle Aurore', on the same day the Germans marched into Paris. Shortly after this Laszlo and Ilsa leave as there is a curfew in Casablanca.

Rick begins to drink heavily. Sam arrives and tries to get him to go to bed or to leave the place altogether. Rick stubbornly orders Sam to play 'As time goes by' again. There is a flashback to Paris with shots of Rick and Ilsa together, enjoying life and filled with happiness. It is clear they are very much in love with one another. She tells him he cannot ask any questions about her past. We see them toasting themselves shortly before the Germans are due to arrive in the city. They arrange to leave by train that night and she asks him to 'kiss her as if it were for the last time'. In the next scene we see Rick waiting at the train station in pouring rain while crowds of people are trying to get out before the Germans arrive. There is no sign of Ilsa. Then Sam arrives with a note in which Ilsa says simply that she cannot join him and he would be best to forget her altogether. He leaves on the train, clearly upset.

The scene returns to the cafe. Rick is drunk. Ilsa arrives, dressed in white. He reacts cynically to her. She begins to tell him about a girl from Oslo who had met a great man whom she worshipped and she thought it was love. She is speaking about Laszlo. Rick is unable to deal with this and asks her were there others in between? She gets up and leaves him.

Laszlo is informed by Strasser that he can leave Casablanca only on condition that he informs on the Resistance members and betrays their names to the Germans. Laszlo refuses and leaves. He learns that Ugarte is dead. Laszlo finds out later that Ferrari might get him a visa on the black market, but this is not possible. Rick meets Ilsa at the market and tells him that Laszlo is her husband and that she was married to him when she met Rick in Paris.

At one stage Rick has a conversation with a young woman from Bulgaria who wants to get a visa to leave. She has no money and speaks to him about love and how much she is prepared to sacrifice for the love of her husband, Jan. Rick is deeply moved because he too loved Ilsa greatly. Shortly after this we see him helping Jan to win money at the gambling table.

Laszlo learns that Rick might have the letters of transit hidden. He goes to Rick to get help in obtaining a visa. Rick refuses, telling him he would not give them to him for a million dollars. Laszlo questions his reasons, and Rick tells him, 'ask your wife'.

Meanwhile, downstairs in the bar, the Germans begin to sing their national anthem. Laszlo moves down and everyone sings 'The Marseillaise'. Strasser is furious and orders that the cafe be shut down. Renault blows his whistle and announces that everyone must leave; the cafe is shut indefinitely. Laszlo returns to the hotel with his wife and explains about Rick's answer. He asks her if she was lonely when he was in the concentration camp and kisses her gently. He leaves. She goes to Rick's room and tries to convince him to give her the letters. She turns a gun on him and he tells her to 'go ahead and shoot, you'll be doing me a favour'. She breaks down and tells him that she still loves him. He learns that back in Paris she had thought that Victor was dead but had heard he had survived the concentration camp just before she and Rick had decided to leave on the train together. She also tells him that she does not know what to do, he must decide for all three of them.

Carl and Laszlo have attended the Resistance meeting. They are followed by the police and Laszlo is slightly wounded. They arrive downstairs in the cafe, while Ilsa and Rick are upstairs. Rick asks Carl to bring Ilsa home to her hotel. Rick and Laszlo have a conversation downstairs at the bar. Laszlo tells Rick that he knows he is in love with Ilsa and to help her escape; he is prepared to stay in Casablanca. The police arrive and arrest Laszlo. Rick remarks that destiny is taking a hand.

The next day Rick goes to Renault and together they form a plan. Rick tells Renault he has the letters and wants to use them to escape with Ilsa. He suggests to Renault that he could make himself professionally important by getting Laszlo on a charge that will imprison him in a concentration camp. Renault agrees. Rick goes and sells his cafe to Ferrari on condition that he keeps all the staff and pays them the same salary. Rick tells Laszlo and Ilsa that he will give them the letters so they can escape. Laszlo arrives at the cafe at night and gets the letters. Renault arrives on the scene and charges Laszlo as an accessory to the murder of the two couriers. Rick turns his gun on Renault and so the plot thickens. Rick forces Renault to telephone the airport. Renault rings Strasser, who is alerted that something is wrong. He in turn rings the police and orders them to go to the airport.

Rick, Renault, Laszlo and Ilsa arrive at night at the airport. She is confused as she thinks that she is leaving with Rick. Rick tells her that her husband needs her and 'we will always have Paris'. Strasser arrives and takes out a gun to stop them from leaving. Rick shoots Strasser, and Victor and Ilsa take their leave of Casablanca. Renault tells the police to 'round up the usual suspects'. He advises Rick to leave Casablanca for a while. The film concludes with both men leaving the airport joking about 'the beginning of a beautiful relationship'.

Themes
Love
Love is a strong theme in *Casablanca*. At the outset of the film Rick has a cynical and negative attitude to love. He has suffered through love and has erected a wall around himself. When Ilsa comes into his cafe he changes dramatically. As he learns the truth about why she did not turn up at the train station, he comes to understand that she did love him but was tied to the fact that she had married Victor Laszlo. It is evident from her behaviour that she still loves Rick. In her marriage to Laszlo it becomes apparent that he truly loves her whereas she is more in awe of his character. Rick is a very honourable man and even though he understands that she will leave Casablanca with him he does not accept this offer as he knows that what they had between them in Paris can never be recaptured.

War

The background of war is always evident in this film. The main characters are intent on gaining their freedom from the German threat that looms over Europe. We witness the brutality of war when we learn how Ugarte died in police custody. We hear about concentration camps through Victor Laszlo, who spent many years interned in one. Major Strasser, a German Nazi, has no scruples about shooting or killing whenever necessary. Ironically, when he turns his gun on Rick to stop Laszlo leaving the country he meets his death through another gun – he is shot by Rick. War is shown to be brutal and demeaning to the people involved.

Courage

There are many instances of courage represented in this film. Initially the film shows us the real courage of Victor Laszlo, who stands up to the Germans and has a strong sense of dignity and heroism. Even though Strasser tries to terrorise him and threatens him with imprisonment, Laszlo is courageous in standing up for his rights. This spirit of courage is shown in a different way through Rick. He suffered greatly after Ilsa abandoned him for no apparent reason. He set up a new life in Casablanca and runs a successful cafe. He is a very just man underneath all his apparent cynicism. When Ilsa returns unexpectedly, he is devastated. His courage emerges when he learns the full truth underlying her life. Rick is loyal to both Victor and Ilsa and manages, through a great deal of ingenuity, to get them both to safety.

Relationships
Rick and Ilsa

We are shown this relationship in two totally different circumstances. Initially we know Rick in his older years when he is cynical about love and relationships. As soon as Ilsa unexpectedly arrives at his cafe we realise that Rick has a capacity to love deeply. Later through the use of flashback we see how Rick truly loved Ilsa. She was faced with a dilemma of falling in love with another man while her husband was alive. When Ilsa returns, Rick knows that the only honourable thing to do is to ensure that she remains committed to Victor, who needs her. Rick is the true hero of this film. A man who was abandoned by the woman he loved for no apparent reason, he manages to survive and even provide her with a visa to safety at the end.

Ilsa and Victor

This relationship seems to be based on one of respect and awe for a great person. Ilsa looks up to Victor and admires him, but she never mentions in the film that she loves him. He, on the other hand, is truly in love with her and is ready to sacrifice himself for this love. We witness this when he tells Rick to get her out safely even though he will have to stay in Casablanca where his life is in danger.

Social setting

The action in this film takes place during World War II. The setting is Morocco in

1941. The Germans are making inroads in many parts of Europe and people are in fear of their lives. Even though Casablanca in northern Africa is governed by the French, there are many threats from the presence of German soldiers. The film deals with various people from different parts of Europe who are hoping to gain visas to get to safety in America. Even though it is wartime there are also opportunities to be entertained in fancy cafes and to enjoy some wine and music. Gambling is another activity carried out in Rick's cafe. The black market was an important reality in World War II and people managed to engage in various types of underhand operations and selling.

Hero
Rick is the true hero of this film. A man who was once abandoned by the woman he loved, he manages to survive and even provides her with a visa to safety at the end.

Heroine
Ilsa is the heroine of this film. She fell in love with Rick when her husband was in a concentration camp. She believed her husband had died and this made it easier to fall in love. She was forced to abandon her relationship with Rick when she heard the truth that Victor was injured but not dead and that he needed her badly.

Villain
The Germans, in particular Major Strasser, are the villains in this film. Strasser is determined to make an impact in Casablanca and threatens people with his presence. He is determined that Victor will not leave Casablanca and get to America safely. His plans are obstructed by Rick's ingenuity.

THE CONSTANT GARDENER
(2011 exam)

Based on the book by John le Carré; directed by Fernando Meirelles

The story
In the opening scene we see Tessa, a white woman, leaving for Loki with Arnold Bluhm, a black doctor. Her husband, Justin Quayle, says goodbye to her and she tells him she will be back in a few days. Then we see the image of an overturned jeep in desert country. Some people arrive in another jeep and remove a body from the overturned jeep. Then the film focuses on a large building in a city with the words 'British High Commission'. The city is Nairobi. A man is seen through a screen and this is Sandy who works in the British Diplomatic Corps in Nairobi. He comes to Justin, who is watering his plants, and tells him that there are reports of a white woman and a black driver who died in Lake Turkana. He also tells Justin that they had spent the night in Lodwar, where they shared a room. The dead man is not Bluhm.

Then there is a flashback to a scene where Justin is giving a lecture to a group of people on behalf of Bernard Pellegrin, a British diplomat and head of the FCO Africa desk. The lecture is interrupted by a young girl who turns out to be Tessa. This is the first meeting between Justin and Tessa. She is angry with the British for attacking Iraq and wants to know what he is going to do about it since he is a diplomat. She is furious at the fact that thousands of innocent people are being killed for barrels of oil. People leave the lecture and they are both left alone. She is apologetic and angry with herself for her rudeness. She invites him for a drink and they begin an affair immediately.

Then the film moves to show Justin and Sandy arriving in the mortuary where a number of people are laid out, among them is Tessa. Justin identifies her, while Sandy is clearly upset. There is another flashback in which Tessa asks Justin to take her to Africa. They go as husband and wife shortly after this as he is working with the British Diplomatic Corps.

The next scene shows us Tessa in the slums of Kibera in Nairobi. She is pregnant and is with Bluhm, a Kenyan doctor. He is giving medicines to people who have AIDS. Shortly after this Justin and Tessa are at home and she asks him to look at her emails. There is a message with the question 'What were you and Arnold doing in the Nairobi Hilton Hotel on Sunday? Does Justin know?' Justin says nothing but asks her about the Nairobi Hilton Hotel. She then tells him that she was meeting someone there last Sunday with Arnold.

There is a reception for the diplomats and their wives. Tessa, who is heavily pregnant, meets a group of diplomats including the Kenyan Health Minister, Dr Nyaba, and Kenneth Curtiss, who is chief executive of Three Bees, a pharmaceutical company in Africa. Tessa is sarcastic to Nyaba about the fact that the medicines have not reached the Kenyan people suffering from AIDS, and wonders have the pills been converted into the limousine he arrived in. Sandy asks Justin to do something about controlling Tessa. It is apparent, however, that Sandy is infatuated with her.

Bluhm tells Tessa that the drug companies are testing the patients for tuberculosis free of charge. Tessa is suspicious and replies that drug companies never do something for nothing.

Tessa loses her baby and is very upset. While in hospital she discovers that a Kenyan women called Wanza Kilulu has been murdered. She believes that Dr Lorbeer was responsible and tells Sandy in confidence. She does not want Justin to get involved as she is concerned for him. Sandy tells her to stop investigating as it will not help Justin's career.

We see Tessa getting emails from a German girl called Birgit and she tells her about the way the drug companies operate. Tessa spends a lot of time working for civil rights with Bluhm, and Justin asks her to stop. She gets upset. Shortly after this we learn that Tessa has sent in a report to Pellegrin and Sandy tells her he has been told to watch all her activities. Sandy tells her about a letter he has received from Pellegrin. She bribes him for the letter by offering to sleep with him at a later stage. He gives her the letter on condition that she returns it safely to the drawer. Then we see Tessa at the computer listening to a Kenyan activist called Grace Makanga, who represents Women For Life. She condemns the fact that the pharmaceutical companies are controlling the government and are giving drugs at such a price.

The film flashes to an image of some men and the death of Tessa. There is a news item announcing the deaths – they name the dead as a father of three and Tessa Quayle, aged twenty-four, the wife of a British diplomat. Then we see Justin and Sandy going to the house where they learn from the servants that the police have taken all Tessa's things away. Sandy begins to search for the letter and Justin discovers a box with mementoes. In the box he finds some photos and a piece of cardboard with the word 'Dypraxa' written on one side and the words 'Wanza Kilulu' on the other. There is also a letter to Tessa from Sandy in which he tells her to run away with him and give up her sham of a marriage because he truly loves her. Justin says nothing to Sandy about the letter. They discover that her laptop and all Tessa's files have been taken.

Justin refuses to have quicklime thrown over her body as nothing can grow on that. Ghita, who works in the British High Commission, comforts him. Justin questions Ghita about the relationship between Arnold and Tessa. Ghita tells him that Arnold was gay. Justin learns from Ghita that the report was sent to the British High Commission and was shown to Kenny Curtiss. Justin goes to the golf course and meets Curtiss along with Tim Donohue, who works as an official in British Intelligence in Nairobi. Curtiss denies ever seeing the report. Justin is sent back to Britain. His passport is kept at security and they tell him there have been forgeries. Justin arrives at a gentlemen's club in London and meets Pellegrin, who warns him that it will do him no good to poke under rocks as he may find nasty things, and suggests he go off and enjoy his sick leave.

Justin meets Ham, who is Tessa's first cousin. Ham's son, Guido, is expert with computers and accesses several files that he had set up with Tessa. Here Justin discovers the full nature of the relationship between the pharmaceutical companies

KDH and Three Bees. It turns out that they both have formed a corporation whereby KDH makes Dypraxa and Three Bees tests it. In the photo advertising KDH, Justin notices that Pellegrin is there along with other people. He also finds a personal file with photos of himself, and Tessa's words to Ham speaking about the promise she made to Sandy and how she had no intention of keeping it – she simply wanted to blackmail the British government. She speaks about her fear of hurting Justin.

Justin returns to the house where he and Tessa lived and breaks down emotionally as he recalls different moments they spent together. He receives a note telling him to stop now or he will get what his wife got. He tells Ham that he wants to continue what she started and proceeds to go to Germany to find Birgit. We see Sandy and the various British diplomats explaining how Justin has gone off the radar and they cannot trace him.

In Germany Justin meets Birgit at the school where she is collecting her young son. Birgit is frightened as her computers have been stolen and tells Justin there is nowhere safe. He learns that Dypraxa cures tuberculosis but it also kills people. He also learns that Dypraxa has not been removed from the market as it would cost millions of dollars to change it. It is cheaper to fix the trials, even if people end up dying. As she is speaking we see several men arrive in various cars all following Justin. He learns that Lorbeer invented Dypraxa and has disappeared but is still in Africa. Justin is badly beaten up in his hotel room and a note is left that this is his last warning: he will join his wife the next time.

Bluhm is found hanging from a tree, having been brutally tortured. Justin returns to Africa. He waits in the garden and sends a note to Sandy, who is entertaining. Justin shows Sandy his letter to Tessa and asks him about the other letter from Pellegrin. Justin learns from Sandy that KDH and Three Bees are both serving British interests in Nairobi and millions of dollars would be lost if they listened to bleeding hearts such as Tessa. Sandy admits that he betrayed Tessa by informing Pellegrin of the fact that she was travelling to Loki.

After this Justin meets Curtiss, who brings him to an area where Wanza Kilulu and sixty-two other Kenyans are buried in quicklime. Their deaths have never been registered. Curtiss tells Justin that he too has been shafted by the High Commission. Justin finds out from Curtiss that Lorbeer is in Sudan, where he is a 'Jesus healer', who has gone to the desert to repent over what he has done. Justin takes Ghita's car and drives. Tim follows him and warns him that they will both be dead by the end of the year. Tim is dying of cancer. Justin tells him he has no home, that his home was Tessa. Tim gives Justin a gun to protect himself.

Justin meets Lorbeer in the desert and tells him he is working as a journalist. Lorbeer speaks about people being driven by guilt. Justin attacks Lorbeer about drug companies and asks him about Tessa. He learns that Tessa had asked Lorbeer to testify on tape. Lorbeer gives Justin a copy of the report. There is an attack from a group of Kenyan warriors and everyone flees. Justin and Lorbeer manage to escape by plane while the Kenyan refugees flee into the wilderness. In the plane Lorbeer tells Justin how Tessa was on her way with Bluhm to show the letter to Grace Makanga, who lives in

Rome. Lorbeer told Crick, the security man of KDH, about Tessa's intentions. Lorbeer tells Justin that Crick will be interested in where Justin is going. Justin replies that he will know already. Justin asks the pilot to drop him off near Lake Turkana. He puts the report in an envelope and addresses it to Grace Makanga in Rome and asks the pilot to post it for him. Justin is set down near Lake Turkana and the plane leaves.

As he walks over the stones we hear a voice speaking from a funeral ceremony about the loss of two valued friends, Tessa and Justin. It is the voice of Pellegrin, praising Justin as courteous, self-effacing, large at heart and a man who chose to take his own life in the same spot as Tessa. The scene moves to the inside of a church where people are gathered together for a memorial service. Ham gets up in the church and begins to deliver an oration. He tells the community gathered there that he will read a non-canonical epistle. He begins to read Pellegrin's letter to Sandy about Tessa's report. In the letter he mentions that Sandy is to shred the report and keep a tighter rein on his resident harlot. 'The issue here is deniability,' he tells Sandy, 'If nobody told us Dypraxa was causing death, we can't be held responsible.' Pellegrin stands up in the church, completely outraged, while the media and community are aghast and follow him with cameras. As he leaves, Ham continues to read, 'if it ever became known that we closed our eyes to the deaths none of us would survive the scandal'. Ham then states that 'it was a bizarre sort of suicide' as Justin's body had eight bullet wounds, none of which came from his own gun. Ham asks the assembled company, 'Who has committed murder?' and answers, 'No one, not the British government, which covers up the offensive corpses, nor the KDH, which has enjoyed record profits this season. There are no murders in Africa, only regrettable deaths.'

The final scene shows Justin sitting calmly beside Lake Turkana throwing away the magazine from his gun. A jeep arrives with several men. He remembers Tessa and begins to speak to her telling her, 'you want me to come home. I am home.' The voice of a man calls 'Mr Quayle' and Justin turns his back to the men while he calls out to Tessa. The film concludes with the noise of the birds flying high in the sky.

Themes
Love
Justin Quayle meets Tessa while he is giving a lecture. They fall in love immediately. They know little about one another but very shortly after they meet they get married and move to Africa. A lot of the film shows us Justin's attempts to come to terms with the sudden death of Tessa, who was murdered, and to understand her character and motivation in her civil rights activities. As the story unfolds, Justin begins to realise how much his wife truly loved him and wanted to protect him from the evil she had found in Africa. The film shows us how Justin is willing to sacrifice his life for the same cause as his wife did.

Corruption
The film is set in Kenya in Africa. It highlights the deep-seated corruption inherent in this country. In the film the corruption stems from the collusion between the British High Commission and the Kenyan government, members of which are bribed. This

collusion springs from a desire to hide the truth underlying the operations of a major pharmaceutical company that has produced a drug called Dypraxa for curing tuberculosis. This drug has not been fully tested and the side-effects can be lethal and have resulted in the deaths of many Kenyans. This fact is covered up by the British High Commission. In addition, a young civil rights activist called Tessa Quayle is murdered when she tries to expose the truth about the situation. Tessa's husband, Justin, manages to uncover the truth surrounding her death. The corruption is clearly exposed when Tessa's cousin Ham reads out a letter from Pellegrin, one of the chief agents involved in hiding the truth.

Loyalty/betrayal
There are many instances of these two themes in the film. Justin shows a profound loyalty to Tessa by trying to discover the truth behind her death. There are hints that she was unfaithful to him, however, he manages to find out that she was truly in love with him when he discovers her files from her cousin Ham.

The British High Commission embodies the theme of betrayal. It betrays the African people by not telling them the truth about the drugs being tested. Sandy even acknowledges to Justin that he betrayed Tessa by telling of her whereabouts and this led to her murder. In the conclusion we see how the truth is fully exposed and justice is done.

Relationships
Justin and Tessa
The relationship between Justin Quayle and his wife, Tessa, is at the centre of the film. They get married very quickly and do not know one another very well. There are many hints from other diplomats that Tessa is having various affairs. Justin discovers that Tessa really loved him and was also a keen civil rights activist who wanted justice for the Kenyan people. He changes in the film and decides to dedicate his life to the interests of justice and good.

Justin and Pellegrin
Another key relationship is between Justin, a minor diplomat based in Nairobi, and Bernard Pellegrin, who runs the FCO office in Africa. Pellegrin has engineered the murder of Tessa so that the truth will not be exposed. He is a hypocrite who tells Justin to stop looking for the truth as nasty things can be found under rocks. He is prepared to murder Justin and call it a suicide. His hypocrisy is exposed at the end by Justin, who gets Ham to read out Pellegrin's letter to Sandy, which reveals that he wanted Tessa killed.

Social setting
The film is set in different locations. Most of the action takes place in the Kibera slums in the centre of Nairobi in Kenya. The people there are poor and their houses are merely galvanised buildings thrown together. Sanitation and food are basic. At the same time there is the pictures given of the British diplomatic lifestyle in Nairobi,

which is affluent and typically colonial. They eat in elegant surroundings and live in large, colonial-style houses. They are governed by money and economic considerations and see Africa as a place to be exploited for their own selfish interests.

The film also shows London and a rich gentlemen's club where the middle class represented in the film enjoy an easy and elegant style of life.

We also see the desert in Sudan when Justin goes to find Lorbeer. This is a dry, hot place where the Masai tribe live in colourful huts and are subject to frequent attacks from neighbouring tribes.

Hero

Justin Quayle, who works in the British Diplomatic Corps in Nairobi, is the hero of this film. He is married to Tessa, who is killed early in the film. He struggles to understand her position as a human rights activist and to find out the reasons leading up to her death. In doing this he overcomes many difficulties and is murdered at the conclusion for continuing his investigations.

Heroine

Tessa Quayle, a human rights activist who works on behalf of the African people, is the heroine of this film. She works relentlessly to uncover the truth that lies behind the huge pharmaceutical companies. She learns that many untested drugs are used on African people, who in turn die. As a result of her investigations, she is murdered.

Villain

Sir Bernard Pellegrin, who is head of the FCO Africa desk, is the villain of this film. He knows that Dypraxa is a drug that has not been fully tested, yet he is more concerned that the British will not lose money. He does not really care about the fact that many Kenyan people will die because of this drug. His corruption is exposed by Justin Quayle at the conclusion.

12 Unseen Poetry

APPROACHING THE UNSEEN POEM

The first thing you must do when tackling an unseen poem is to try to understand its meaning. The tone and the choice of words will help to convey the poem's meaning. You will find that the more times you read the poem, the more its meaning will become clear to you.

Some modern poetry has no clear and unequivocal meaning, and in fact is not meant to have a prescribed and definite meaning. In many cases the meaning can be very obscure, so don't worry about understanding the meaning immediately.

Remember, a poem can have many different interpretations, and that is part of the beauty of poetry. It is important to take risks when reading and trying to understand a poem's meaning.

A poem attempts to communicate some emotion or emotions to the reader through a particular choice of words and structure. To understand the content or meaning of a poem more deeply, we need to examine the following:
- ideas: the content or subject matter
- persona
- language.

Ideas
1. State the idea or attitude expressed in each component part or in each verse.
2. Are there key words or word repetitions strategically placed in order to express the main ideas? (Remember, poetry is emotion and may communicate through syntax, word repetition or image association rather than logic.)
3. Examine why the verses are structured in the particular way that they are.
4. Try to understand the relationship between the different parts of a poem; this will help to reveal its structure.
5. The theme or themes can be elicited or drawn out by grasping how the particular ideas or responses are developed within the poem.

Persona
1. Who is speaking in the poem? Is it the poet himself, or is he pretending to be someone else?

2. To whom is he speaking? To a particular person or to a general audience?
3. What do we learn about the poet from the poem?

The language of poetry

When you analyse the style of a poem – that is, the language, tone, point of view and techniques used – it will help you to gain a deeper understanding and interpretation of the poem.

The particular way in which language is used in a poem helps to give a shape and structure to the poem's thought and meaning.

The language of poetry is made up of:
- imagery
- words
- sound
- rhyme
- grammar
- alliteration
- metre
- onomatopoeia.

Imagery

Imagery is any form of descriptive writing. Imagery focuses the meaning of the poem as a whole. It can also function to create atmosphere and establish a certain pattern within a poem. A poet can make use of language in many different ways to create imagery or word pictures. Don't just identify imagery; be able to say what its function in poetry is.

Imagery creates atmosphere, establishes a pattern within a poem and focuses the meaning of a poem as a whole. Imagery is effective when it is central to the poem's meaning. When studying imagery in a poem, know how to identify the following:
- metaphor
- simile
- symbol.

Both *metaphor* and *simile* compare one thing with another. In a metaphor, this similarity is implied, while a simile shows the comparison using the words 'like' and 'as'. Similes are closer to ordinary speech, while metaphors are more condensed and economical.

Simile: The fog descended like a blanket.
Metaphor: The blanket of fog descended.

A *symbol* is a word that stands for or points to a reality beyond itself. For example, some flowers can symbolise the shortness of life. Some other examples:
- sunrise: a new beginning
- water: purity
- the sea: eternity
- garden: order

- spring: new life and energy
- autumn: maturity, fulfilment, growth, fertility
- winter: old age and death
- rose: maturity
- skull: death
- river: life.

When you are examining symbols, an act of imagination is required before the meaning becomes fully clear. Aim at capturing the way in which a symbol glows or echoes with meaning. The statement or ideas expressed may not make sense on the surface level. The sense or meaning of symbols must be inferred from some association, comparison, contrast or inversion of images and ideas that are used in the poem.

Take, for example, the following lines from T. S. Eliot's poem 'The Waste Land':

> Unreal City,
> Under the brown fog of a winter dawn,
> A crowd flowed over London Bridge, so many,
> I had not thought death had undone so many.

The fog and the winter dawn have many different meanings. They could refer to the spiritual apathy and stagnation that were a feature of the time when Eliot was writing the poem.

When you are studying the imagery in a poem, ask yourself the following questions:
- What does it say?
- Why is it used?
- Does it have connotations or sound effects?
- Does it fit into the context?
- How well does it do its task?

Words
Examine the way words work within a poem.

Appropriateness
Are the words that are used poetic, colloquial or abstract? If so, why? Do the words have connotations or associations? For example:

> I stared and stared
> And Victory filled up
> The little rented boat.

The idea in the lines above is that the poet feels a sense of victory as she sits in this boat.

> There was a sunlit absence.

The poet refers to the absence of some person who was a source of joy.

Allusions

An allusion is a reference to another book, event, person or place. The allusion may be implied or hinted at. Sometimes the effect of using allusion may be to make something that is being said more significant, more ambiguous or more amusing.

Collocation

This occurs through an explosive, unexpected or sometimes contradictory combination of words, for example:

> 'Hope' is the thing with feathers –
> That perches in the soul –
> And sings the tune without the words –
> And never stops – at all –

Repetition

The repetition of words can give emphasis to the power of the poem. Repetition occurs whenever a key word or phrase is repeated at different points:

> No argument, no anger, no remorse,
> No dividing of blame.
> No grief for our dead love, no howling gales.

Rhythm

Rhythm can be used in poetry to add to the mood and atmosphere, and therefore it can help to convey the meaning more clearly. Effective rhythm is where stress falls on the crucial or important words. In the best poetry the rhythm and meaning of the words appear as one and not two things, for example:

> Cut grass lies frail:
> Brief is the breath
> Mown stalks exhale.
> Long, long the death.

Ask yourself whether it is significant that these thoughts and feelings have been expressed in this particular rhythm.

A line can end in two ways: either *end-stopped* with an *end rhyme*, or it can run on into another line in a flow of thought. End rhyme occurs when two consecutive lines rhyme, or alternate lines rhyme. Look at the following lines, which are an example of end rhyme:

> If I were a dead leaf thou mightest bear, [a]
> If I were a swift cloud to fly with thee; [b]
> A wave to pant beneath thy power, and share [a]
>
> The impulse of thy strength, only less free [b]
> Than thou, O uncontrollable! If even [c]
> I were as in my boyhood, and could be [b]

The comrade of thy wanderings over Heaven, [c]
As then, when to outstrip thy skiey speed [d]
Scarce seemed a vision; I would ne'er have striven [c]

As thus with thee in prayer in my sore need. [d]

(Percy Bysshe Shelley, 'Ode to the West Wind')

In the above poem, each letter a, b, c, d indicates a different aspect of end rhyme.

Rhythm sometimes exists to link words and ideas. It can also be used for a particular purpose, for example it can suggest speed, calm, anger or monotony.

The absence of rhythm can suggest fear, worry or aimlessness. Uneven rhythm can also be used for a particular purpose, for example:

How the old Mountains drip with Sunset
How the Hemlocks burn –
How the Dun Brake is draped in Cinder
By the Wizard Sun –

How the old Steeples hand the Scarlet
Till the Ball is full –
Have I the lip of the Flamingo
That I dare to tell?

The above lines are taken from a poem by Emily Dickinson. The rhythm is uneven. It serves the function of building up an atmosphere in nature before the poet herself intrudes into the poem.

Alliteration

This is the repetition of the initial consonant sound. When you are dealing with an unseen poem, discuss the effect of alliteration: don't just give examples. Ask yourself whether or not it produces a distinctive tone and whether or not it is regularly spaced:

I met a Lady in the Meads
Full beautiful a fairy's child . . .

With pitchforks, faint forked lightning's, catching light . . .

O wild west wind, thou breadth of Autumn's being . . .

The alliteration here enacts the awe of the poet in the presence of such a mighty force.

Assonance

This is the repetition of identical vowel sounds. Look, for example, at the effect of assonance in the following lines from Tennyson:

Lo! in the middle of the wood,
The folded leaf is woo'd from out the bud

> Sun steep'd at noon, and in the moon
> Nightly dew-fed; and turning yellow
> Falls, and floats adown the air.

The combined effect of the assonance of the *o* sound creates an impression of rich abundance in nature.

Onomatopoeia
This is where the word conjures up the sound: *wheeze*, *buzz*.

> watch the crisping ripples on the beach
> Liplapping of Galilee

Ambiguity
Ambiguity in poetry means the use of a word or words to mean two or more different things. Many times a poet can enrich the meaning of a poem by using words that are ambiguous. Ambiguity can highlight the many nuances or levels of meaning that can be found in poetic language. Look at the following lines:

> The grass divides as with a comb –
> A spotted shaft is seen –
> And then it closes at your feet
> And opens further on . . .

The above statements about the grass dividing and then closing and opening at your feet are an example of ambiguity. How exactly does the grass divide? Why does it close at your feet and then open further on?

Effects of sound
Don't just give examples, show the effect. For example, harshness can be conveyed by the use of consonants *b*, *t*, *k*.

> Blight and famine, plague and earthquake, roaring deeps . . .
> Clanging fights, and flaming towns, and sinking ships.

A sense of smoothness can be conveyed by the use of certain vowels, and also by the *s* sound:

> There is sweet music here that softer falls.

Grammar
Consider some of the grammatical devices used in poetry:
- The omission of 'and', verbs or commas. Ask yourself why?
- Adding 'and', commas, verbs or capital letters when not usual. Ask why?
- Short sentences. What is their purpose?
- Long sentences. Anger? Boredom? Movement?
- Unusual syntax. Look at the purpose.

- Word compounds, e.g. world sorrow, blue-bleak, leafy-with-love. What are they saying? Why are they used?
- The unusual use of words:

> Have passed I thought, a whip lash
> Unbraiding in the sun
> When stooping to secure it
> It wrinkled, and was gone.

- Nouns made into verbs. Why?
- Coining of words. Why?

Metre
- A very short line can express emotion, joy, anger or hatred.
- A very long line – what effect does it have?
- Run-on lines can express movement, speed, growth or development.

METHOD OF ANSWERING QUESTIONS ON AN UNSEEN POEM

Remember that a poem is made up of content or subject matter. This content is shaped in a particular way, and the shape of a poem is known as its structure or form.

1. Aim first of all to give a general summary of what the poem is about and the different stages in the poem.
2. Read the poem through several times to grasp some idea of the meaning.
3. Examine the title of the poem and see what relation it may have to the content.
4. Examine what type of poem it is. Is it narrative, an argument, a philosophical insight into life, an ode, a lyric, a sonnet?
5. If the poem is a narrative, understand the main events. When you understand why the events follow one another in a particular way, you will understand how the poem is designed. There are three elements common to poems that tell stories: expectation, surprise and reversal.
6. If the poem is a meditation on life, get the general meaning of what is being said.
7. If the poem is an argument, follow the main stages. Ask yourself why the argument moves from one stage to the next. Look at the conclusion of the argument. Is it logical? Is it effective? Has it achieved what it set out to do? Are you convinced? Identify the main points and the different stages.
8. Look at the words and see whether they carry symbolic or emotive meaning. Ask yourself why this is so. Look for a particular tone. Tone is the voice, mood or outlook of the poet.
9. Show how figures of speech contribute to the poem. Remember, figures of speech can be metaphors, symbols, personification, similes, etc. Poems often convey their meaning by implication, suggestion or word connotations or associations, and not necessarily through explicit statement.
10. Be aware of your reaction to the poem. What thoughts and feelings do the words stir up in you? Remember that a poem does not have to make complete sense.

Often the power of poetry comes from its ability to establish or suggest many different levels of meaning and many possibilities.

Sample questions and answers

Courtesy
Hilaire Belloc

Of Courtesy, it is much less
Than Courage of Heart or Holiness,
Yet in my walks it seems to me
That the Grace of God is in Courtesy.

On Monks I did in Storrington fall,
They took me straight into their hall:
I saw three Pictures on a wall,
And Courtesy was in them all.

The first the Annunciation;
The second the Visitation;
The third the Consolation,
Of God that was Our Lady's Son.

The first was of Saint Gabriel:
On wings a-flame from Heaven he fell:
And as he went upon one knee
He shone with Heavenly Courtesy.

Our Lady out of Nazareth rode –
It was her month of heavy load:
Yet was her face both great and kind,
For Courtesy was in her Mind.

The third it was our Little Lord,
Whom all the Kings in arms adored;
He was so small you could not see
His large intent of Courtesy.

Our Lord, that was Our Lady's Son,
Go bless you, People, one by one:
My rhyme is written, my work is done.

Sample questions

1. From your reading of the above poem, explain briefly what the main features of courtesy are.
2. Study the rhyming scheme in the above poem and comment on how the particular rhyme of the poem helps to develop the main ideas.
3. Do you like the above poem? In your answer, take into account the way the poet has organised his thought, and the use of imagery.

Sample answers

1. The writer maintains that courtesy is less than courage or holiness, but that it contains the grace of God. To illustrate this idea, the poet shows how he saw courtesy in the three pictures that represent the life of Our Lady – the Annunciation, the Visitation and the Consolation or birth of her Son. Courtesy is seen in the Angel Gabriel as he announces the message to Our Lady that she will be the mother of God. Our Lady's face reflects courtesy as she carries Our Lord in her womb while she is pregnant. The image of Our Lord in the stable is another example of courtesy according to the writer.

2. The rhyming scheme in the above poem is interesting and original. It is irregular. The function of this type of irregular scheme could be to highlight the fact that the poet is trying to discover what exactly courtesy is.

   In the first stanza, the word 'less' rhymes with 'Holiness', which has two syllables.

   In the second stanza, however, the words at the end of each line rhyme: fall, wall, hall, all. The ordered structure in the rhyming pattern reflects the fact that all three pictures hanging in a monk's hallway showed the same thing – courtesy. In this stanza the poet has begun to express an image of what courtesy means for him.

   In the third stanza, the rhyming scheme is slightly irregular:

   annunciation
   visitation
   consolation
   son

   Perhaps the poet is saying that, through this type of rhyming scheme, courtesy can be seen in both the life of Our Lady and that of her Son.

3. Yes, I like this poem because it is a simple representation of what courtesy means to the poet. He uses the number of words to create a graphic and clear picture of the different ways in which he sees courtesy reflected. We can visualise Gabriel kneeling down before Our Blessed Lady. We can also see Our Lady heavy with the weight of pregnancy as she rides on the donkey: 'it was her month of heavy load'. We also see how vulnerable and small the child was, yet he was able to reflect courtesy.

   The concluding stanza is made up of only three lines. This is interesting because it ties up with the ideas expressed by the poet, that the work that he set out to do is now completed.

The Mother
Patrick Pearse

I do not grudge them: Lord, I do not grudge
My two strong sons that I have seen go out
To break their strength and die, they and
A few,
In bloody protest for a glorious thing,
They shall be spoken of among their people,
The generations shall remember them,
And call them blessed;
But I will speak their names to my own heart
In the long nights;
The little names that were familiar once
Round my dead hearth.
Lord, thou art hard on mothers:
We suffer in their coming and their going;
And tho' I grudge them not, I weary, weary
Of the long sorrow – And yet I have my joy:
My sons were faithful, and they fought.

Sample questions
1. What is the tone of the above poem? Support your answer by reference to the poem.
2. What do you consider to be the main theme of this poem? Support your answer by reference to the poem.
3. From your reading of the above poem, what type of people do you think these sons were? Make reference to the poem to support your answer.

Sample answers
1. The tone of the poem is a mixture of joy and sorrow. The poet's voice is filled with a sincere faith and assurance that God will look after this mother. The poem opens with some clear words spoken by the mother. It is a type of prayer to God, where the mother generously offers her two sons. She sees their death as blessed, and a 'glorious thing'. She knows that she will be sad when they are gone, and that she will mourn them. The tone of the conclusion is hopeful and optimistic, however. She knows her sons remained faithful to their cause, which is obviously Ireland, and that they fought for their country.
2. In my opinion the main theme of this poem is the generosity of the mother as she faces the fact that her sons will die for a noble cause – fighting for the freedom of their country. The mother addresses God directly by telling Him that she does not grudge her two strong sons. She knows that the cause for which they fight is a good one, that generations will remember them and speak about them, and they will be considered blessed. The mother acknowledges that she will undoubtedly suffer

sorrow over the loss of her two sons. Her joy will overcome this sorrow, however, because she knows that her sons were faithful and that they fought.
3. Her two sons were strong and courageous. They were prepared to go out, 'to break their strength and die'. They were rebels for a 'glorious cause', which was obviously the freedom of their country. They were united together and clearly very much loved by their mother. They were faithful to their cause as they did not give up: 'my sons were faithful and they fought'.

In Memoriam
Alfred Lord Tennyson

Be near me when my light is low,
    When the blood creeps, and the nerves prick
    And tingle; and the heart is sick,
And all the wheels of Being slow.

Be near me when the sensuous frame
    Is racked with pangs that conquer trust;
    And Time, a maniac scattering dust,
And life, a Fury slinging flame.

Be near me when my faith is dry,
    And men the flies of latter spring,
    That lay their eggs, and sting and sing,
And weave their petty cells and die.

Be near me when I fade away,
    To point the term of human strife,
    And on the low dark verge of life
The twilight of eternal day.

Sample questions
1. Sum up the main points in the above poem.
2. From your reading of the above poem, what type of person would you consider the poet to be? Support your answer by reference to the poem.
3. Pick out two images that you find significant in expressing the thought of the poet. Comment on why you consider these images to be effective.

Sample answers
1. The poet is obviously praying to God to be near him when he is dying, 'when his light is low'. In stanza one, he prays that God will be with him when his body has broken down physically and he has slowed down, 'all the wheels of being slow'. In stanza two, the poet continues this prayer. This time he asks God to help him when

he begins to lose his trust and to doubt, when the 'sensuous frame is racked with pangs that conquer trust'. He feels that he needs protection from God because he sees that life is like a maniac scattering dust, or confusing him, in other words. He prays that God will be near him when he finds it hard to believe, 'when my faith is dry', and when he finds himself surrounded by men who are only mean, petty and bitter, 'lay their eggs that sting and sing'. In the final stanza the poet asks God to be near him when he actually dies, 'fade away'. He believes that death is the end of all difficulties and the dawning of a new life:

> To point the term of human strife,
> And on the low dark verge of life
> The twilight of eternal day.

2. The poet is a man of faith and confidence in God. The whole poem is a prayer. In each stanza he addresses God with the faith and confidence of a child, 'Be near me'.

   The poet is also a realistic person – he realises that men are petty, bitter and negative. He also realises that he will suffer physically with pangs of conscience, 'pangs that conquer trust'.

3. (a) 'And Time, a maniac scattering dust'

   The idea in this image is that time is like a madman spreading dust around him and blocking people's vision of what is right and wrong, and confusing them deliberately. The poet feels that when he is sick and unable to reason clearly, he wants God to protect him from the brutal reality of time, which will only confuse him more.

   (b) 'And all the wheels of Being slow.'

   This is a very vivid image of the human body. The poet visualises the body's mechanisms like wheels. It is a rich metaphor to describe the human body. In this very vivid image, the poet show us an image of what the human body will be like when it is sick and unable to function properly; he sees the functions of the body as similar to wheels which have slowed down.

Fittings
Anne Dean

Under mother's eye, I stood undressed
In the dressmaker's room
While she pinned me into next summer.

I heard her breathing
Through pins she held between her teeth
As she tucked and darted

Shaped me, revealing little. 'Space to grow'
Her voice behind clenched jaws.
I worried she'd swallow a pin,

Felt prickling over my body,
A tightness under my arms.
On her knees, she measured

Hem length from floor to crease
Against a ruler. 'Enough for letting down . . .'
Muffled by cloth.

She worked her way around the skirt,
Followed the line on the paper pattern.
I imagine a new self.

Her machine rattles through my dreams,
Crafts and stitches French-seams.
'Made to last.'

On her hanger the dress looks right.
Soft cotton drops over my shoulders.
They step back. 'Look at yourself.'

I hesitate, and glance back at them.
Pushed towards the long mirror,
I see myself. Tilted.

Sample questions
1. Write a short note on the two different points of view in the poem. Which do you consider to be more effective? Give reasons for your answer.
2. Choose two examples of the effective use of images in this poem. Write an explanation of your understanding of the imagery in each one.
3. Write a brief commentary on your reaction to this poem.

Sample answers
1. *The mother's viewpoint*: The mother is anxious to get the measurements right for this new summer dress. She is absorbed in the whole process of measuring the child correctly. She is concerned that there will be enough space to grow and enough material left in order to let the dress down if necessary. The mother is also keen to sew the dress as soon as possible; she sews on French-seams which are made to last.

   The child's viewpoint: The child sees herself standing in a dressmaker's room under the eye of her mother. Her mother is pinning her into a new dress for next summer. The child worries that her mother will swallow a pin. As the mother measures her from top to toe, the child begins to imagine a new self. The child hears the sewing machine rattling through her dreams as the mother sews through the night. The child thinks the dress looks right as it hangs on the hanger. The child hesitates before looking at herself in the mirror. She is pushed towards the mirror and sees herself 'tilted'.

I feel that the child's viewpoint is more effective because it gives us a real insight into the whole process of being fitted for a new dress. The child's vision of the whole situation is reflected in each stanza. As she stands in the dressmaker's she hears the mother breathe; later on, she hears the machine 'rattling through her dreams'. The child is unsure and awkward in her new dress and so she sees herself in the mirror as 'tilted'.

2. 'While she pinned me into next summer.'
This image is a good one to describe how a child is being fitted into a new summer dress. The image in the phrase 'pinned into next summer' shows us how the dress is being made especially to fit this child.

'Pushed towards the long mirror,
I see myself. Tilted.'

The child is not sure about how she will appear in her new dress, and so when she looks into the mirror she sees herself tilted or at an angle. In other words, the idea in this clever image is to highlight how unsure or awkward the child feels in this new garment.

3. My viewpoint about this poem is that it gives us a realistic vision from the point of view of a child about her experiences of being fitted for a new dress. It is a simple poem yet cleverly expressed. Each stanza shows us the child's reaction to the fitting and at the same time, the mother's busy preoccupation with fitting the child. The language used by the poet is simple and easy to follow. Each stanza develops the idea in what is expressed before. The use of the child's voice throughout the poem makes it a very realistic and dramatic piece of writing.

13
Prescribed Poetry

In this chapter there are sample poems by some of the prescribed poets on the course. The method of answering questions is outlined. In each case, carefully study the questions and the approach taken in answering them.

Approaching the question

- **Stage 1:** Rephrase or rewrite the question.
- **Stage 2:** Take a stance on the question. Decide to agree, disagree or partly agree.
- **Stage 3:** Begin a rough draft of your answer. Write down seven or eight points that will form the framework of your answer. These points must be on different aspects of the question and must contain quotations or references. They will form the basis of each of the paragraphs of your answer. Remember, a good answer must be structured into several different paragraphs and all must develop the question asked.

The concluding paragraph must tie up all your ideas and refer back to the question. In addition, a good conclusion makes a definitive statement on the question.

Sample questions and answers

Study the following poems and the sample questions and answers that follow.

> *Spring*
> Gerard Manley Hopkins
> (2011 exam)
>
> Nothing is so beautiful as Spring—
> When weeds, in wheels, shoot long and lovely and lush;
> Thrush's eggs look little low heavens, and thrush
> Through the echoing timber does so rinse and wring
> The ear. It strikes like lightnings to hear him sing;
> The glassy peartree leaves and blooms, they brush
> The descending blue; that blue is all in a rush
> With richness; the racing lambs too have fair their fling.

> What is all this juice and all this joy?
> A strain of the earth's sweet being in the beginning
> In Eden garden.—Have, get before it cloy
> Before it cloud, Christ, lord, and sour with sinning,
> Innocent mind and Mayday in girl and boy,
> Most, O maid's child, thy choice and worthy the winning.

Sample questions
1. From your reading of the first stanza (page 208), why does the poet claim that nothing is as beautiful as Spring?
2. What is the tone of the first stanza?
3. Explain the question that the poet asks in stanza two (page 209).
4. What type of person do you imagine the poet to be from your reading of the above poem?

Sample answers
1. The poet explains that nothing is so beautiful as spring because he sees all the world of nature filled with a rich sense of wonder and beauty. He speaks about the long, lovely, lush weeds, and how the singing of the thrush does 'rinse and wring the ear'. He means that the music fills the hearer with a sense of joy and wonder. He also speaks about his surroundings, which are like 'blue is all in a rush'. This is a happy and peaceful image where the poet pays tribute to the glory and wealth of nature.
2. The tone of the first stanza is filled with awe and wonder. The poet simply praises the glory and richness of the world of nature.
3. The poet asks in the second stanza about the source of all this richness and joy in the natural world. He thinks that it may come from 'the beginning' when the world was first created. He seems to draw a parallel with the Garden of Eden when God gifted humankind with huge wealth and happiness and beauty.
4. Hopkins seems to be a person who loves the natural world and creation. He sees beauty in everything, even in weeds. He opens the poem by praising the world in springtime and stating how:

   > Nothing is so beautiful as Spring—
   > When weeds, in wheels, shoot long and lovely and lush;

   The poet is also an observant person. He notices how the thrush's eggs are like 'little low heavens', because they are so pretty and beautiful they remind him of heaven.
      Hopkins is an original poet. This is evident from his use of imagery. He describes how the song of the thrush actually rinses and wrings the ear. He is talking about the capacity of the thrush's song to inspire and to delight the ear with music.
      Hopkins is a deep thinker. He asks the question about the root or source of this

joy and vitality in the natural world. He believes in God and in his goodness. Hopkins also sees the capacity of humankind to offend God by sinning and to lose its innocence. Hopkins is a humble man who recognises the power and glory of God and who is inspired to write about this power and wonder in poetry.

Child of Our Time
Eavan Boland
(2010 and 2011 exams)

Yesterday I knew no lullaby
But you have taught me overnight to order
This song, which takes from your final cry
Its tune, from your unreasoned end its reason;
Its rhythm from the discord of your murder
Its motive from the fact you cannot listen.

We who should have known how to instruct
With rhymes for your waking, rhythms for your sleep,
Names for the animals you took to bed,
Tales to distract, legends to protect
Later an idiom for you to keep
And living, learn, must learn from you, dead,

To make our broken images rebuild
Themselves around your limbs, your broken
Image, find for your sake whose life our idle
Talk has cost, a new language. Child
Of our time, our times have robbed your cradle.
Sleep in a world your final sleep has woken.

Sample questions
1. From your reading of the above poem what type of person would you say the poet is?
2. Explain the meaning of the second stanza.
3. Comment on some images used by the poet to express the main theme in this poem.
4. What do you think is the main point made in this poem? Discuss the tone used by the poet to convey this point.

Sample answers
1. The poet seems to condemn violence and to suggest that peace is the only way forward in times of war. She mentions how the child's death is 'unreasoned', and how people must now find a 'new language' outside of violence.

2. The poet is speaking about the adult world, and the people who are running society. She is talking to a young child who has been killed in a bomb and she is saying how adults are the ones who now must learn from this death. She makes the statement that, while adults are usually the ones who teach younger people about rhymes and stories and language, now the situation is reversed: the child will teach the adult generation a lesson on the futility of violence.
3. One of the main themes in this poem is the whole futility or pointlessness of war and violence. Boland uses many images to express this fact. She describes the child's death as 'unreasoned'. She speaks about the fact that political talk has amounted to nothing and now new things have to be learned from the child's death:

>   find for your sake whose life our idle
> Talk has cost a new language.

Boland uses the image of 'a new language' to highlight the need for peace, and the need for a change in mentality towards war and violence.
4. The main point made by this poem is the fact that a young child has died as a result of violence and that this death should not have happened. Boland speaks about the death of the child as happening in the modern world, 'Child of our time'. The poet also states that with this death of a young child the people who are running society must now stop and think about finding a new way forward, a 'new language'. She is speaking about the need for peace and for the end of violence:

> To make our broken images rebuild
> Themselves around your limbs,

Boland's tone is calm and reasoned. She is not passionate or over emotional. Instead, she uses a balanced and reasonable tone to express her sorrow at the untimely death of this child. She uses a controlled and calm tone to ask for a change in mindset and for other ways to operate in society besides violence and warfare.

The Wild Swans at Coole
William Butler Yeats
(2010 and 2011 exams)

The trees are in their autumn beauty,
The woodland paths are dry,
Under the October twilight the water
Mirrors a still sky;
Upon the brimming water among the stones
Are nine-and-fifty swans.

> The nineteenth summer has come upon me
> Since I first made my count;
> I saw, before I had well finished,
> All suddenly mount
> And scatter wheeling in great broken rings
> Upon their clamorous wings.
>
> I have looked upon those brilliant creatures,
> And now my heart is sore.
> All's changed since I, hearing at twilight,
> The first time on this shore,
> The bell-beat of their wings above my head,
> Trod with a lighter tread.
>
> Unwearied still, lover by lover,
> They paddle in the cold
> Companionable streams or climb the air;
> Their hearts have not grown old;
> Passion or conquest, wander where they will,
> Attend upon them still.
>
> But now they drift on the still water,
> Mysterious, beautiful;
> By what lake's edge or pool
> Delight men's eyes when I awake some day
> To find they have flown away?

Sample questions
1. Do you like this poem? Give reasons for your answer.
2. Write a short note on what you learn about the poet from this poem.

Sample answers
1. Yes, I like this poem very much. The poet sets out a beautiful autumnal scene in Coole Park, where he sees fifty-nine swans on the lake one evening. He constructs the poem in five stanzas and draws an interesting contrast between their beauty and his consciousness of old age in himself.

    Yeats clearly admires the swans for their elegance and beauty and in many ways he could be using them to symbolise his quest for immortality. The swans are powerful and passionate birds for Yeats. Perhaps he is also using the picture of the swans and the whole impact of the scene to symbolise poetic inspiration.

2. Yeats tells us that it is nineteen years since he first saw the swans floating on the lake at Coole. It is clear that Yeats is conscious of his old age and compares this to

the swans' beauty and dynamism. In stanza three, he states that his heart is sore. The stanza develops by suggesting some reasons for this suffering in Yeats. He feels that all is changed, and he remembers that when he first heard the swans he was a younger and more energetic man: 'All's changed since I, hearing at twilight . . . Trod with a lighter tread.'

Yeats sets the scene deliberately in an autumnal setting. This could symbolise his own consciousness of increasing old age and also the decline of his poetic inspiration. The concluding stanza seems to reinforce this idea. Yeats poses the question of whether, as he hopes, the swans will delight the eyes of other men, when he awakes one day to find they have flown away. Perhaps he suggests that as an old man he will no longer need poetic inspiration.

Examination Papers

14

LEAVING CERTIFICATE EXAMINATION, 2009

English – Ordinary Level – Paper I

Total Marks: 200

Wednesday 3 June

- This paper is divided into two sections,
  Section I COMPREHENDING and Section II COMPOSING.
- The paper contains **three** texts on the general theme of CONNECTIONS.
- Candidates should familiarise themselves with each of the texts before beginning their answers.

- Both sections of this paper (COMPREHENDING and COMPOSING) must be attempted.
- Each section carries 100 marks.

SECTION I – COMPREHENDING

- Two questions, A and B, follow each text.
- Candidates must answer a Question A on one text and a Question B on a different text. Candidates must answer only one Question A and only one Question B.
- **N.B.** Candidates may NOT answer a Question A and a Question B on the same text.

SECTION II – COMPOSING

- Candidates must write on **one** of the compositions 1–7.

SECTION I
COMPREHENDING (100 marks)

TEXT 1
YouTube – CONNECTING OUR WORLD

Irish Independent journalist, Gemma O'Doherty, interviewed Chad Hurley. He, along with his partners, Steve Chen and Jawed Karim, came up with an idea which has connected millions of people on the website, YouTube. The following edited extract is based on that interview.

Q1. How did YouTube come about?
YouTube started with such a simple idea. We had videos we wanted to share with our families and friends but found there wasn't really a way of doing that on the internet. We thought it would be interesting to see if we could figure out a way that would make it simple to share home-made video material. My friend Steve Chen and I put our heads together and started coming up with new ways of putting video onto the net. We wanted to give our website mass appeal, to make our website easy to use, without the need for any special software.

Most importantly we did not charge people for the service. Within months the site was flooded with videos and there was no shortage of viewers willing to watch them. They were able to send each other links to the website. We were in the right place at the right time. People had started getting their own devices, like mobile phones and digital cameras, which enabled them to make videos to share with one another. We knew we were on to something special.

Q2. Why is YouTube so popular?
The website has become the first stop for young people who want to watch a video on the internet. Thanks to YouTube, the dream of creating television on demand suddenly became a reality. Every single minute, ten hours of new material ranging from shaky home videos to concert clips, is put onto the website. It is a place where ordinary people can be turned into celebrities with an audience of 100 million viewers.

Q3. What makes YouTube so successful?
This is a multi-tasking generation. Young people are capable of dealing with multiple things at once. They're not just sitting behind their computer; at the same time they may be watching TV or talking on their mobile phone or reading a magazine. The internet revolution is all about connecting people. If you look at

the success of social networking, like Facebook or text messaging or email, it's all about communication. That has been the key to YouTube's success. It's a great way to connect with other people. What we're seeing with this generation is the sharing of ideas, thoughts and experiences.

Q4. How do you protect your website from misuse?
We are fully aware that the website has the potential to be dangerous. We have made it clear what's acceptable to put on YouTube and what's not. Content that is violent or hateful or generally unsuitable we can remove in a matter of minutes.

Q5. What does the future hold for YouTube?
People are always going to want quality information and entertainment be it from newspapers, television or magazines and certainly that demand is not going to disappear. YouTube is adding to the choice. We are continuing to work on our website which is still so young. The speed of connection to the website will continue to improve. It will be increasingly possible to connect from wherever you are at any time. It's a chance for different cultures to talk to each other. Every day YouTube gets bigger and as a result I'm working harder!

N.B. Candidates may NOT answer Question A and Question B on the same text.

Questions A and B carry 50 marks each.

Question A

(i) Having read the entire interview, what do you think are the advantages and disadvantages of YouTube? Support your answer with reference to the text. (15)

(ii) The picture that accompanies this text shows YouTube inventor Chad Hurley, Planet Earth and computer screens. Do you think this is a suitable picture to accompany the interview? Give reasons for your answer. (15)

(iii) In this interview, what does Chad Hurley tell us about the public's response to the development of YouTube? (20)

Question B

You have won a competition entitled 'Be a Celebrity for a Day'. Write out **two diary entries** or **two blog entries** about your experience. (50)

TEXT 2
THE FAMILY'S FIRST TELEVISION

In the following adapted extract from 44, A Dublin Memoir, *Peter Sheridan describes the arrival of the family's first television set on New Year's Eve, 1959. Peter, his brothers, Johnny and Shea and sister Ita help their father and Uncle Paddy to get it working.*

1. New Year's Eve, 1959. A light snowfall. We were waiting for our first images on our new television. Da said we'd be watching pictures from the BBC by five o' clock. I watched my father and his brother Paddy attach the aerial to the chimney and in no time the cable was lowered down the back wall, taken in through the kitchen window and plugged into the back of the television set. The entire family sat in a big semi-circle and stared at it. Ma was in the armchair by the fire with Frankie asleep in her arms. Da reached out to turn it on. His hand was still blue with the cold. He couldn't grip the switch. He blew on his fingers and tried again. The click sounded like an explosion. A small dot appeared in the centre of the screen. It was magic. The dot disappeared and we all let out a sigh of disappointment. Just as quickly the whole screen lit up and we all sighed again with excitement. But to our disappointment, no picture filled the screen – only a snow of black and white dots appeared. Da took off his woollen cap and threw it in my lap. "Get that on, son, you're going up to the aerial."

2. The roof was like a scene from Mars. Da had rigged up a light and had it hanging from the chimney stack. This cast huge shadows over the snow. Every time they moved the light, the shadow of the aerial seemed like a giant centipede about to enter our house.

Da and Uncle Paddy warmed their frozen hands on candles they had set in bean cans. They looked like zombies who'd been attacked by the abominable snowman. I knew not to look down. To look straight ahead, like Da told me. I was shaking with fear. I reached the chimney and felt the fishbone aerial against the top of my head. Each time I slid up those few feet, the aerial swayed gently under my weight. "Now son, listen to me, very gently reach up your hand and turn the aerial towards England." I'd have flown to England if he'd asked me. I turned it in a straight line. Da sent the message down the line of communication he had established.
"Have we a picture?"
Johnny at the top of the ladder shouted down to Ita at the bottom.
"Have we a picture?"
Ita ran into Shea who was in charge of the tuning.
"Have we a picture?"
Shea turned the button fully one way, then the other. Word came back up the line.
– "Snow."
– "Snow."
– "Snow."
– "Snow."

3. "There's your problem. There's your problem, right there. The church is blocking your signal," Paddy said to Da. "The church stands directly between you and a perfect picture."

Da saw it immediately.

"The signal is going to hit them houses and bounce over there." Paddy turned the light southwards. "It's going to re-form over there, do a little jazz dance and work its way into us from the direct opposite side."

Paddy turned the light towards me. The two of them shouted at me with one voice.

"Turn it around son, turn it around."

I turned the aerial in the complete opposite direction. Word went down the line. Word came up the line.

– "There's a picture!"
– "There's a picture!"
– "There's a picture!"
– "There's a picture!"

4. Half an hour into 1960 we all sat staring at the television. The sound was perfect. A man was describing the celebrations in Trafalgar Square. There was definitely something on the screen. Outlines that looked like human beings. I went right up close but all I could see were dots and lines. Paddy touched something at the back of the set and there it was – a perfect picture. Well, nearly perfect. Lots of snow but a definite picture. We all clapped. It was a woman on a horse. She looked majestic. We stayed glued to the television. The music blared out and the Queen inspected the guard. Da and Paddy stood behind us.

I couldn't wait for the rest of the 1960s to begin.

N.B. Candidates may NOT answer Question A and Question B on the same text.

Questions A and B carry 50 marks each.

Question A

(i) What do you learn about the Sheridan family from your reading of the extract? Support your answer with reference to the extract. (15)

(ii) This extract is full of detailed description. Choose your favourite detail/description from the passage and explain why you liked it. (15)

(iii) How does the writer create an atmosphere of suspense and excitement in paragraph 2 of the extract? (20)

Question B

Imagine you are the young Peter Sheridan. Write the **letter** he might have written to his grandmother describing the events that took place in his house on New Year's Eve, 1959 and his role in them.

(50)

TEXT 3

These images represent different types of connections

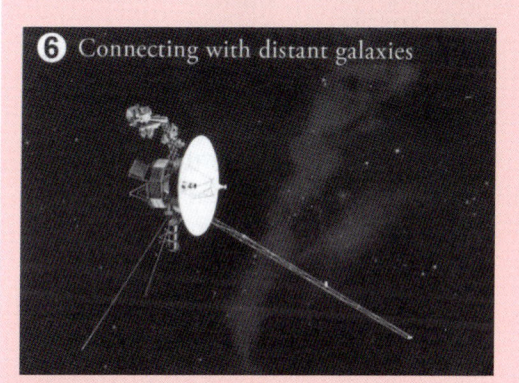

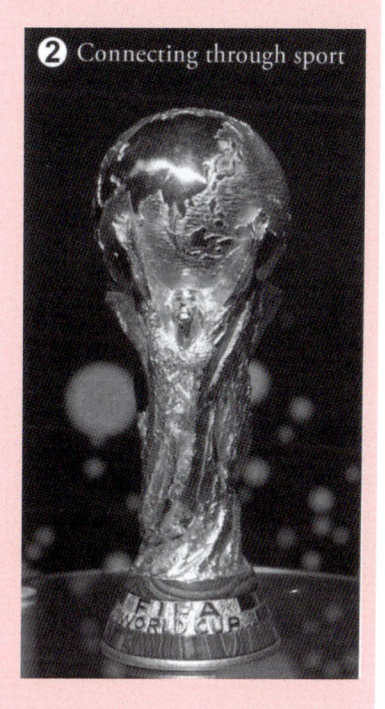

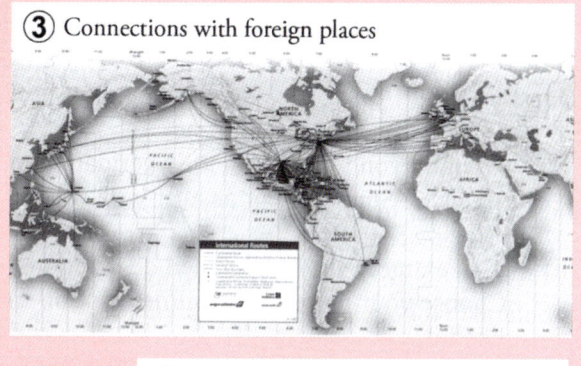

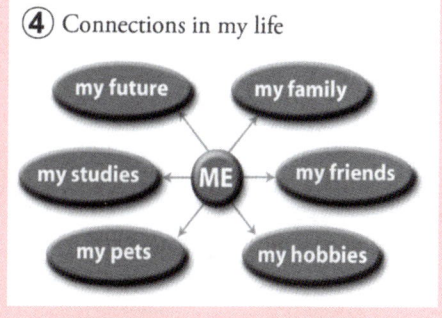

① Connecting with friends

② Connecting through sport

⑥ Connecting with distant galaxies

③ Connections with foreign places

⑤ Connecting with the past

④ Connections in my life

- my future
- my family
- my studies
- ME
- my friends
- my pets
- my hobbies

N.B. Candidates may NOT answer Question A and Question B on the same text. Questions A and B carry 50 marks each.

Question A

(i) Choose **one** of the images from Text 3 and explain why you think **it is** or **is not** a good illustration of that type of connection. (15)

(ii) If you were asked to replace **one** of the images illustrating a connection in Text 3, which one would you choose to remove?

Describe the image you would use as a replacement.

(**N.B.** The caption should remain the same.) (15)

(iii) Which **one** of the different types of connection represented in Text 3 do you find most interesting? Explain your answer. (20)

Question B

Write the short **talk** you would give to your class on **one** of the following topics:

– letter writing is a thing of the past

– the internet can be a fascinating place

– there is nothing in newspapers to interest young people (50)

SECTION II
COMPOSING (100 marks)

Write a composition on **any one** of the following.

Each composition carries 100 marks.

The composition assignments below are intended to reflect language study in the areas of information, argument, persuasion, narration and the aesthetic use of language.

1. "We were in the right place at the right time." (TEXT 1)
   Write about a time when you found yourself in the right place at the right time.

2. "This is a multi-tasking generation." (TEXT 1)
   Write an article for a magazine about what it is like being a teenager in the twenty-first century.

3. "New Year's Eve… A light snowfall." (TEXT 2)
   Write a personal account of your favourite memories of Christmas and the New Year.

4. "They looked like zombies who'd been attacked by the abominable snowman."
   Write a short story inspired by the above sentence. (TEXT 2)

5. "I couldn't wait for the rest of the 1960s to begin." (TEXT 2)
   Write a talk you would give to your classmates about what you imagine life will be like in the year 2060.

6. "Connections with foreign places" (TEXT 3)
   Write a narrative or short story inspired by image 3.

7. Look at the images in Text 3. (TEXT 3)
   Write a personal account of an experience that showed you the importance of connections.

LEAVING CERTIFICATE EXAMINATION, 2009

English – Ordinary Level – Paper 2

Total Marks: 200

Time – 3 hours 20 minutes

Candidates must attempt the following:

- **ONE** question from SECTION I – The Single Text
- **ONE** question from SECTION II – The Comparative Study
- **THE QUESTIONS** on the Unseen Poem from SECTION III – Poetry
- The questions on **ONE** of the Prescribed Poems from SECTION III – Poetry

SECTION I
THE SINGLE TEXT (60 MARKS)

Candidates must answer on **ONE** text (**A–I**).

A   CAT'S EYE – Margaret Atwood
Answer **all** of the questions.

1. (a) Based on your reading of the novel, describe the relationship between Elaine Risley and Mrs Smeath. (10)

    (b) What kind of character was Elaine's brother, Stephen? Support your view by reference to the novel. (10)

    (c) Describe briefly **one** event from *Cat's Eye* that you thought was particularly memorable, and explain why you found it to be so. (10)

2. Answer **ONE** of the following: [Each part carries 30 marks]

    (i) "Cordelia is a fascinating character." Do you agree with this view of her? Support your answer by reference to the novel.

    OR

    (ii) "What if…"
    Suggest **one** change you would make to the storyline of *Cat's Eye*. Describe what you think would happen as a result of that change.

    OR

    (iii) You have been asked to talk to Fifth Year students about the novel you have studied for your Leaving Certificate. Write out the short talk you would give them on *Cat's Eye*.

B   REGENERATION – Pat Barker
Answer **all** of the questions.

1. (a) In your own words, outline Siegfried Sassoon's attitude to the war. (10)

    (b) Which character did you admire most in *Regeneration*? Explain your choice by reference to the novel. (10)

    (c) What do you think is the saddest moment in the novel? Briefly describe what happens and explain why it is so sad. (10)

2. Answer **ONE** of the following: [Each part carries 30 marks]

(i) What is your opinion of Dr. Yealland and the methods he uses to treat his patients? Explain your view by reference to the text.

OR

(ii) Have your views on war changed in any way as a result of reading *Regeneration*? Explain why or why not, referring to the text in support of the points you make.

OR

(iii) Imagine that you are a nurse working in Craiglockhart. Write a letter home, describing what day-to-day life is like for the patients in the psychiatric hospital.

C CIRCLE OF FRIENDS – Maeve Binchy
Answer **all** of the questions.

1. (a) Describe what happens when Eve visits Simon Westward to ask for money to help pay for her college fees. (10)

   (b) Select one scene or moment in the novel that made you feel particularly sympathetic towards Benny. Briefly describe the scene, and explain your response to it. (10)

   (c) "Jack Foley is a very selfish character." Do you agree or disagree with this statement? Give reasons for your answer. (10)

2. Answer **ONE** of the following: [Each part carries 30 marks]

   (i) Choose **one** of the following issues that *Circle of Friends* made you think about:
   - Friendship
   - Women's rights
   - Disappointment
   Explain how this issue affected **one** character in the story.

   OR

   (ii) If you were asked to play the part of one of the characters from *Circle of Friends* in a new film adaptation of the novel, which character would you choose? Explain your choice by reference to the novel.

   OR

   (iii) Based on your reading of *Circle of Friends*, do you think that Maeve Binchy is a good story-teller? Give reasons for your opinion.

D JANE EYRE – Charlotte Brontë
Answer **all** of the questions.

1. (a) Describe what happened to Jane when she was locked in the Red Room. (10)

(b) Based on your knowledge of the novel, describe the type of person you imagine Mrs Reed to be. (10)

(c) Did you like or dislike the character of Helen Burns? Explain your view. (10)

2. Answer **ONE** of the following: [Each part carries 30 marks]

(i) "As a novel, *Jane Eyre* presents readers with a very negative and depressing view of life."

Do you agree with this statement? Give reasons for your answer, supporting them by reference to the text.

OR

(ii) Imagine that Jane was teaching you in Thornfield Hall.
Write a letter to one of your friends in which you describe your impressions of Jane.

OR

(iii) "All the male characters in *Jane Eyre* are selfish and cold-hearted." Discuss this view with reference to at least **one** of the male characters in the novel.

E **SPIES** – Michael Frayn
Answer **all** of the questions.

1. (a) Why do Stephen and Keith suspect that Mrs. Hayward (Keith's mother) is a German spy? Refer to the novel in your answer. (10)

(b) Do you agree that Keith is a very unpleasant boy? Explain your answer by reference to the novel. (10)

(c) Did the ending of *Spies* surprise you? Give reasons for your answer. (10)

2. Answer **ONE** of the following: [Each part carries 30 marks]

(i) From the following statements, choose **one** which in your opinion best describes the story. Give reasons for your choice:
- *It is a story about childhood*
- *It is a story about war*
- *It is a story about growing up*

OR

(ii) "Dear Michael…"
Write a letter to Michael Frayn in which you tell him what you thought of *Spies*. Support the points you make by reference to the novel.

OR

(iii) In your opinion, would *Spies* make a good film? Refer to the novel in support of your answer.

F   PHILADELPHIA, HERE I COME! – Brian Friel
Answer **all** of the questions.

1. (a) Describe what happened during the visit of the Americans (Aunt Lizzy, Uncle Con and Ben Burton) to the O'Donnell household. (10)

   (b) In your opinion, was Gar a good son to S.B. O'Donnell? Give reasons for your answer. (10)

   (c) What do you think is the most amusing scene in the play? Describe what happens and explain what made the scene so amusing. (10)

2. Answer **ONE** of the following: [Each part carries 30 marks]

   (i) "Lack of communication is the main problem for the characters in *Philadelphia, Here I Come!*". Do you agree?
   In your answer, you should refer to **one or more** of the characters in the play.

   OR

   (ii) Imagine you are Madge, the housekeeper in the O'Donnell home. Write the letter you would send to Gar a week after he left for Philadelphia.

   You should refer to characters and/or events from the play in your letter.

   OR

   (iii) "Gar's friends, the Boys, are more to be pitied than laughed at."
   Do you agree with this view of Tom, Ned and Joe? Support your answer by reference to the play.

G   THE CURIOUS INCIDENT OF THE DOG IN THE NIGHT-TIME – Mark Haddon
Answer **all** of the questions.

1. (a) Describe the scene early in the novel when Christopher is arrested and brought to the police station. (10)

   (b) Do you like or dislike Christopher's mother, Judy Boone? Explain your answer. (10)

   (c) What kind of a relationship does Christopher have with Siobhan, his teacher at school? Refer to the novel in your answer. (10)

2. Answer **ONE** of the following: [Each part carries 30 marks]

   (i) Imagine that Christopher's father, Ed Boone, kept a diary. Write the diary entry Ed Boone might have written after Christopher discovered the hidden letters from his mother. Support your answer with reference to the novel.

OR

(ii) What do you think is the most important lesson about life that can be learned from *The Curious Incident of the Dog in the Night-time*? Refer to the novel in your answer.

OR

(iii) From your reading of the novel, would you like to have had Christopher as a friend? Give reasons for your answer.

H   THE CRUCIBLE – Arthur Miller
Answer **all** of the questions.

1. (a) Why is Reverend Parris so upset and angry at the beginning of the play? (10)

    (b) In your view, was Elizabeth Proctor a good wife to John Proctor? Explain your answer, by reference to the play. (10)

    (c) Which scene in the play is the most dramatic and memorable, in your opinion? Give reasons for your answer by reference to the text. (10)

2. Answer **ONE** of the following: [Each part carries 30 marks]

    (i) "Arthur Miller's play, *The Crucible*, is so cruel that it is unsuitable for study by Leaving Certificate students."
    Discuss this view, referring to events from the play in your answer.

    OR

    (ii) This play is set in Salem in 1692. Would you like to have lived there at that time? Support the points you make by reference to the play.

    OR

    (iii) "Abigail Williams is the real villain of Miller's play, *The Crucible*." Write your response to this statement, supporting your answer by reference to the text.

I   MACBETH – William Shakespeare
Answer **all** of the questions.

1.
    (a) Describe what happens when Macbeth and Banquo first meet the witches in the early part of the play. (10)

    (b) Did you feel sympathy for Lady Macbeth at any time during the play? Give reasons for your answer, based on your knowledge of the text. (10)

    (c) From the following statements, choose **one** which, in your opinion, best describes what the play is about. Give reasons for your choice.
    - *It is a play about power*
    - *It is a play about evil*
    - *It is a play about love* (10)

2. Answer **ONE** of the following: [Each part carries 30 marks]

   (i) What is your opinion of the actions and behaviour of Macduff throughout the play, *Macbeth*? Support the points you make by reference to the text.

   OR

   (ii) *Macbeth* continues to be one of the most performed and popular of Shakespeare's plays. Do you think it deserves to remain so popular today? Give reasons for your answer by referring to your own experience of studying and/or watching the play in performance.

   OR

   (iii) Imagine you were asked to direct a new film based on Shakespeare's play, *Macbeth*. Which two actors would you cast in the main roles of Macbeth and Lady Macbeth? Explain your choices with reference to the play.

SECTION II
THE COMPARATIVE STUDY (70 MARKS)

Candidates must answer **ONE** question from **either A** – Social Setting, **or B** – Theme.

In your answer you may not use the text you have answered on in **SECTION I** – The Single Text.

N.B. The questions use the word **text** to refer to all the different kinds of texts available for study on this course, i.e. novel, play, short story, autobiography, biography, travel writing and film. The questions use the word **author** to refer to novelists, playwrights, writers in all genres and film directors.

A   SOCIAL SETTING

1.
   (a) Write a paragraph in which you outline what you liked (**or** disliked) about the social setting in **one** text from your comparative course.   (30)

   (b) Compare the social setting in the text you have described in part (a) above with the social setting in another text you have studied.   (40)

   OR

2. Imagine that you, as a reader, could visit the world or social setting of the comparative texts you have studied.

   (a) Describe what you found interesting about the social setting in **one** text.
   (30)

(b) Explain how the social setting in the second text is more (**or** less) interesting than the one already described in (a) above. (40)

B THEME
Before beginning your answer to either of the two questions on THEME, you should name a <u>theme</u> that you are going to discuss.

1. You have been asked to talk to your class about the theme of the comparative texts you have studied.

    (a) Describe **one** key moment in the text where the theme is clearly evident. (30)

    (b) Compare the moment described in (a) above with a moment in another text where **the same theme** is also clearly shown. (40)

    OR

2. (a) Choose a theme from **one** of the texts on your comparative course and say why it did (**or** did not) make the text entertaining. (30)

    (b) Choose the **same theme** from another text and say why it made that text more (**or** less) entertaining than the one discussed in (a) above. (40)

SECTION III
POETRY (70 MARKS)

Candidates must answer the questions on the Unseen Poem **and** the questions on **one** of the Prescribed Poems – A, B, C, D.

UNSEEN POEM (20 marks)
In this poem, the writer Robert Hershon, tells of a moment in a restaurant with his adult son. Read the poem at least twice and answer the questions following it.

> **SENTIMENTAL MOMENT**
> Don't fill up on bread
> I say absent-mindedly
> The servings here are huge
> My son, whose hair may be
> receding a bit, says
> Did you really just
> say that to me?
> What he doesn't know
> is that when we're walking
> together, when we get
> to the curb*
> I sometimes start to reach
> for his hand.
>
> ** edge of the street*

1. (a) What impression does this poem give you of the way the father feels towards his son? (4)

   (b) What words or phrases from the poem give you this impression? (6)

2. The writer chose the title *Sentimental Moment* for this poem. In your view, what other title might he have chosen? Explain your choice by referring to the text of the poem. (10)

PRESCRIBED POETRY (50 marks)

You must answer on **ONE** of the following poems: (**A – D**)

A   AT GRASS

    The eye can hardly pick them out
    From the cold shade they shelter in,
    Till wind distresses tail and mane;
    Then one crops grass, and moves about
    – The other seeming to look on –
    And stands anonymous again.

    Yet fifteen years ago, perhaps
    Two dozen distances sufficed
    To fable them: faint afternoons
    Of Cups and Stakes and Handicaps,
    Whereby their names were artificed
    To inlay faded, classic Junes –

    Silks at the start: against the sky
    Numbers and parasols: outside,
    Squadrons of empty cars, and heat,
    And littered grass: then the long cry
    Hanging unhushed till it subside
    To stop-press columns on the street.

    Do memories plague their ears like flies?
    They shake their heads. Dusk brims the shadows.
    Summer by summer all stole away,
    The starting-gates, the crowds and cries –
    All but the unmolesting meadows.
    Almanacked, their names live; they

    Have slipped their names, and stand at ease,
    Or gallop for what must be joy,
    And not a fieldglass sees them home,
    Or curious stop-watch prophesies:
    Only the grooms, and the groom's boy,
    With bridles in the evening come.
                           Philip Larkin

1. (a) What are the poet's first impressions of the retired racehorses? Refer to the first stanza in support of your answer. (10)

   (b) What kind of lives did the racehorses live fifteen years ago? Support your answer by reference to the poem. (10)

   (c) Choose one phrase or line from the poem that you find particularly appealing. Explain your choice. (10)

2. Answer **ONE** of the following: [Each part carries 20 marks]

   (i) How does Larkin convey the world of the racecourse in the third stanza? Refer to the text in your answer.

   OR

   (ii) The following statements suggest Philip Larkin's attitude to the racehorses:
   – He admires them
   – He feels sorry for them
   – He is fascinated by them

   Choose **one** statement from the above list that is closest to your own understanding of the poem. Explain your choice, supporting your answer by reference to the text.

   OR

   (iii) Imagine you are to make a video of *At Grass* to show to your Leaving Certificate class. What visual and/or sound effects would you use in the production? Explain your choices by reference to the poem.

B   ON PASSING THE NEW MENIN GATE

Who will remember, passing through this Gate,
The unheroic Dead who fed the guns?
Who shall absolve the foulness of their fate –
Those doomed, conscripted, unvictorious ones?
Crudely renewed, the Salient holds its own.
Paid are its dim defenders by this pomp;
Paid with a pile of peace complacent stone,
The armies who endured that sullen swamp.

Here was the world's worst wound. And here with pride
'Their name liveth for ever', the Gateway claims.
Was ever an immolation so belied
As these intolerably nameless names?
Well might the Dead who struggled in the slime
Rise and deride this sepulchre of crime.

Siegfried Sasson

1. (a) What, in your opinion, is the poet's attitude towards the monument commemorating the dead?
    Support your answer by reference to the poem. (10)

   (b) Why, in your view, does Sassoon describe the war dead as *unheroic* and *unvictorious*?
    Support your answer by reference to the poem. (10)

   (c) What words and phrases in this poem, in your opinion, best convey the awful experiences of the soldiers in the First World War?
    Explain your answer. (10)

2. Answer **ONE** of the following: [Each part carries 20 marks]

   (i) From your understanding of the poem, write a piece where you argue that Sassoon is either:
    – proud of the men who died

   OR

    – angry at the massive waste of life

    Support your answer by reference to the poem.

   OR

   (ii) On the gate is written, "*Their name liveth for ever*".
    Imagine you are a relative of one of the war-dead. Based on your reading of the poem, write a piece in which you explain the kind of memorial that would best commemorate your relative and his fellow soldiers.

   OR

   (iii) You are to make a video in which this poem is spoken. Describe the sound effects, music, images, etc. you would use to illustrate the reading of the poem.

C FILLING STATION

Oh, but it is dirty!
– this little filling station,
oil soaked, oil-permeated
to a disturbing, over-all
black translucency.
Be careful with that match!

Father wears a dirty,
oil-soaked monkey suit
that cuts him under the arms,
and several quick and saucy

and greasy sons assist him
(it's a family filling station),
all quite thoroughly dirty.

Do they live in the station?
It has a cement porch
behind the pumps, and on it
a set of crushed and grease-
impregnated wickerwork;
on the wicker sofa
a dirty dog, quite comfy.

Some comic books provide
the only note of color –
of certain color. They lie
upon a big dim doily
draping a taboret
(part of the set), beside
a big hirsute begonia.

Why the extraneous plant?
Why the taboret?
Why, oh why, the doily?
(Embroidered in daisy stitch
with marguerites, I think,
and heavy with gray crochet.)

Somebody embroidered the doily.
Somebody waters the plant,
or oils it, maybe. Somebody
arranges the rows of cans
so that they softly say:
ESSO—SO—SO—SO
to high-strung automobiles.
Somebody loves us all.
     Elizabeth Bishop

1. (a) What impression of the filling station and its inhabitants do you get from reading the first two stanzas of the poem? Refer to the text in support of your answer. (10)

(b) *"Somebody loves us all."*
In your opinion, does this line provide a good ending to the poem? Explain your answer. (10)

(c) What impression of the poet, Elizabeth Bishop, do you get from reading this poem? (10)

2. Answer **ONE** of the following: [Each part carries 20 marks]

(i) "Good poetry creates vivid pictures in our minds." In your opinion, is this true of *Filling Station*? Support your view by reference to the text of the poem.

OR

(ii) Imagine you are Elizabeth Bishop. Write a diary entry, based on your reading of the poem, in which you describe your experience of stopping at this filling station.

OR

(iii) Which of the following statements is closest to your own view of the poem:
- *Life is full of surprises*
- *Everyone needs love*
- *We shouldn't judge by appearances*

Explain your choice, supporting your answer by reference to the text.

D NAMING MY DAUGHTER

Beside my desk, I had pinned
A list of possible names for my unborn child,
Adding to it at intervals
As the months swelled slowly on.

She was born without colour
Among the yellow daffodils
And the greening trees of a wet March.

I chose none of those names for my daughter.
I gave her instead
The Caribbean name of Rain:
Wanting something soft, familiar and constant
To touch and touch again
Her thin coverlet of earth.

Rosita Boland

1. *(a)* How does the poet show that she is looking forward to the birth of her child? Support your answer by reference to the poem. (10)

(b) Write out **one** phrase or line from the poem that you find particularly appealing. Explain what you especially like about it. (10)

(c) Why did Rosita Boland choose the "Caribbean name of Rain" for her daughter? Support your view by reference to the poem. (10)

2. Answer **ONE** of the following: [Each part carries 20 marks]

(i) Imagine you have been asked to suggest a poem for a new collection entitled *Family Love*. Explain why you would choose the poem, *Naming My Daughter* as part of the collection.

OR

(ii) Which **one** of the following statements would best describe your view of the poem?
- It is a poem about love
- It is a poem about disappointment
- It is a poem about nature

Explain your choice using reference to the text.

OR

(iii) Write a short letter to the poet, Rosita Boland, telling her about how this poem made you feel. Refer to the text of the poem in your answer.

Acknowledgments 2009 Examinations

For permission to reproduce copyright material in these examination papers, the publishers gratefully acknowledge:

'Interview with Chad Hurley' by Gemma O'Doherty reproduced by permission of *The Irish Independent*. Extract from *44, A Dublin Memoir* by Peter Sheridan reproduced by kind permission of Pan Macmillan. 'Sentimental Moment' by Robert Hershon reproduced by kind permission of Robert Hershon. 'At Grass' from *The Less Deceived* by Philip Larkin reproduced by kind permission of Marvell Press. 'On Passing the New Menin Gate' by Siegfried Sassoon. Copyright Siegfried Sassoon by kind permission of the Estate of George Sassoon. 'Filing Station' from *The Complete Poems, 1927–1979* by Elizabeth Bishop. Copyright © 1979, 1983 by Alice Helen Methfessel. Reprinted by permission of Farrar, Straus and Giroux, LLC. 'Naming my Daughter' by Rosita Boland reproduced by kind permission of the author c/o The Gallery Press, Loughcrew, Oldcastle, County Meath, Ireland.

The publishers have made every effort to trace all copyright holders, but if they have inadvertently overlooked any, they will be pleased to make the necessary arrangements at the first opportunity.